U•X•L Graphic Novelists

U·X·L Graphic Novelists

S-W
Volume 3

Tom Pendergast and Sara Pendergast
Sarah Hermsen, Project Editor

U·X·L

An imprint of Thomson Gale, a part of The Thomson Corporation

THOMSON
GALE

Detroit • New York • San Francisco • New Haven, Conn. • Waterville, Maine • London • Munich

THOMSON
GALE

U·X·L Graphic Novelists

Tom Pendergast and Sara Pendergast

Project Editor
Sarah Hermsen

Rights Acquisition and Management
Tim Sisler, Margaret Abendroth

Imaging and Multimedia
Dean Dauphinais, Mike Logusz

Product Design
Jennifer Wahi

Composition and Electronic Prepress
Evi Seoud

Manufacturing
Rita Wimberley

For permission to use material from this product, submit your request via Web at http://www.gale-edit.com/permissions, or you may download our Permissions Request form and submit your request by fax or mail to:

Rights Acquisition and Management Department
Thomson Gale
27500 Drake Rd.
Farmington Hills, MI 48331-3535
Permissions Hotline:
248-699-8006 or 800-877-4253, ext. 8006
Fax: 248-699-8074 or 800-762-4058

LIBRARY OF CONGRESS CATALOGING-IN-PUBLICATION DATA

Pendergast, Tom.
  UXL graphic novelists / Tom Pendergast and Sara Pendergast; Sarah Hermsen, project editor.
      v. cm.
  Includes bibliographical references and index.
  Contents: v. 1. A-H – v. 2. K-R – v. 3. S-W.
  ISBN 1-4144-0440-9 (set : alk. paper) – ISBN 1-4144-0441-7 (v. 1 : alk. paper) – ISBN 1-4144-0442-5 (v. 2 : alk. paper) – ISBN 1-4144-0443-3 (v. 3 : alk. paper)
  1. Cartoonists–Biography–Dictionaries. 2. Comic books, strips, etc.–Dictionaries.
I. Pendergast, Sara. II. Title.
  NC1305.P46 2007
  741.5'69730922–dc22
  [B]   2006013711

This title is also available as an e-book.
ISBN 1-4144-0620-7
Contact your Thomson Gale sales representative for ordering information.

Printed in China
10 9 8 7 6 5 4 3 2 1

Table of Contents

Reader's Guide

Graphic Novelists contains biographical profiles of 75 notable people involved in the creation of graphic novels, a diverse and rapidly changing field. They represent the diversity of style, content, and intended audience of one of the most popular literary forms of the early twenty-first century. The novelists—who wrote for a variety of different ages, from pre-teen to adults—and their works represent three broad categories: super-hero or action-oriented works; manga; and "independent" work, a broad category of graphic novels that simply fit nowhere else, and includes fiction, nonfiction, comedy, drama, romance, and others.

The study of graphic novelists is an emerging field. Many of the graphic novelists we have profiled are as yet little known outside a narrow circle of interest, and there is still real debate about what a graphic novel is and what it can be. This is thus the rare reference book that jumps into a field while it is still fresh. Many of the graphic novelists profiled—24 of 75—agreed to be interviewed by us or our contributing writers, and the conversations that we have had with them were an invaluable addition to the book. The people profiled in this collection play a variety of roles in the creation of graphic novels. Some are authors; some are illustrators or artists; most are author/artists who have created both the words and the artwork in their books. Some even bind, market, and sell their own works, and operate their own Web site. Some work other jobs, and prepare their graphic novels in the evenings and weekends. Most are full-time creators, and for those who write and illustrate, their job requires long and sometimes tedious hours of drawing.

Some of the graphic novelists featured are tremendously popular among young adults, yet they have also created works that deal with more violence, drug use, and sexuality than is considered appropriate for middle school and high school readers. The more explicit works that are not widely read by young adults, or that are specifically marketed to adults are not discussed in detail.

Each entry contains a Best-Known Works section that provides a short listing of the creator's best-known graphic novels, in addition to other works that may be pertinent to their career as a graphic novelist. Also included are numerous sidebars that offer additional insight into the creative process, important collaborators and publishers, and conventions used in the creation and publication of graphic novels. The For More Information section provides a listing of sources consulted in the creation of the entry, as well as additional sources known to provide substantive information about the entrant or about topics discussed in the sidebar. Highlighting the text are over one hundred color and black-and-white photos as well as a words to know section defining terms used throughout the set, and a comprehensive subject index.

Acknowledgements

Several skilled writers assisted in creating a number of essays, including Rob Edelman, Tina Gianoulis, Jim Manheim, and Chris Routledge. The Sno-Isle Regional Library system's graphic novel collection was an important resource. Thanks also goes to the enthusiastic work of Conrad and Louisa Pendergast. Especially important to this set were the invaluable suggestions made by the advisory board to guide the content and structure of the book. They include:

Philip Charles Crawford: Library director, Essex Junction High School, VT; author of *Graphic Novels 101: Selecting and Using Graphic Novels to Promote Literacy for Children and Young Adults*; author of the pamphlet "Using Graphic Novels in the Classroom" (http://scholastic.com/librarians/printables/downloads/graphic-novels.pdf); regular reviewer of graphic novels for professional journals; and frequent speaker at library and literature conferences. **Essays***: Neil Gaiman; Dave McKean; Grant Morrison.

Kathleen Fernandes: Assistant manager of adult and teen services, Sno-Isle Libraries, Marysville, WA.

Kat Kan: Former young adult librarian and freelance graphic novel consultant and writer, whose column "Graphically Speaking," has appeared in *Voice of Youth Advocates* since 1994. **Essays***: Mike Kunkel; Hayao Miyazaki; Scott Morse; Trina Robbins; Stan Sakai.

Nicole Pelham and **Danielle Pelham**: Co-founders of NDP Comics, Seattle, WA, an artists group that publishes American manga and offers classes in manga drawing in the Pacific Northwest. The Pelham sisters have taught over 300 classes at such places as the University of Washington, the Seattle Children's Museum, the Bumbershoot Music Festival, the Seattle Buddhist temple, and anime conventions. **Essays***: Clamp.

*Indicates essays written for *Graphic Novelists*.

Comments and Suggestions

We welcome your comments on *U•X•L Graphic Novelists* as well as your suggestions for people and topics to be featured in future editions. Please write to: Editor, *Graphic Novelists*, U•X•L, 27500 Drake Road, Farmington Hills, Michigan, 48331; call toll-free: 800-877-4253; fax to: 248-699-8097; or send e-mail via www.gale.com.

Introduction

Midway through 2001 ICV2.com, a Web site that tracks the comic book industry, took note of a surprising new trend: sales of graphic novels were beginning to represent a significant percentage of all comic book sales. What's more, graphic novels were far more likely to appear in the place where most Americans buy their books: the large chain bookstores such as Barnes & Noble, Borders Books, Books-A-Million, B. Dalton, and other giant retailers. In succeeding years this trend—at first apparent only to those immersed in the comic book industry—became widespread and unmistakable. In 2002, graphic novel sales in the United States reached $100 million, with half the books being sold in specialty comics stores, half in regular bookstores. A year later, bookstore sales alone topped $105 million, while the specialty stores sold $60 million. In 2004 sales soared to $207 million, outstripping those of comic books, and expectations were that in 2005 sales would top $300 million.

Surging sales told only part of story. Across the United States, and in many European and Asian countries, bookstores and libraries were experiencing (and driving) the graphic novel boom. Large bookstores began to set aside sizeable sections for graphic novels, and their shelves overflowed with a diverse mix of works, from superhero fare from comic book giants DC Comics and Marvel, to manga titles from the likes of Viz and TokyoPop, to an eclectic mix of autobiography, fiction, and nonfiction from a range of publishers, large and small, committed to expanding the boundaries of the graphic novel form. At Borders alone, graphic novel sales rose 100 percent each year from 2002 to 2004. Librarians struggled to keep up with patron demands for new titles.

Kathleen Fernandes, assistant manager of adult and teen services for Sno-Isle Libraries in Washington's Puget Sound area, reported that Japanese manga titles were the most widely circulating books in the teen collection.

Magazines used by librarians to help guide their purchasing decisions began to pay attention to graphic novels as well. Beginning in 1994, *Voice of Youth Advocates (VOYA)* began a regular column called "Graphically Speaking," written by Kat Kan. By the late 1990s *VOYA*, *Booklist*, *Library Journal*, *School Library Journal*, and others began regularly to review new graphic novel releases. Mainstream magazines also took note: in 2001 *Time* magazine created a regular feature, written by Andrew Arnold, called "*Time.comix*"; and in 2005 *Newsweek* offered a lengthy and glowing testimonial to the growing importance of graphic novels. Perhaps the most thriving source of information about graphic novels, however, is the Internet, where multiple Web sites dedicate their efforts to reviewing comic books and graphic novels, and interviewing comics creators (see Where To Learn More section for listing of some of these online sources).

What is a graphic novel?

Ask anyone in the graphic novel industry—creators, publishers, reviewers—to tell you what a graphic novel is, and you'll likely find yourselves in the midst of a maelstrom. Any inclination to call graphic novels a genre—which implies similarity in style or content, as in the genres comedy or science fiction—quickly runs aground. There is a dizzying variety of content found in graphic novels. In this collection alone you will find autobiography, science fiction, westerns, comedy, romance, and action-adventure. If there is one thing that the graphic novel has shown, it is that it is capable of taking on any number of kinds of stories. Moreover, stylistic differences abound.

Calling the graphic novel a form of storytelling works somewhat better, for it accentuates the structure rather than the content. Clearly, graphic novels have a distinct form—in simplest terms, they combine pictures with words to tell a story. The only problem with this definition is that this form of storytelling has been around for ages and has gone by the term "comics" or "comic books." There is no meaningful or valid way to distinguish the form of a comic book from that of a graphic novel, as many experts feel that there is no functional difference between the ways stories are told in comic strips, comic books, and graphic novels.

Yet somehow, the sense that a graphic novel is something different and apart remains. The difficulties in distinguishing graphic novels from other forms of sequential art give credence to the suggestion that the term graphic novels is an ingenious device used by marketing departments at large publishers to boost sales. Such an approach to defining the graphic novel holds that it is a story told in comic book form, but packaged as a trade paperback, with higher print standards, better binding, and more pages than a comic book. This definition allows graphic novels to include a collection of comic strips about a common set of characters; a collection of comic book-length stories (that is, thirty-two-page stories) brought together in a longer narrative; and a single, sustained storytelling effort. This definition probably comes closest to describing the actual application of the term graphic novel in the world today, for it is the only one to acknowledge that graphic novels, as they are bought and sold in the marketplace today, are in essence long comic books.

A short history of the graphic novel

While few can agree on what exactly a graphic novel is, there is wide agreement that the book that started the graphic novel boom in the United States was Will Eisner's *A Contract with God,* published in 1978. Eisner joked that when he approached a publisher about the book, which brought together four stories about tenement life during the Great Depression (1929–41; period of severe economic hardship in the United States), he told them it was a "graphic novel" because he knew they would never publish a comic book of this length on this topic. Eisner was a comics creator who had made his name with the *Spirit* comic book series in the 1940s. But Eisner wanted more from his art than was available at the time: he wanted comics to take on serious subject matter, to deal with issues in a longer form, and to reach readers beyond their teenage years. These hopes have animated the field ever since.

Eisner's work was not without precedent. Belgian artist Hergé had been creating *TinTin* stories in Europe since the 1930s and these were published as "graphic albums," the European corollary to the graphic novel. In Japan, Osamu Tezuka initiated the field of modern manga in the 1950s, and his works and the works of many other Japanese manga-ka (manga creators) were collected into tankobon (or graphic novels) beginning in the 1960s. In the United States, a growing underground comics, or comix, movement in the 1960s and 1970s prompted many other comic book writers to try to move away from the dominant trend toward superheroes and industry limitations on content imposed in the 1950s when prominent parents and educators became alarmed that comics might contribute to juvenile delinquency. Titles such as George Metzger's *Beyond Time and Again,* serialized from 1967 to 1972; Richard Corben's 1976 *Bloodstar;* and Jim Steranko's 1976 *Chandler: Red Tide* all pushed the boundaries of regular comics and explored more mature and complicated material. But it was Eisner's work that seemed to indicate a new world of possibility.

By the mid-1980s a flood began that has since continued unabated. Two works introduced in 1986 began the modern trend: Frank Miller's *Dark Knight Returns,* an interpretation of the Batman legend, and Art Spiegelman's *Maus: A Survivor's Tale,* a family memoir of the Holocaust that depicted Jews as mice, Nazis as cats, Poles as pigs, and Americans as dogs. Within a year, Alan Moore's *The Watchmen* was released as a graphic novel to great acclaim. The works by Miller and Moore breathed new life into a superhero genre that many thought was dying, and their long, fully developed stories focused more intently on characterization than ever before. Though initially released serially, they bore the marks of a graphic novel in their depth, complexity, and ability to sustain a narrative. *Maus* demonstrated to a broad public that a graphic novel could be personal, political, and poignant; it became the first graphic novel to win a major book prize when it won a special Pulitzer Prize in 1992.

Since 1986, a number of graphic novelists have continued to work in the superhero field, using larger-than-life characters with extraordinary powers as the focal point for storytelling that is sometimes merely amusing and escapist, and sometimes quite profound. Many of them are featured in this collection. For all their innovations in length and characterization, superhero graphic novels remained trapped within the rules of the superhero universe (which were sometimes quite carefully spelled out by the corporate publishers who owned the characters). It was in the so-called "independent" comic book world that creators truly began to explore new approaches to style, form, and narrative structure. Independent graphic novel creators have typically worked outside the mainstream comics industry, creating works that express their unique and sometimes intensely personal vision.

Over the years, independent graphic novelists have been those most responsible for pushing the boundaries of what is possible in the graphic novel form (though the superhero books still sell more). Wendy and Richard Pini, with their *Elfquest* series, and Colleen Doran, with *A Distant Soil,* explored the world of fantasy; Los Bros Hernandez (Jaime and Gilbert Hernandez) told rather realistic stories of Hispanic life in their series of graphic novels called *Love and Rockets*; Paul Chadwick blurred the boundaries between superhero and social/political commentary in multiple volumes of *Concrete*; Larry Gonick delved into such tough topics as history, physics, and sex education in his *Cartoon Guide* series of non-fiction graphic novels; Scott McCloud used comics to figure out how comics worked in *Understanding Comics*—the list could go on and on. These independent works have raised the intellectual standard for the industry: many are read by adults and reviewed in serious magazines and newspapers. (A number of them are intended for adults, with truly mature themes and images).

The great majority of these pioneering independent graphic novelists either self-published or worked with small, dedicated publishing firms that backed their vision. But by the late 1990s, the publisher Dark Horse Comics had grown from its meager beginnings to become one of the largest publishers, and it continued to back the work of independent graphic novelists. Other independent publishers expanded the quality and number of their offerings. Even more significantly, major New York publishing houses (Random House in particular) began to recognize the legitimacy of graphic novels, and published Chris Ware's strangely brilliant work *Jimmy Corrigan: The Smartest Kid on Earth* in 2000 and Marjane Satrapi's groundbreaking *Persepolis,* the story of a girl coming of age in Iran during its Islamic Revolution, in 2003. By the mid-2000s the graphic novel boom had created the economic conditions that allowed creators of work that would once have been ignored to land their projects with a major publisher promising wide distribution.

Outside influences

The comic book and graphic novel industry in the United States has long been remarkably contained. Other than René Goscinny and Albert Uderzo's *Asterix the Gaul* series and Hergé's *TinTin* series, few graphic novels from Europe reached American shores for many years, and fewer still from other countries. (Great Britain, with its shared language, is the exception.) All that began to change in the 1990s, when Japanese manga (comic books) became the latest Japanese import to transform an American industry. Japan had a long tradition of embracing comics books and graphic novels (called tankobon in Japan), and such works made up 20 percent of the Japanese publishing industry in the 2000s. Since the 1960s, Japan had exported animated cartoons, or anime, to the United States, but in the 1990s they also began to export manga.

The first manga series to gain real attention in the United States was Kazuo Koike's *Lone Wolf and Cub,* a samurai action tale first issued in English translation in 1987, then later reissued in its entirety by Dark Horse beginning in 2000. For a time, Japanese works trickled into the United States, intriguing fans with their very different storytelling and artistic techniques. By the late 1990s teen readers had discovered manga, and demand soared. Two publishers—VIZ and TOKYOPOP—began translating and importing huge numbers of manga. In 2001, TokyoPop became the largest-selling publisher of graphic novels with 23.6 percent of the market, thanks to sales of Naoko Takeuchi's *Sailor Moon.* Fans were soon exposed to all varieties of manga, from the shonen action-adventure stories for boys to the shojo tales of romance for girls. They became familiar with the strange time lag in publication—a series might begin publishing in the United States years after it finished its run in Japan—and with the unique conventions and styles of manga (see Manga section for an introduction to this branch of graphic novels). By the mid-2000s, manga made up a large percentage of the graphic novels available in most chain bookstores, where they are especially popular with pre-teen and teenaged girls, long a neglected market. Moreover, publishers are beginning to publish American manga (manga-style stories created by English speakers) and to import manga from China and South Korea. (For more on manga, see "Manga: A Primer.")

The future of the graphic novel

In 2005, the future for the graphic novel looked extremely bright. Sales of graphic novels were at their highest levels ever; graphic novelists were increasingly being signed with large, prosperous publishing houses; numerous movie adaptations—and not just of superhero stories—were being made, building on the success of such box-office hits as *Ghost World, American Splendor, Sin City,* and *Hellboy;* and several comics creators worked to explore the potential of the Internet as a medium for telling stories.

It may be too soon to say that graphic novels have secured a stable place on bookstore shelves and lifted comics from the margins of literary expression. As fans of the comics industry know all too well, there have been several booms over the years, followed by long stretches of disinterest and flagging sales. Yet the advances of the last several decades are undeniable: graphic novelists have produced a range of works for readers of all ages and all interests, and the quality of the writing and the art has improved dramatically. Once thought of as a medium only capable of telling light stories about powerful men in tights, graphic novels have now shown themselves capable of addressing the widest range of human experience, with the interaction between words and art contributing to the power of the stories that are told.

◼ ◼ ◼

Works Consulted

Books

Gravett, Paul. *Manga: Sixty Years of Japanese Comics.* London: Laurence King Publishing, 2004.

McCloud, Scott. *Understanding Comics.* Northampton, MA: Kitchen Sink Press, 1993; reprinted, New York: HarperPerennial, 1994.

Sabin, Roger. *Comics, Comix & Graphic Novels: A History of Comic Art.* London: Phaidon Press, 1996.

Schodt, Frederik L. *Manga! Manga! The World of Japanese Comics.* Tokyo: Kodansha, 1983.

Periodicals

"Comic Relief: Take That, Batman. Graphic Novels Are Moving Out of the Hobby Shop and into the Mainstream." *Newsweek International* (August 22, 2005): p. 58.

Kean, Danuta. "Get Ready for Manga Mania." *The Bookseller* (November 19, 2004): p. 22.

Wolk, Douglas. "Graphic Novel Sales Even Better Than Expected." *Publishers Weekly* (June 21, 2004): p. 18.

Web Sites

Arnold, Andrew. "The Graphic Novel Silver Anniversary." *Time.* http://www.time.com/time/columnist/arnold/article/0,9565,542579,00.html (accessed on June 9, 2006).

Bussert, Leslie. "Comic Books and Graphic Novels: Digital Resources for an Evolving Form of Art and Literature." *Association of College and Research Libraries.* http://www.acrl.org/ala/acrl/acrlpubs/crlnews/

backissues2005/february05/comicbooks.htm (accessed on June 9, 2006).

Cohn, Neil. "Reframing Comics." *Comixpedia*. http://www.comixpedia.com/index.php?name=Sections&req=viewarticle&artid=554&page=1 (accessed on June 9, 2006).

Couch, Chris. "The Publication and Formats of Comics, Graphic Novels, and Tankobon" (December 2000). *Image & Narrative*. http://www.imageandnarrative.be/narratology/chriscouch.htm (accessed on June 9, 2006).

Duffy, Jonathan. "Return of the Dark Art." *BBC Online*. http://news.bbc.co.uk/1/hi/uk/442081.stm (accessed on June 9, 2006).

George, Milo. "In Depth: The Eddie Campbell Interview." *Graphic Novel Review*. http://www.graphicnovelreview.com/articles/issue1/campbell_interview.php?mode=full (accessed on June 9, 2006).

ICv2. http://www.icv2.com (accessed on June 9, 2006).

Poitras, Gilles. *The Librarian's Guide to Anime and Manga*. http://www.koyagi.com/Libguide.html (accessed on June 9, 2006).

Manga

Most people familiar with American comic books and graphic novels immediately recognize that Japanese comic books—called manga—don't play by the same rules. They begin at the end, the characters have huge eyes, and scenes seem to go on forever, often with no words. Japanese manga is, in fact, a sophisticated and well-developed form of storytelling, every bit as rich and complicated as the comic book/graphic novel tradition that developed in the West. It just operates on a different set of conventions and with a different history.

Manga and Japanese literary tradition

Japan has a long history of sequential art, a term used by American comics creator Will Eisner to describe a sequence of artistic images that are united with words to tell a story. As early as the twelfth century, Japanese artista and illustrators had created small comic panels to offer information, convey humor, or make political statements. But Japanese manga—which in literal translation means "involuntary pictures"—as it exists today really got its start in the years after World War II (1939–45), when the nation first encountered American comic books. Japanese writer and artist Osamu Tezuka—often called the "Father of Manga" or "God of Manga"—was deeply moved by American comic books. In the decades after the war, he took this form, which had been primarily aimed at children and young adults, and infused it with the visual lessons he had learned from watching American movies to tell long, complicated stories of real substance. As a result, he created modern manga as we know it today.

Tezuka's great artistry won many readers, first among young people, and later among adults. Soon others followed in his footsteps, exploring new styles of art and storytelling. Slowly, the manga industry grew. Manga was easy to read and cheap to print, a virtue in a nation that was slowly recovering from the devastation of war. Manga stories were created for every imaginable audience. Manga magazines offered initial opportunities for young artists, many who got their first exposure by winning a contest. If their stories were popular the manga-ka, or manga creators, were offered a continuing story. The most popular manga-ka became very rich. Today, manga is a respectable form of reading material in Japan, where manga magazines and graphic novels sell millions and millions of copies every year. In contrast to the West, the manga industry in Japan is so popular that it is larger than the country's film industry.

Reading from right to left

Like all books in Japan, manga is read from right to left—exactly the opposite of reading material in the West. On a graphic novel page, your eye starts at the top right, moves leftward to the end of the panel, and proceeds in a zig-zag down the page. When translated versions of Japanese manga were first imported into the United States in the late 1990s, some publishers decided that their readers weren't ready for this unfamiliar reading format and they "flipped" the story, rearranging it so that it read from left to right. But discerning readers soon realized that flipping distorted some of the artwork, making it appear that the artist didn't know how to arrange a scene. As Western manga readers grew more sophisticated, they demanded that publishers offer manga "unflipped." By the mid-2000s, the major manga publishers offered most of their manga in the original, right-to-left format. (Manga created by Americans, however, follows American left-to-right conventions.)

From magazines to tankobon

In Japan, almost all manga are first published in manga magazines. These thick, cheaply printed black-and-white magazines bring together short installments of many different stories. Some of the stories are just a page in length, while others range up to twenty pages long. The magazines are sold on newsstands and even in vending machines all over Japan and are hugely popular with readers of all ages. Paul Gravett, in his *Manga: Sixty Years of Japanese Comics*, noted that in 2002 there were 281 manga magazines published in Japan. If a story from a magazine catches on and becomes a fan favorite, many episodes are collected together and published as a tankobon, the Japanese equivalent of the graphic novel. If a story is very popular, it may go on for years and years, resulting in dozens of volumes of tankobon. Though translated manga magazines have had some success in Western markets, the two-hundred-page tankobon is the primary form in which Western readers get their manga.

Manga genres

Unlike American superhero comic books—which many people assume are created primarily for adolescent boys—manga artists create works for a variety of different markets. The biggest segment of the Japanese manga market, shonen manga is focused on action and adventure, sports, and high-tech robots and other vehicles, and is marketed primarily to boys up to high school age. The second-biggest—and fastest growing—segment of the market is shojo manga, or manga for girls. Shojo titles tend to focus on romance and relationships, with some tales embrace action and fantasy as well. Kodomo manga is created for very young children. Japanese adults also read manga: both josei manga (for women) and seinen manga (for men) create more mature versions of the stories told to their younger counterparts, and both forms adopt a greater variety of artistic styles and a far more mature treatment of sexuality than in the titles for younger readers. These large categories of manga just begin to touch on the variety of specialty manga being published: in Japan, there are manga for gay and lesbian readers, and manga that focus specifically on religion, mechanized robots, magical girlfriends, and other such topics.

Sound effects

Modern Japanese writing is a combination of three different scripts: kanji, or Chinese characters, and hiragana, a Japanese syllabary (set of characters that represent syllables), make up the bulk of the writing, while katakana, another syllabary, is used to represent sounds ("splash," for example), ideas (a light bulb indicating a thought), and words from other languages. In translation, kanji and hiragana are easily rendered in different languages, but katakana proves more difficult. It is often integrated into the artwork, rather than part of a word balloon. It is very difficult to remove the katakana from the artwork, or to translate it directly into another language, without destroying the overall balance of the images. Publishers have tried several different approaches to dealing with these Japanese sound effects; some have left them intact and provided a glossary of terms at the back of the book, but this can be cumbersome; others have replaced the sound effects with translated words, but this seriously alters the artwork. Perhaps the best solution to the problem has been to provide small subtitles or footnotes, so that the reader can enjoy the original artwork and easily access the meaning of the words.

Big eyes, small mouth, and other manga conventions

One of the first things people notice about manga is the unique way characters are portrayed: girls (and sometimes boys) have huge, expressive eyes, and most characters have small noses and mouths. While a number of explanations for this style have been offered—that eyes are the window into the soul, or that big eyes are a romantic contrast to the smaller eyes of Japanese people—the origins of the style are fairly straightforward. Osamu Tezuka, who introduced the style, simply wanted to model his characters on some of his favorite American cartoon characters, Betty Boop and Bambi. Other manga-ka followed and expanded on Tezuka's lead. In shojo (girl) manga especially, eyes grew larger and larger, and the mouth shrunk in comparison. These large eyes were good at conveying emotion and feeling, and were used to draw readers into the emotions of his characters.

Manga artists use an array of artistic conventions to give readers clues to the emotions of characters. The number of teardrops falling from a character's eyes are used to indicate the intensity of feeling, and a large drop of sweat on the forehead indicates confusion, stupidity, or relief. When a male character develops a nose bleed, this is usually an indication that he is feeling lust for a girl. A large, cross-shaped mark on the forehead is used to indicate the throbbing of veins, as when a person is angry. In shojo manga, specific flowers are often used to refer to specific emotional states, and flames, sparkles, and starbursts contribute to the drama of the story.

American readers are sometimes surprised to see some nudity in Japanese manga created for young people. Japanese culture tends to be more accepting to occasional nudity than American culture, and the display of the buttocks is often used as a joke. Female breasts are sometimes displayed even in manga for young adults, though the display of male and female genitalia are extremely rare.

Mysterious manga-ka

Unlike American authors—who frequently give interviews and discuss their upbringing and education—Japanese manga-ka (manga creators) tend to hide the details of their private life. Quite often, manga-ka do not release the year of their birth, divulging instead their blood type, which is thought to give a clue to their personality, somewhat like a Zodiac sign in the West. A common practice among manga-ka is to include brief personal notes within the text of their manga, but these notes are usually very cryptic, revealing little about their life. Tomoko Taniguchi, a manga author who we interviewed for this collection, noted that many Japanese authors "want to stay mysterious in order to let our work stand on its own."

American manga ... and beyond

Manga has become a huge cultural phenomenon in the United States in the first years of the twenty-first century. Some observers have compared the manga craze to the "British Invasion" of the 1960s, when British rock bands led by The Beatles had a huge surge in popularity in the United States. Like that invasion, the manga craze has encouraged American artists to follow in the trends initiated by the Japanese. Fred Gallagher's *MegaTokyo* Internet comic strip, launched in 2000, is considered the first American manga, but it is hardly the last. A number of American graphic novelists have begun releasing works in the manga style, and in 2005 the publisher TOKYOPOP began to release a manga comic strip called "Peach Fuzz" to appear in American newspapers. Other publishers, including Antarctic Press and Seven Seas Entertainment, have published manga stories written in English. Perhaps the best gauge of the American adoption of manga can been seen in schools and libraries, where young people have avidly embraced the manga drawing styles.

Manga from other countries is also beginning to appear in American bookstores. Chinese manga (manhua), with versions of *Crouching Tiger, Hidden Dragon* and *Shaolin Soccer*, and Korean manga (manwha) are beginning to appear in the United States, and fans are coming to appreciate both the similarities and differences between these and Japanese manga. Clearly, manga has become a force to be reckoned with in American publishing.

.

Graphic Novel Publishers

The following is an annotated list of the major publishers of graphic novels in the United States. Graphic novelists featured in the book are indicated by bold face type.

Dark Horse Comics

Founded in 1986 by Portland, Oregon-based comics fan Mike Richardson, Dark Horse Comics has distinguished itself over the years for its support of independent comic book and graphic novel creators. Dark Horse first came to attention when it published **Paul Chadwick**'s *Concrete* series, and it later published works by award-winning authors including **Frank Miller**, **Mike Mignola**, **Stan Sakai**, **Sergio Aragonés**, **Neil Gaiman**, comic book legend **Will Eisner**, and many others. Dark Horse began publishing translations of Japanese manga in 1994, including the work of such notable manga creators as **Kosuke Fujishima**, **Kazuo Koike**, and **Osamu Tezuka**.

Addresses: *Office*—Dark Horse Comics, 10956 SE Main Street, Milwaukie, OR 97222. *Web Site*—www.darkhorse.com.

Del Rey

Judy-Lynn del Rey started Del Rey Books as a publisher of science fiction and fantasy with her husband Lester del Rey in 1977. In 2004 Del Rey, an imprint of Random House, entered into an agreement with Kodansha, one of Japan's largest manga publishers, to publish English translations of some of Kodansha's books. The success of the venture catapulted Del Rey to the top of manga industry in the United States by early 2005, with two of its first four titles—Ken Akamatsu's *Negima* and **CLAMP**'s *Tsubasa*—becoming the year's top two bestselling manga.

Addresses: *Office*— Random House, Inc., 1745 Broadway, New York, NY 10019. *Web Site*—http://www.randomhouse.com/delrey/manga.

DC Comics

DC Comics, founded in 1935, soared to prominence when it introduced the character Superman in 1938, followed not long after by Batman. In the years that followed, DC Comics has continued to develop the superhero genre. To keep its oldest characters—including The Flash, Wonder Woman, Green Lantern, the Justice League of America (JLA)—fresh, DC Comics employed a number of talented writers, including **Frank Miller** and **Chuck Dixon**. While the company remained best known for its iconic superheroes, it did not shy away from innovation and introduced such award-winning books as *Watchmen* by **Alan Moore** and Dave Gibbons and *Sandman* by **Neil Gaiman**.

Addresses: *Office*—DC Comics, 1700 Broadway, 7th Fl., New York, NY 10019-5905. *Web Site*—www.dccomics.com.

Fantagraphics

Starting with the publication of *The Comics Journal* in 1976, Fantagraphics Books has grown to become a leading publisher of comics and graphic novels. The publisher's focus has been on works that exhibited the high literary and artistic standards of literature, poetry, and historical and political writing. Among the notable creators published by Fantagraphics are R. Crumb, **Gilbert and Jaime Hernandez**, **Daniel Clowes**, **Joe Sacco**, and **Chris Ware**.

Addresses: *Office*—Fantagraphics Books, 7563 Lake City Way NE, Seattle, WA 98115. *Web Site*—http://www.fantagraphics.com.

Image Comics

Founded in 1992 by seven of Marvel Comics' best-selling artists, Image Comics quickly grew to become a powerhouse among comics publishers. Image made a name for itself publishing creator-owned works in almost every genre, most notably *Spawn* by **Todd McFarlane**, one of Image's original founders.

Addresses: *Office*—Image Comics, 1942 University Ave, Suite 305, Berkeley, CA 94704. *Web Site*—www.imagecomics.com.

Kodansha

Started in 1909 by Seiji Noma as a publisher of magazines, Kodansha Ltd. began publishing books in 1949 and has since grown to become one of the largest publishers in Japan. The company remains privately owned and managed by the Noma family. In Japan, Kodansha published the works of such manga creators as **CLAMP, Fuyumi Soryo, Kosuke Fujishima**, and **Miwa Ueda**, among others.

Addresses: *Office*—c/o Kodansha America, Inc., 575 Lexington Ave., New York, NY 10022. *Web Site*—www.kodansha.co.jp; English site: http://www.kodanclub.com.

Marvel Comics

Founded as Timely Comics in 1939, Marvel grew under the supervision of such influential editors as Stan Lee and Archie Goodwin to dominate the U.S. comics industry as one of the two largest publishers. Known for its superhero and action comics, Marvel Comics created its stories around its several thousand proprietary characters, including such superheroes as Spider-Man, X-Men, and the Fantastic Four. Among the many authors and artists who have worked for Marvel are **Garth Ennis, Mike Mignola, Grant Morrison**, and **Alex Ross**.

Addresses: *Office*—Marvel Entertainment, Inc., 417 5th Avenue, New York, NY 10016. *Web Site*—http://www.marvel.com.

Oni Press

Founded in 1997 by Bob Schreck and Joe Nozemack, Oni Press was created to publish comics for people who like to read. The books by Oni encompassed a wide range of genres including drama, romance, horror, and mystery by creators such as **Lea Hernendez, Ted Naifeh, J. Torres**, and **Andi Watson**.

Addresses: *Office*—Oni Press, 1305 SE MLK Blvd., Suite # A, Portland, OR 97214. *Web Site*—http://www.onipress.com.

Pantheon

A division of Random House, Pantheon published a range of graphic novels and memoirs by authors such as **Daniel Clowes, Matt Groening, Marjane Satrapi, Art Spiegelman, Alex Ross**, and **Chris Ware**. The entrance of Pantheon into graphic novel publishing was widely considered as a sign that the graphic novel had gained mainstream respect.

Addresses: *Office*—Random House, Inc., 1745 Broadway, New York, NY 10019. *Web Site*—http://www.randomhouse.com/pantheon/graphicnovels/home.html.

Slave Labor Graphics

Started in 1985 by Dan Kado, Slave Labor Graphics grew into SLG Publishing in order to publish comics and graphic novels for mature audiences under the imprint Slave Labor Graphics and those for younger audiences under the Amaze Ink imprint. In 1995 **Andi Watson** became the first creator to publish under the imprint Amaze Ink.

Addresses: *Office*—SLG Publishing, P.O. Box 26427, San Jose, CA 95159-6427. *Web Site*—http://www.slavelabor.com/index2.html.

TOKYOPOP

Founded by Stuart Levy in 1996, TOKYOPOP has become a leader in the publishing and distribution of manga and anime in the United States. TOKYOPOP publishes Japanese manga in English translation by such creators as **CLAMP** and **Yukiru Sugisaki**. In addition, TOKYOPOP has developed a number of manga created by English-language authors and artists. In 2006 TOKYOPOP introduce the first American manga comic strip to American newspapers with "Peach Fuzz."

Addresses: *Office*—TOKYOPOP, 5900 Wilshire Blvd., Ste. 2000, Los Angeles, CA 90036-5020. *Web Site*—www.tokyopop.com.

Top Shelf Productions

Founded in 1997 by Brent Warnock and Chris Staros, Top Shelf has gained a reputation for publishing thoughtful, even arty graphic novels for more mature readers; titles in this vein include *Blankets* by **Craig Thompson**, *The Barefoot Serpent* by **Scott Morse**, and *Tricked* by Alex Robinson. **Alan Moore**, best known for creating *Watchmen*, has also published some of his experimental work with Top Shelf.

Addresses: *Office*—Top Shelf Productions, PO Box 1282, Marietta, GA 30061-1282; Top Shelf Productions, PO Box 15125, Portland, OR 97293-5125. *Web Site*—www.topshelfcomix.com.

VIZ Media, LLC

Owned by three of Japan's leading manga and anime companies—Shueisha Inc., Shogakukan Inc., and Shogakukan Production Co., Ltd. (ShoPro Japan)—VIZ Media is one of the largest publishers and distributors of manga in English translation. Head-quartered in San Francisco, California, VIZ Media, publishes manga in graphic novels and such magazines as *Shonen Jump* and *Shojo Beat*. VIZ has translated and published the work of such Japanese creators as **Akira Toriyama**, **Hiroyuki Takei**, **Masashi Kishimoto**, and **Yu Watase**, among others. VIZ also distributes anime videos, DVDs, and audio soundtracks, and in 2005 became the first manga publisher to team up with a large U.S. distributor when it signed an agreement with Simon and Schuster.

Addresses: *Office*—VIZ Media, LLC, P.O. BOX 77010, San Francisco, CA 94107. *Web Site*—http://www.viz.com.

Words To Know

A

anime: Japanese animated cartoons on television or film, often based on manga.

C

coloring: A stage in the production of a comic book or graphic novel that involves adding color to the penciled and inked drawings. This stage can be accomplished by hand or with a computer.

comix: A term used to refer to underground comics, a branch of comic books that flourished in the 1960s and 1970s in reaction against mainstream comics and was more adult-oriented in its themes and subject matter.

creator-owned comic: A comic that is wholly owned by the comic creator, who retains all rights to licensing, movie reproduction, and future use. Creator-owned comics were created to escape the influence of major publishers who paid comic book creators a flat fee for their work, thus depriving creators from profits derived if their work became popular.

F

fan service: In manga, these are illustrations inserted into the story that do not have any relation to the narrative but are there as a service to fans of certain characters or elements in the story.

fanzine: An amateur magazine created by and circulated among fans of comics, movies, and television.

G

graphic album: The European, specifically French, equivalent of the graphic novel.

I

inking: A stage in the production of a comic book or graphic novel that involves tracing on top of pencil drawings with a brush or pen filled with India ink, usually black, in order to emphasize certain elements of the drawing.

L

lettering: A stage in the production of a comic book or graphic novel that involves adding word balloons and other letters to the drawn page. Lettering was once done solely by hand but is now often done on the computer.

M

manga: The Japanese equivalent for comic books; the literal translation of the term is "involuntary pictures." Unlike American comics, however, Japanese manga read from right to left on the page. It first became known for its immediately recognizable human characters with large eyes and small mouths and mechanized robot warriors.

manga-ka: A creator of manga, or Japanese comics.

P

penciling: An early stage in the production of a comic book or graphic novel that involves the creation of the initial drawings. Later stages include inking, lettering, and coloring.

S

sequential art: The combination of pictures and words to tell a story; this phrase is sometimes used in place of comic book.

shojo: A form of manga for girls that focuses on romance and relationships.

shonen: A form of manga for boys that focuses on action and adventure.

T

tankobon: The Japanese equivalent of a graphic novel, a tankobon typically brings together a manga series that has had initial success in magazine publication.

U•X•L Graphic Novelists

Joe Sacco. *Fantagraphics Books.*

■ ■ ■

Joe Sacco

Born October 2, 1960 (Malta)
Maltese author, illustrator, journalist

"The main benefit [to comics] is that you can make your subject very accessible. You open the book and suddenly you're in the place."

Joe Sacco is one of the leading proponents of the union between comic book art and journalism. His central theme is war, which he spotlights in his graphic novels. He is not concerned with combat heroics. Instead, he recounts the plights and fates of individuals caught up in the chaos of battle. He explores the personalities of those responsible for instigating war, but primarily he focuses on war's survivors, and how they get on with their lives while processing their memories of combat and killing.

Sacco's drawings are in black and white, which serves to accentuate the grim tone of his subject matter. Often appearing in his work is his own image, observing the activities around him. He draws himself with oversized lips and vacant eyes. More often than not, he looks bewildered or scared.

Best-Known Works

Graphic Novels

Spotlight on the Genius That Is Joe Sacco (1994).

Palestine: A Nation Occupied (1994).

War Junkie (1995).

Palestine: In the Gaza Strip (1996).

Safe Area Gorazde: The War in Eastern Bosnia 1992–95 (2000).

The Fixer: A Story of Sarajevo (2003).

Notes from a Defeatist (2003).

War's End: Profiles from Bosnia (2005).

"Mr. Sacco seeks to make complex political and historical conflicts understandable to a mass audience," observed Robert K. Elder, writing in the *New York Times* in 2000. Sacco explained to the *Guardian* the qualities comics offer: "The main benefit is that you can make your subject very accessible. You open the book and suddenly you're in the place. Maybe there's also a guilty pleasure as people think back to their childhood days reading comics and they think, 'This might be fun, it might be an easy way to learn something about this.' It's a very subversive medium, it's appealing but what's in the comic itself could be very hard, even difficult, material."

Indeed Sacco has used comics to offer up some tremendously difficult content. Rebecca Tuhus-Dubrow noted in the online *January Magazine* in 2003, "Like Art Spiegelman before him, Sacco uses comics to deliver familiar content in an unfamiliar form, disarming us of our numbness to images of war and privation. Visual novelty aside, Sacco's focus—preferring the anecdotal to the panoramic [specific tales versus wider scope]—excavates details that seldom make it to the news or the history books." Added Dave Gilson, writing in *Mother Jones* in 2005, "By presenting his first-hand reporting from hot spots like Gaza, Sarajevo, and Iraq in gritty black-and-white comics, Sacco has won over serious fans of comics and nonfiction alike... Sacco's work is often called 'comic journalism,' but that label doesn't fully capture how he's managed to simultaneously blend and defy both genres."

Early years form artistic sensibility

Joe Sacco was born on October 2, 1960, in Malta. His father was an engineer, and his mother was a teacher. He began drawing at age six, and throughout his childhood viewed art as a hobby. He was, however, fascinated by life and survival in war zones, with his interest sparked by his parents' reminiscences of the bombing of Malta during World War II (1939–45; war in which Great Britain, France, the Soviet Union, the United States, and their allied forces defeated Germany, Italy, and Japan).

In the early 1970s, Sacco and his parents came to the United States. They settled first in Los Angeles, and then relocated to Portland, Oregon. His adolescence was uneventful. "A lot of [underground comic book artists] spent their high school years feeling alone and alienated," he told *Time* magazine's Joel Stein. "I had pretty good teen years.... I was short and all, but I wasn't picked on."

Sacco graduated from the University of Oregon in 1981, where he majored in journalism. "I took one class in journalism school on cartoons, but it wasn't about drawing them so much as looking at them and appreciating them in some way," he told Howard Price, in an interview on the *Comic Book Resources* Web site. "We had a couple of exercises where we had to draw some things, but it wasn't a drawing class. I've never taken any art classes after junior high school."

Creates unique career in journalism

Sacco spent most of the 1980s working primarily as a writer, editor, and copy editor. Some of his jobs—writing for a journal published by the National Notary Association, for example—simply bored and frustrated him. Others—a stint with the magazine *The Comics Journal*—were more challenging. In 1983, he published several romance comics in his native Malta. In 1985 and 1986, he was one of the publishers and editors of the *Portland Permanent Press,* an alternative humor magazine. He also briefly edited *Centrifugal Bumble-Puppy,* a comics anthology.

Up to this point, Sacco was dissatisfied with the progress of his journalism career, and he decided to become a full-time cartoonist. In the late 1980s, he traveled through Europe with the rock band the Miracle Workers and recorded his experiences in sketches and words. He began writing and drawing *Yahoo,* a comics magazine published between 1988 and 1992. In *Yahoo,* Sacco put forth his views on a range of subjects. "In the Company of Long Hair" recalled his experiences while touring with the Miracle Workers. In "When Good Bombs Happen to Bad People," he recounted the history of aerial bombing that targets civilian populations.

Sacco had come to view himself not as an artist but as a journalist whose reportage consisted of words and images. He had long been dissatisfied with what he perceived as the narrow, one-dimensional manner in which the mainstream media reported on current events. His aim was to travel to, spend time in, and report on the sounds and sights of the world's hot spots. "The whole point of my life, or of my career anyway," he told Robert K. Elder of the *New York Times,* "is to get the general public interested. There's a cumulative hope that the more people know, the better the democracy is going to be."

Develops creative process

Through the years, Sacco developed his own research style. His primary task while traveling is to seek out unusual stories and form relationships with the individuals connected to the stories. He conducts countless interviews while taking notes and photographs and making rudimentary sketches. He told *January* magazine, "If I'm writing about the Middle East, I have to go there, and if possible, stay long enough to get a real feeling for what's going on." Upon arriving home, Sacco organizes his notes, writes his stories, and completes the bulk of his drawing. His primary influences range from the legendary underground comic artist R. Crumb (1943–), to writers George Orwell (1903–1950), the author of *Animal Farm* and *1984*, and Michael Herr, an acclaimed journalist who covered the war in Vietnam; to famed eccentric journalist Hunter S. Thompson (1937–2005).

Reports Palestinian plight

Sacco developed an interest in the Middle East and, for two months in 1991 and 1992, traveled to Jerusalem, the West Bank, and the Gaza Strip. This journey resulted in *Palestine,* a nine-part comic book series published in 1993, in which he scrutinizes the plight of Palestinians under Israeli occupation. Sacco spotlights the experiences and views of a range of refugees; some are cynical and radical, while others are more accepting of their situation. While offering their testimony, he adds his own personal observations.

With the publication of *Palestine,* Sacco won his first major acclaim. Gordon Flagg, writing in *Booklist* in 1996, dubbed the series "The first major work of comics journalism," adding that, "Although Sacco's sympathies, expressed through the first-person narration, are definitely with the Palestinians, the work overall is far too nuanced to be deemed propaganda [or material that is supposed to influence people's opinions]." *Palestine: A Nation Occupied,* consisting of stories from the first five issues of *Palestine,* was published in 1994. A follow-up, *Palestine: In the Gaza Strip,* featuring material from the final four issues, came out in 1996.

During this time, Sacco also began publishing compilations of his early work. One was *War Junkie,* a collection of short pieces in which he explores a range of themes, from the political (in which he spotlights the nature and effect of warfare) to the autobiographical (in which he recalls his European tour with the Miracle Workers). In particular, Sacco won praise for his war stories. *Publishers Weekly* called "More Women, More Children, More Quickly," an account of Sacco's mother's childhood memories of life in Malta during World War II, as "a tour de force, capturing the extraordinary hardship and terror experienced by a child caught in the midst of total war." In 2003, Sacco again reused much of this material in *Notes from a Defeatist,* another compilation.

Focuses on Bosnian War

After his experiences in the Middle East, Sacco was drawn to the civil war in Bosnia, where rival Muslims, Serbs, and Croats battled for control of this portion of the former nation of Yugoslavia. He traveled to the region during a four-week period in 1995 and 1996, when the war was in its final stages. Sacco embedded himself in Sarajevo, the Bosnian capital, where he spent time hanging out in bars and restaurants and forming relationships with the war's survivors. He also journeyed to Gorazde, a small town that was besieged by Serbian nationalists (devotion to the interests or culture of a specific nation) and was the locale for some of the war's most heated battles.

In 2000, 2003, and 2005, respectively, Sacco published three authoritative, highly acclaimed accounts of the war: *Safe Area Gorazde: The War in Eastern Bosnia 1992–95*; *The Fixer: A Story from Sarajevo*; and *War's End: Profiles from Bosnia*. In *Safe Area Gorazde*, he recounts the conflict through the reminiscences of his interviewees and explores how neighbors become enemies, all in the name of nationalism. His stories are wrought with irony, as he reports on the plight of starving adolescent girls who express their yearning for normalcy by imploring him to bring them Levi's 501 blue jeans. At its most vivid, his reportage charts genocidal massacres perpetrated on Bosnians by Serbian nationalists.

Time labeled *Safe Area Gorazde* an "epic comic book," adding, "Like Art Spiegelman's *Maus*, Sacco's book juxtaposes the pop style of comics with human tragedy, making the brutality of war all the more jarring." "Who would have imagined that the best dramatic evocation of the Bosnian catastrophe would turn out to be a book-length comic strip written by an American of Maltese origin who arrived in the Balkans only in late 1995, after the shooting had largely stopped, and stayed just four weeks?" observed David Rieff in the *New York Times Book Review*. "And yet Joe Sacco...has produced a work that improbably manages to combine rare insight into what the war in Bosnia felt like on the ground with a mature and nuanced political and historical understanding of the conflict."

Offers unique perspectives

The Fixer: A Story from Sarajevo is the real-life account of Neven, a Sarajevo native and former soldier and guerilla fighter who escorts Westerners through the war-torn region. Sacco had worked with Neven while researching *Safe Area Gorazde* and came to realize that the guide's own multifaceted life was substance for a graphic novel. "He's an interesting character," Sacco told *Publishers Weekly*, "and using him allowed me to tell the story of how journalists often have to rely on totally uncreditable people who have their own agendas. It's a story that isn't told very much. The book makes it clear that you can never trust Neven, you can never know what's really true. He's not a sympathetic character but he can be a poignant character." In its review of *The Fixer*, *Publishers Weekly* observed that "Sacco marvelously weaves in his own feelings of uneasiness and awe at his guide's grim life story . . . Sacco's finely wrought, expressively rendered b&w drawings perfectly capture the emotional character of Sarajevo and the people who struggle to live there."

War's End: Profiles from Bosnia consists of two war stories, "Christmas with Karadzic," in which Sacco and other journalists attempt to interview the infamous Serbian leader and war criminal Radovan Karadzic (1945–), and "Soba," in which a Sarajevo-born artist and ex-soldier attempts to deal with his recollections of the horrors of war. Reviewers praised the work's brutal honesty and Andrew D. Arnold, author of a long-standing column on graphic novels for *Time* magazine, added that Sacco's "Hogarthian black-and-white images and vibrant characterizations make for some of the most vivid and dramatic comics being published today."

For More Information

Periodicals

Armstrong, Rebecca. "Drawn to Slaughter; What Drives Joe Sacco to War? Why Would a Guy 'Who Just Likes Drawing Stuff' Risk Everything for a Comic Book? And Can We, Asks Rebecca Armstrong, Really Trust Him?" *Independent* (November 7, 2004).

Arnold, Andrew D. "5 Fantastic Graphic Novels: These Books Are Topical, Complex and Well Written. They're Also Illustrated." *Time* (June 13, 2005).

Bennett, Kathleen E. "Joe Sacco's *Palestine*: Where Comics Meets Journalism." *Stranger* (1994). Also available online at http://www.info goddess.com/comix/joe.sacco.int.html (accessed on January 10, 2006).

Blincoe, Nicholas. "Cartoon Wars: By Dramatising Events in Comic-Book Form, Joe Sacco's *Palestine* Exposes the Fantasy of the Israeli Occupation." *New Statesman* (January 6, 2003).

Campbell, Duncan. "I Do Comics, not Graphic Novels: Whether He's Depicting War Crimes in Bosnia or Musing on Palestinian Tea, Joe Sacco Is One of the Most Original Cartoonists Working Today." *Guardian* (October 23, 2003).

Elder, Robert K. "The Agony in Bosnia, Frame by Comic Book Frame." *New York Times* (October 18, 2000).

Flagg, Gordon. "Palestine: In the Gaza Strip." *Booklist* (January 1, 1996).

Flagg, Gordon. "War's End: Profiles from Bosnia." *Booklist* (June 1, 2005).

Gilson, Dave. "Joe Sacco: The Art of War." *Mother Jones* (July-August 2005).

Jefferson, Margo. "No Frigate Like a Book." *New York Times Book Review* (September 1, 2002).

Reid, Calvin. "Joe Sacco, Comics Journalist." *Publishers Weekly* (November 24, 2003).

Rieff, David. "Bosnia Beyond Words: Joe Sacco Recalls the Horrors of the Balkans in a Comic-Book Format." *New York Times Book Review* (December 24, 2000).

Stein, Joel. "What's Going On? Joe Sacco's *Safe Area Gorazde* Is a Comic-Book Look at a Horrible War." *Time* (May 1, 2000).

"The Fixer: A Story from Sarajevo." *Publishers Weekly* (November 24, 2003).

"War Junkie." *Publishers Weekly* (June 12, 1995).

Web Sites

Groth, Gary. "Joe Sacco, Frontline Journalist." *The Comics Journal.* http://www.tcj.com/aa02ws/i_sacco.html (accessed on May 3, 2006).

Price, Howard. "Joe Sacco Interview." *CBR.* http://www.comicbookresources.com/news/newsitem.cgi?id=618 (accessed on May 3, 2006).

Tuhus-Dubrow, Rebecca. "Joe Sacco." *January Magazine.* http://www.januarymagazine.com/profiles/jsacco.html (accessed on May 3, 2006).

Yoshiyuki Sadamoto

Born January 29, 1962 (Tokushima, Japan)
Japanese author, illustrator

Yoshiyuki Sadamoto is the internationally acclaimed character designer and author of the *Neon Genesis Evangelion* manga series, an adaptation of the hugely popular anime series of the same name. Like so much of the story he has been charged with converting to print, Sadamoto is somewhat mysterious. Little is known about him, and the author's notes that he contributes to some of the manga volumes are deliberately vague and mysterious. With the success of his manga series, and the growing popularity of his other works in Japan, it may be that Sadamoto will become much better known in years to come.

"They say that a story's hero will serve as a mirror by which you may always see the artist. And I'm not saying it isn't true. It's just, you know, sometimes it's more like a funhouse mirror."

Helps found Gainax

Yoshiyuki Sadamoto was born on January 29, 1962, in Tokushima, Japan, a seaport on Shikoku Island, southeast of Tokyo. He attended Tokyo Zokei University, an innovative university established in 1966. The university was founded to promote Zokei, the idea that art and design should be synthesized and integrated with fast-changing technological developments in modern culture. Around 1980, while he was a university student, Sadamoto joined with several of his friends—Hideaki Anno, Takami Akai, and Shinji Higuchi—to form an animation studio called Daicon Film. The students introduced their first anime (animated cartoon) in 1981, but it was a rough effort. In 1983, they introduced a more polished work at the 22nd annual Japan National Science Fiction Convention. They began to gain attention and work, and were known for producing short films that parodied some of the other trends in Japanese anime, especially the mechanized robot shows that were popular in Japan. In 1985, the anime studio changed its name to Gainax.

Best-Known Works

Graphic Novels

Neon Genesis Evangelion. 9 vols. 1996–2004 (Japanese); 2002–04 (English).

Other

Der Mond: Newtype Illustrated Collection (2000).

Sadamoto has also provided character design for a variety of anime, manga, and video projects, including *Wings of Honneamise, Nadia: The Secret of Blue Water, FLCL, .hack/SIGN, .hack/GU,* and *Gunbuster 2.*

Over the years, Gainax has produced a number of anime works, including television series and feature films. Among its early popular works are *Wings of Honneamise,* a feature-length film released in 1987, and *Nadia: The Secret of Blue Water,* a 39-episode television series that appeared in Japan in 1990 and 1991. Gainax soared in popularity with the television series *Shin Seiki Evangelion,* which was directed by Anno based on characters that were created and drawn by Sadamoto. *Shin Seiki Evangelion* (which became *Neon Genesis Evangelion* when it was translated for English-speaking audiences) aired from fall 1995 to spring 1996 and was later replayed, becoming hugely popular among teenagers and adults. It formed the basis for the manga versions that would come later.

In the United States, those involved with a hugely popular television series like *Shin Seiki Evangelion* would be interviewed on television and profiled in magazines. In Japanese culture, however, it is customary for people not to divulge details about their personal lives. For this reason, relatively little is known about Sadamoto, and that which is known is somewhat mysterious. Some of the best sources for information about an author are the notes in the back of manga volumes, but even those can be obscure. For example, in the note by Sadamoto in *Neon Genesis Evangelion,* Volume 8, he writes: "They say that a story's hero will serve as a mirror by which you may always see the artist. And I'm not saying it isn't true. It's just, you know, sometimes it's more like a funhouse mirror." He goes on to tell a story about his mother finding out that he has stolen from her purse and tying him to a foundation pole in a half-built house in his neighborhood so that everyone would know what he had done. In a similar note in the back of

Volume 9 of the series, he writes: "I admit I have an unfathomable fascination with romance—and whether your object of affection be a pop star on TV or a two-dimensional drawing, you may count upon the pitiful genetic programming of that degenerate creature called man to rise to the fore. Hence my careless life of cars, women, and manga." Fans of his work who wish to know more about the author have been left to debate the meaning of such vague comments. Perhaps as intended, the focus must be on the work, not the author.

From anime to manga

The appearance of *Shin Seiki Evangelion* on Japanese television in the mid-1990s created a sensation, for a variety of reasons. For the previous five years, the more popular anime had moved away from distinctly Japanese styles and closer to American cartoons. *Shin Seiki Evangelion* returned to more traditional Japanese styles, featuring mecha (or mechanized robots controlled by humans), extensive exploration of characters' emotions, and people drawn with angular bodies and spiky hair. *Shin Seiki Evangelion* was also unique in its treatment of psychological issues. Director and creator Hideaki Anno (1960–) had spent time in therapy for depression, and the series was filled with characters who battled depression or a sense of isolation from others, and who struggled to develop a better understanding for their friends. Finally, the series drew on a variety of symbols not typically seen in Japanese anime. Anno used Christian imagery, such as the cross and characters called Adam and Eva, as well as symbols from the Jewish faith. Fans of the series have debated whether these religious symbols were crucial to understanding the story, providing clues to deeper meaning; or whether they were used on a superficial basis, simply to add to the multiple layers of mystery that made the series so popular.

The plot of the series is complicated. The story is set in the year 2015, fifteen years after a global catastrophe destroyed much of Earth's population. In Tokyo-3, built on the remnants of the original city, a group of teenage students—all born after the disaster—are trained to operate giant robotic mechanisms called Evangelions, or Evas, and to do battle against giant alien Angels. But who are the Angels, and what is the ultimate goal of the mysterious group leading the fight against them? This remains uncertain. The last two episodes of the original television series left many viewers confused, even angry. Were the humans on Earth destined to merge into a single, all-powerful soul, or were they to maintain their individuality? In 1997, Gainax released films offering answers to the mysterious ending, *Death and Rebirth* and *The End of Evangelion,* but these only stirred up more debate.

The controversy and mystery helped make a huge success of *Evangelion.* In fact, the series has been called "one of the most influential and controversial series in the history of Japanese animation," by NPR radio host Madeleine Brand on *All Things Considered.* Sadamoto begin working on the manga, or print, version of the story soon after the anime version first aired. In Japan, manga titles are first issued in the wildly popular weekly and monthly magazines, and later collected into *tankōbon,* which bring together all the stories in a series. Sadamoto's version of the *Evangelion* story was issued in nine volumes in Japan. By September 1997, individual episodes of the series were being published, under the title *Neon Genesis Evangelion,* in the United States and Great Britain. Beginning in 2002, Viz Communications took advantage of the booming popularity of manga in English-speaking markets and began to release graphic novels that mirrored the nine volumes of *tankōbon* published in Japan. These graphic novels were hugely popular in the United States, and the original television series first appeared on U.S. television as several isolated episodes in 2003 and then in its complete run in the fall of 2005.

Neon Genesis Evangelion, manga style

Sadamoto's version of *Neon Genesis Evangelion* was directly based on the TV series, but Sadamoto brought a different sensibility to the story. The setup was the same: teenage students were tapped by NERV, a paramilitary organization, to train on and pilot 120-foot-tall biomechanical fighting units, known as Evas. The main character in the series is Shinji Ikari, whose father, Gendo Ikari, is the supreme commander of NERV. He is joined early on by two female pilots, Rei Ayanami, a beautiful albino student who is curiously distant, and Asuka Langley Soryu, whose feisty personality is a mask for her loneliness and misery. Later, Shinji's friend Toji Suzuhara also becomes a pilot, as does the mysterious "fifth child," Kaworu Nagisa, a boy who bears a striking resemblance to Rei Ayanami. Rounding out the cast are Major Misato Katsuragi, a NERV leader who shares an apartment with Shinji, and several of Shinji's friends from school.

Sadamoto's story displays a near-perfect balance between the various elements of manga. He is a skilled designer of mecha, and the various manga and enemy Angels are shown with great detail when they are sitting still and in a range of dynamic action scenes. Sadamoto also shows a sure hand with humor: in Volume 3, for example, Toji gives Shinji a hard time for staring at Rei and Shinji gets him back by stuffing his fingers up Toji's nostrils. Silly teen antics like this occur throughout the series, helping to lighten a mood that sometimes grows heavy. Sadamoto's real strength, however, lies with characterization. Though those new to manga often complain that all the characters look alike, Sadamato creates characters with distinct physical appearances: Shinji has mussed black hair and has a worried look on his face, for example, while Rei, depicted on color covers with pale white skin, light blue hair, and red eyes, nearly always bears a blank look on her face, which makes her rare moments of emotion all the more striking.

In the end, the teen pilots who are at the center of the book share an emotional bond: all have lost their mothers in mysterious circumstances, and all face feelings of pain and sadness as a result. Shinji's pain is compounded by the fact that his father, who commands all of the Eva pilots, seems to not care for him at all. In Volume 5, Shinji finds his father standing at his mother's grave and tries to talk to him. But his father rebuffs the attempt, telling his son: "Don't try to think we can understand each other....People are such sad creatures." All the characters, teens and adults, share the fatalism that comes from living in a society where mysterious and powerful Angels threaten the future of life on Earth. This sense that their life may be cut short sometimes pushes the characters to be more open about their feelings than they otherwise might. In Volume 6, for example, Shinji urges Asuka to tell Mr. Kaji that she loves him, reminding her that "there's no telling what might happen to us tomorrow." With his depictions of teenage crushes, sadness, friendships, anger, and humor, Sadamoto manages to convey the complexity of the issues facing the characters.

Beginning with Volume 5 of *Neon Genesis Evangelion*, Sadamoto began to take the story in a direction that was different from the anime version. Fans of the series were thrilled to see that one of the show's original creators might offer an alternative ending, and in an endnote to Volume 9 manga scholar Carl Gustav Horn noted that Sadamoto himself had suggested that the manga series might run to twelve volumes. However, the last volume to be published, Volume 9, came out in 2004; by the end of 2005, there was no indication that another volume was coming.

American readers (or perhaps their parents) initially may be shocked by some aspects of *Neon Genesis Evangelion*. Several scenes, for example, include both male and female nudity. Also, characters regularly use more mature language than is expected for their age. In general, Japanese culture tends to be more permissive about showing the human body and allowing swearing in literature for young readers. Many manga readers have become accustomed to these and other conventions imported from across the Pacific.

Beyond *Neon Genesis Evangelion*

Neon Genesis Evangelion is not Sadamoto's only work, just the only manga work to be translated into English. He has been involved in character design for numerous projects released in Japan by Gainax over the years, including *FLCL* and *Gunbuster 2*. The project that is most likely preventing Sadamoto from continuing the *Neon Genesis Evangelion* saga, however, is *.hack*, a series of anime shows and video games that explore a world in which a computer virus cripples the Internet and a mysterious new Internet emerges to capture the attention of millions around the world—and to trap many within its virtual reality. Sadamoto's status as a rising star in the Japanese art world was confirmed in 2000 with the release of *Der Mond*, a lavish, full-color collection of Sadamoto's artwork from *Evangelion* and several other series. Though such a work is not uncommon in Japan, where manga and anime art is extremely popular, the issuing of an English translation of the work in 2001 was a clear sign that Sadamoto's stardom had reached well beyond the shores of his native land.

For More Information

Books
Sadamoto, Yoshiyuki. *Neon Genesis Evangelion*. 9 vols. San Francisco, CA: Viz, 2002–04.

Periodicals
Raiteri, Steve. *Library Journal* (January 2003): p. 85.

Web Sites
Era, Ikiria. "Breaks the Familiar Formula." *Comicreaders.com: Manga*. http://www.comicreaders.com/modules.php?name=News&file=article&sid=1515 (accessed on May 3, 2006).

Gainax. http://www.gainax.co.jp/ (accessed on May 3, 2006).

.hack. http://www.dothack.com (accessed on May 3, 2006).

Roberts, Alison L. "Yoshiuko Sadamoto's *Der Mond*." *Absolute Zero*. http://www.absolute-0.com/art_manga/der_mond.htm (accessed on May 3, 2006).

"Yoshiyuki Sadamoto." *Anime News Network*. http://www.animenewsnetwork.com/encyclopedia/people.php?id=17 (accessed on May 3, 2006).

Other
Brand, Madeleine. "Two New DVD Releases of *Neon Genesis Evangelion*" (transcript). *All Things Considered*. National Public Radio (March 19, 2004).

Stan Sakai. *Courtesy of Stanley Sakai.*

Stan Sakai

Born May 25, 1953 (Kyoto, Japan)
American author, illustrator

"Working on an independent comic gives me total control of all aspects of the creation."

Stan Sakai created the award-winning American comic series *Usagi Yojimbo,* about an anthropomorphic (humanlike) rabbit samurai who hires himself out as a bodyguard during a difficult, dangerous period in seventeenth-century Japan. Based on the life of a real Japanese swordsman, Miyamoto Musashi, *Usagi Yojimbo* has garnered Sakai a great deal of respect in the comics industry for his in-depth research and dedication to the craft. Over the more than two decades since beginning his series, Sakai has won praise from international organizations for his accurate depictions of Japanese history and for the quality of his work, yet the series is not translated into Japanese, nor is it written in the style of Japanese manga. Sakai's *Usagi Yojimbo* is a uniquely Western-style comic. Indeed, Sakai's career is firmly rooted in American comics; he is the award-winning inker for Sergio Aragonés's *Groo the Wander* series, the longest-running humorous comic series in history.

Best-Known Works

Graphic Novels

Usagi Yojimbo: Summer Special #1 (1986).

Usagi Yojimbo Book 1: The Ronin (1987).

Usagi Yojimbo Book 2: Samurai (1989).

Usagi Yojimbo Book 3: The Wanderers Road (1989).

Usagi Yojimbo Book 4: Dragon Bellow Conspiracy (1990).

Usagi Yojimbo Book 5: Lone Goat and Kid (1992).

Usagi Yojimbo Book 6: Circles (1994).

Usagi Yojimbo Book 7: Gen's Story (1997).

Usagi Yojimbo Book 8: Shades of Death (1997).

Space Usagi (1998).

Usagi Yojimbo Book 9: Daisho (1998).

Usagi Yojimbo Book 10: Brink of Life and Death (1998).

Usagi Yojimbo Book 11: Seasons (1999).

Usagi Yojimbo Book 12: Grasscutter (1999).

Usagi Yojimbo Book 13: Grey Shadows (2000).

Usagi Yojimbo Book 14: Demon Mask (2001).

Usagi Yojimbo Book 15: Grasscutter II (2002).

Usagi Yojimbo Book 16: The Shrouded Moon (2003).

Usagi Yojimbo Book 17: Duel at Kitanoji (2003).

Usagi Yojimbo Book 18: Travels with Jotaro (2004).

Usagi Yojimbo Book 19: Fathers and Sons (2005).

Blends Japanese and American cultures

Sakai's blending of Western sensibilities with Japanese culture is easily traced to his upbringing. Stan Sakai was born in Kyoto, Japan on May 23, 1953. His father, Akio Sakai, was a *nisei*, a second-generation Japanese American born in Hawaii, who served in the U.S. military and was stationed in Kyoto after World War II (1939–45; war in which Great Britain, France, the Soviet Union, the United States, and their allied forces defeated Germany, Italy, and Japan). He married Teruko, a Japanese woman; Stan was their second son, and he and his older brother call themselves *sansei*, third-generation Japanese Americans. Three years after Stan was born, the Sakai family moved back to Honolulu, Hawaii, and he grew up in Kaimuki.

In Hawaii, the Japanese American community, which comprised about half of Hawaii's population at that time, was strong and vibrant. There were Japanese stores and restaurants in the neighborhood, the Kapahulu Theater showed Japanese movies (the theater offered samurai movies every Saturday afternoon), one of the local television stations showed Japanese programs, and several radio stations offered Japanese programming. Along with the Japanese American culture, Hawaii offered a wide variety of cultures from the indigenous and other immigrant groups, so Sakai's early life was rich with various languages, foods, music, and customs.

Like many *nisei* and *sansei,* Sakai grew up speaking mostly English, although he did attend Japanese language school in eighth grade. He loved watching the Japanese movies, especially the *chambara,* the samurai action films. He also liked some of the television programs aired for children in the early 1960s, such as *Kaze Kozo* (a series about a boy ninja) and anime (animated manga) such as *Princess Knight* (a series done by **Osamu Tezuka** [1928–1989; see entry]). Sakai also counted Akira Kurosawa's *The Seven Samurai* (1954) among his favorite movies, citing later in life that Kurosawa's (1910–1998) epic scope on screen dramatically influenced his own art.

Sets sights on a career in comics

Sakai recalled fond memories of reading comic books. He told Karon Flage of *Sequential Tart,* "I always read comics, even when my parents threw out my comic book collection." He and his older brother especially enjoyed *The Fantastic Four* and *Spider-Man.* The vivid combination of art and adventure inspired Sakai and his brother to draw their own comics, and Sakai would later note Steve Ditko, who did the art on *Spider-Man* and other Marvel titles, as another strong influence on his own art. Sakai told Flage, "When I realized people actually made a living doing comics, I knew what I wanted to be when I grew up."

Sakai took a roundabout route to a career in comics, however. In high school, he took the usual college preparatory classes, Japanese language classes, and a single art class during his sophomore year. He graduated in June 1971, and he then attended the University of Hawaii at Manoa, where he majored in drawing and painting. He graduated in spring 1975 with a bachelor of fine arts degree. In 1977, he married Sharon Ota, a friend since elementary school; they had two children, Hannah and Mark. After college, Sakai worked as a production manager for a silk screening company. When the company moved to Pasadena, California, he and Sharon transferred there.

In Pasadena, Sakai began working toward a different career. From 1978 to 1980, he attended the Art Center College of Design in Pasadena as a part-time student. He started to work as a free-lance artist after leaving the silk screening company, doing book illustrations, magazine advertising, album covers, anything to keep working. In the early 1980s, comics fanzines (fan-produced magazines and amateur publication associations (APAs) flourished, and Sakai submitted stories to various fanzines and APAs just to get published.

Sakai's entrance into the comics industry came when he met **Sergio Aragonés** (1937–; see entry) a comic artist working for *Mad* magazine. While teaching a class about calligraphy in the early 1980s, Sakai displayed a talent that caught the eye of Aragonés, who hired Sakai to do the lettering for his new comic book series *Groo the Wanderer.* They became good friends, and Sakai noted Aragonés as another major influence on him, not just for art, but for the way he would research a topic before doing a story. *Groo* was a humorous comic series about a Conan-type barbarian (but even less intelligent), yet Aragonés took story details seriously. Sakai was still doing the lettering for *Groo* in 2005.

Develops his own comic

After several attempts at publishing various comic creations, Sakai finally landed a contract in 1984, when Steve Gallacci published Sakai's first comic story featuring his Usagi Yojimbo character in the anthology *Albedo Anthropomorphics.* Sakai based his character on a real-life swordsman from Japanese history: Miyamoto Musashi (c. 1584–1645). Musashi lived at the beginning of the Tokugawa Era in the seventeenth century. Sakai was inspired by a number of Japanese movies about Musashi, in particular the *Samurai Trilogy,* directed by Hiroshi Inagaki (1905–1980), which chronicled Musashi's transformation from farmer to master swordsman to philosopher. Musashi was a farmer who studied the way of the sword and became a feared assassin. The turmoil of his life led Musashi to seek inner peace, and he became a philosopher, artist, and author. His *The Book of Five Rings* is hailed as a masterpiece on samurai strategy.

Usagi Yojimbo becomes an epic tale of a masterless samurai and his journey to inner peace. Usagi Yojimbo starts the series as the bodyguard to Lord Mifune, but upon the lord's death becomes a masterless samurai who wanders the countryside offering protection to various people that he meets and honing his efforts toward

Factually Based Characters

The host of characters Stan Sakai introduces in *Usagi Yojimbo* over the years have been based on careful research, and many are patterned after true historical figures. While Sakai's humanlike characters are dramatic themselves, the people on whom they are based are some of the most colorful characters from Japanese history and popular culture. Tomoe Ame, Sakai's female cat warrior, is based on Tomoe Gozen, a famed female warrior who lived in the twelfth century during the Gempei War (Japan's civil war). Tomoe was the spouse of Lord Kiso Yoshinaka, and when they were cornered by an enemy army in Uji Province (outside Kyoto) it was she who jumped on her horse, attacked the opposing army, and cut off the general's head. Sakai has noted that the name for the character also comes from a favorite Japanese candy called Tomoe Ame.

Lord Hikiji is based on Date Masamune, a powerful lord who lived around the turn of the seventeenth century. He aspired to become Shogun (a samurai general) himself, and sent the first delegation of samurai to Europe. Other characters are based on characters from Japanese popular culture: Lone Goat and Kid are based on **Kazou Koike's** (1936–; see entry) Lone Wolf and Cub, Ogami Itto and his son Daigoro, who starred in several popular movies and in their own manga series in Japan. Zato-Ino, the blind swordspig, is based on one of the most popular Japanese movie characters, Zato-Ichi, the blind swordsman who targets his opponent through using only his keen hearing. Gennosuke Murakami, or Gen, the bounty hunter, is based on the Japanese actor Toshiro Mifune (1920–1997) made famous in the movie *Yojimbo*; Sakai drew Gen to behave just like the movie character, down to his constant beard shadow, the way he scratches himself under his kimono, and the way he manipulates people and events.

inner fulfillment. Throughout the series, Sakai introduces many characters that are based on real people.

Sakai based Usagi Yojimbo on a real person; however he drew his character not as a man, but as a rabbit. The idea came to him when he was doodling around, trying to get the look of the character. He particularly liked one of his drawings of a rabbit with its ears tied into a *chonmage*, the samurai's topknot. Rabbits feature prominently in Japanese folklore and legends, so Sakai decided to stick with the rabbit, which he named Miyamoto Usagi (*usagi* is the Japanese word for rabbit). Sakai decided to draw his other characters as animals too. As he explained to Flage in *Sequential Tart*: "Using anthropomorphic characters gives me more freedom in writing as well as art. I base the stories in feudal Japan but they are written with a Western perspective. I don't think I could do this if I was using human characters."

Following the example of his friend Sergio Aragonés, Sakai researched the history and culture of Japan during the Tokugawa Era, which lasted from 1600 to 1868. While the stories are fictional, the background is deeply rooted in history, which Sakai reinterprets for Western readers. Sakai's research into Japan's culture and history resulted in many fascinating background details in his stories, including seaweed farming, kite-making (Sakai said that research took two years), sword-making, pottery-making, and also various ghost legends. He told Jennifer Contino of *The Pulse*, "Believe me, the readers watch that the research is right. The story *Demon Mask* involved Usagi playing a game of Go. I got that game confused with Go-Moku, a game I played as a kid and which we called Go. They both use the same game board and pieces but the strategies are different. I heard about that mistake in e-mails from as far away as Germany. I bought a couple of books on Go, looked up the American Go Association, went to a tournament, talked to some players, and corrected that mistake when it was reprinted in the trade collection." Sakai's attention to research and the incorporation of so many historical and cultural details in his stories has led to use of his books in school curricula; the University of Portland selected one of Sakai's *Usagi Yojimbo* stories as a resource on samurai culture in its Japanese history classes.

Develops a fan base

As Sakai developed *Usagi Yojimbo* into an ongoing series, he bounced from one publisher to another. Seattle-based Fantagraphics first signed Sakai to write *Usagi Yojimbo* as a continuing comics series. When Fantagraphics decided to focus on publishing only adult-oriented material in 1996, Sakai took *Usagi Yojimbo* to Mirage Studios, the publisher of the popular *Teenage Mutant Ninja Turtles* comics. Mirage published a couple of years' worth of comics issues of *Usagi Yojimbo* as well as Sakai's *Space Usagi,* a mini-series about a descendant of Usagi Yojimbo living in the far future. The publisher then shut down the publications division, and Sakai began working with Dark Horse Comics.

In 1998, Dark Horse published all of the Mirage Studios issues of *Usagi Yojimbo* and *Space Usagi.* The group started to publish a limited series of *Usagi Yojimbo* comics, but decided instead to make

Sakai's *Space Usagi* was a miniseries about a descendant of Usagi Yojimbo living in the far future. *Dark Horse Comics.*

it a continuing series. In 2004, Sakai and Dark Horse Comics celebrated the twentieth anniversary of *Usagi Yojimbo* with a deluxe hardcover book, *The Art of Usagi Yojimbo.* Throughout the series' more than two decades of publication, Sakai has maintained total creative control over his work; the only thing he doesn't do with

Usagi Yojimbo is coloring, which is handled by long-time colleague and friend Tom Luth (1954–), who also colors *Groo*.

Usagi Yojimbo has been translated into about a dozen languages, including Croatian, but it has never been translated into Japanese. As Sakai told Cecelia Goodnow of the *Seattle Post-Intelligencer,* "There has never been an American comic book that has made a dent in the Japanese market." While *Usagi Yojimbo* is set in Japan, it follows the stylistic and storytelling conventions of American comics. Some readers and librarians have mistakenly called *Usagi Yojimbo* manga, but it isn't.

Receives high praise

Sakai's work has been honored with the Eisner Award, the highest honor in the comics industry, numerous times. His first Eisner Award nominations for *Usagi Yojimbo* and for his lettering work on *Groo* came in 1993. And they kept coming: he was nominated for Eisner Awards, mostly for Lettering and Best Writer/Artist, in 1993, 1994, 1995, 1997, 2000, 2002, 2004, and 2005. In 1996, he won Eisner Awards for Best Lettering for *Groo* and *Usagi Yojimbo,* and for Talent Deserving of Wider Recognition for *Usagi Yojimbo.* He won another Eisner Award in 1999 for Best Serialized Story for *Usagi Yojimbo* issues 13–22, the *Grasscutter* storyline.

Other awards were also heaped on him. In 1990, Sakai received a Parent's Choice Approval award for "Skillful weaving of facts and legends into his work," and the foundation recommended *Usagi Yojimbo* for ages seven and up. The Parent's Choice Foundation is a nonprofit organization dedicated to evaluating books, movies, software, and other media to determine their suitability for children. In 1991, the San Diego Comic-Con International gave Sakai the Inkpot Award for Lifetime Achievement in the Field of Cartooning. In 2002, he won a Reuben Award for Best Comic Book from the National Cartoonists Society, and that year the Young Adult Library Services Association's Popular Paperbacks Committee selected *Usagi Yojimbo Vol. 12: Grasscutter* for its Graphic Novels list.

Sakai has received international awards from other countries: He won the Spanish Haxtur Award in 1999 for Best Short Story for the "Noodles" storyline in *Usagi Yojimbo,* and for the *Grasscutter* storyline he won the Haxtur for Best Script in 2000. The Utopia Comic Book Convention in Mexico City held its first convention in November 2003 and created the Silver Pen Award; Sakai was among the first winners that year.

Continues to enjoy his work

Asked if he had ever thought about giving up on writing *Usagi Yojimbo*, Sakai told Karon Flage of *Sequential Tart*: "I have never felt that way. Nor have I ever thought of taking a hiatus from the series. I do everything, so I can vary the kind of stories that I want to tell. I can do mysteries then switch to a fantasy with ghosts and monsters then do a historical drama. After more than 16 years, I'm still never bored with Usagi." He told Cecelia Goodnow that Usagi has "matured as a warrior and a person. I've matured, too." Fans didn't tire of the story either; all of the *Usagi Yojimbo* trade volumes were continuously being reprinted through 2005.

In addition to his work on *Usagi Yojimbo*, Sakai kept himself busy with other projects as well. He has written and illustrated some shorter works, most notably the illustration work for the backup story "Riblet," for Jeff Smith's *Stupid, Stupid Rat Tails*, a *Bone* prequel volume. He also wrote and illustrated "Urchins," a story about young Anakin Skywalker, in *Star Wars Tales #14*, published by Dark Horse Comics in December 2002. One book that Sakai would like to publish is *Nilson Groundthumper*, one of his first stories, in which Usagi originally appeared as a secondary character. He told *Graphic Novelists* that if he ever has time, he might try to work on this story again. In 2005, he was still lettering *Groo the Wanderer* for Sergio Aragonés and the *Spider-Man* Sunday comic strips that Stan Lee had been writing for more than twenty years. He told Flage, "Lettering is actually relaxing in many ways. It is more mechanical than creative and uses another part of my brain. I guess it proves the whole left brain/right brain theory. Anyway, I enjoy lettering and it lets me work with terrific creators such as Sergio, Mark Evanier, and Stan Lee." An easygoing and humble man, Sakai also spent a lot of time going to schools and libraries to promote reading and to talk with children and teens about comics.

■ ■ ■

For More Information

Periodicals
Kan, Katharine. "Graphically Speaking: An Interview with Stan Sakai." *Voice of Youth Advocates* (April 2003).

Web Sites
Chun, Gary C. W. "A Man and His Samurai Rabbit" (July 15, 2001). *Honolulu Star-Bulletin*. http://starbulletin.com/2001/07/15/features/story6.html (accessed on May 3, 2006).

Contino, Jennifer. "Yojimbos, Rabbits, & Legends: Nineteen Years and Three Publishers Later, Usagi Yojimbo Is Still Going Strong" (February 6, 2003). *The Pulse.* http://www.livejournal.com/users/usagigaijin/10780.html (accessed on May 3, 2006).

Epstein, Daniel Robert. "Stan Sakai Talks Usagi Yojimbo" (2005). *Underground Online Comics Channel.* http://www.ugo.com/channels/comics/features/stansakai/default.asp (accessed on May 3, 2006).

Flage, Karon. "The Way of the Samurai: Stan Sakai" (March 2001). *Sequential Tart.* http://www.sequentialtart.com/archive/mar01/sakai.shtml (accessed on May 3, 2006).

Goodnow, Cecelia. "Usagi Yojimbo Creator Comes Back to Where It All Began" (October 3, 2005). *Seattle Post-Intelligencer.* http://seattlepi.nwsource.com/books/242952_sakai03.html (accessed on May 3, 2006).

Moondaughter, Wolfen. "'Bun' Anniversaire! Stan Sakai" (October 2004). *Sequential Tart.* http://www.sequentialtart.com/archive/oct04/ssakai.shtml (accessed on May 3, 2006).

"Stan Sakai." *Usagi Yojimbo Dojo: Stan Sakai.* http://usagiyojimbo.com/sakai.html (accessed on May 3, 2006).

Thompson, Kim. "Stan Sakai Interview" (Fall 1996). *The Comics Journal #192.* http://www.groo.com/sakaiint2.html (accessed on May 3, 2006).

Other

Additional material for this entry was obtained through an e-mail interview with Stan Sakai on October 21, 2005.

Marjane Satrapi. *AP Images.*

■ ■ ■

Marjane Satrapi

Born November 22, 1969 (Rasht, Iran)
Iranian author, illustrator

Growing up in Iran, Marjane Satrapi saw few comic books and never imagined that she would become a comic artist. However, she lived through an extraordinary childhood that taught her a great deal about the power of government and religion and the value of family and freedom. From an early age, Satrapi learned that life is filled with complexities and contradictions, and when she became an adult, living in a city far from her homeland, she began to tell the stories of her youth, her family, and her country. By then she had discovered the medium of the graphic novel, and it seemed perfectly suited to describing the world through the eyes of a child. The books she produced—published in English as *Persepolis: The Story of a Childhood* and *Persepolis 2: The Story of a Return*—would do much more than educate readers about the effects of revolution, war, and repression in Iran. Translated into more than a dozen languages, they would bridge every culture and

Best-Known Works

Graphic Novels

Persepolis: The Story of a Childhood. 2001 (France); 2003 (United States).

Persepolis 2: The Story of a Return. 2002 (France); 2004 (United States).

nation with stories of the enormous challenges faced by ordinary people and everyday courage in the face of injustice.

Grows up in tumultuous times

Satrapi was born on November 22, 1969, in the city of Rasht in northwestern Iran and grew up in the capitol city of Tehran. She came from a historically prominent family: Her mother's grand-father, Nasreddine Shah, was once an emperor of Iran. Members of the Satrapi family were intellectual, and they placed a high value on education, culture, and travel. The family encouraged independence and a questioning spirit in Marjane, giving her the one comic book she enjoyed, an explanation of the principles of Marxism called *Dialectical Materialism.* Young Marji was educated at a French school in Tehran.

Though her parents both came from the upper class, they did not support the dictatorial regime of the shah of Iran, which ruthlessly limited the rights of common people. Instead, they developed open-minded and liberal attitudes. They supported political changes that would bring a democratic government to their country. Satrapi was ten years old when the shah was overthrown by a revolution that was quickly taken over by Islamic religious extremists. The new government was an Islamic Republic, and it instituted strict new rules against free expression, especially against any expression that countered strict Islamic teachings. Within a year, the neighboring country of Iraq thought to take advantage of an Iran weakened by revolution and attacked. The war between Iraq and Iran lasted eight years, from 1980 to 1988, adding bombings and other wartime deprivations to the repression of the conservative religious regime.

With the creation of the Islamic Republic in 1979, the richly varied culture of Iran was quickly overwhelmed by the repressive policies of Islamic fundamentalists who had strict rules governing every aspect of daily life. For the Satrapi family, this meant seeing friends and family members jailed or executed. Even social gatherings became hidden events, given sudden political importance because they were forbidden. For young Marjane, the new regime meant constant restrictions, prompting her rebellious spirit to resist. In 1984, fearful that their daughter would get into serious trouble, or, worse, lose her independent spirit, the Satrapis sent Marjane to Austria to attend a French school in Vienna. At the age of fourteen, she left her home and everyone she had ever known to live in a strange country.

Struggles to adapt to life outside Iran

As an expatriate (someone who has left his or her native land), Satrapi faced a new set of problems. Although she was free from the restrictive rules that had been placed on Iranian society, she felt a different sort of confinement caused by isolation and loneliness. To the girl who had lived for four years under war and tyranny, the young Europeans she met seemed shallow and naive. Even other Iranian expatriates seemed able to separate themselves from the horrors Satrapi felt so vividly. However, she wished to fit in to the unfamiliar new culture, so she tried to leave her Iranian identity behind and become just another rebellious European student.

While attending the French high school in Vienna and later studying illustration in Strasbourg, Satrapi also learned about radical politics, drugs, and sex. Though she made new friends and had a boyfriend for two years, she never really lost her deep sense of isolation at being away from her home, family, and culture. She finished school and passed her baccalaureate, a final exam in the French education system, but her personal life was in chaos. The breakup of her relationship left her depressed and desperate, and she ended up broke, alone, and homeless for several months.

In 1988, after four years in Austria, Satrapi returned home to Iran. Once again, her experience was full of contradictions. While overjoyed to be back in the arms of her loving family, she was overwhelmed by the changes in her homeland. Iran had been devastated by eight years of war, and was still worn under the restrictive rule of the fundamentalists. Once again, Satrapi felt that she did not fit anywhere comfortably. The years away had separated her from her Iranian friends, and her rebellious nature brought her into constant friction with the authorities.

Fighting her way out of suicidal depression, Satrapi studied graphic arts in Tehran and found radical friends who helped ease her isolation. In 1991, she married her boyfriend Reza, though her parents were reluctant to see her settle in Iran. They loved their daughter and hoped that she would return to Europe where she could live a less restricted life. Within a few years, she had divorced, and, as her parents had wished, she went to live in France.

Begins career in comics

In Paris, Satrapi began her career as an illustrator and writer of children's books. In 1997, she began to share studio space with a group of young comic artists called L'atelier des Vosges. As she told stories of her youth to her new friends, they began to encourage her to draw her experiences in comic book form. Having read some of the powerful work of comic artists like **Art Spiegelman** (1948–; see entry), Satrapi began to feel that the graphic novel could be the perfect format to convey the complexity of her childhood experiences.

At first Satrapi had little confidence in her ability to draw the people in her stories. Her art training in Iran had been hampered by the conservative regime's strict standards of modesty. Unlike most drawing classes that include nude models, Satrapi's Iranian drawing class employed female models wearing full-length veils and long dresses that entirely concealed their bodies. Male models offered more opportunities for the student artist, because in long-sleeved shirts and long pants their arms and legs could be seen. However, female students were discouraged from looking directly at male models, so learning to draw human figures became difficult. Satrapi developed a simple, black-and-white style of drawing that resembled rough woodcut prints. The stark style was perfectly suited to recounting the memories of a child and the devastation of a society.

Writes her life story

Satrapi combined story and art to create two graphic novels based on her life experiences. Named for the ancient Persian capital of Iran, *Persepolis* and *Persepolis 2* were first published in France in four volumes. They became immediately popular and were translated from the original French into German, Dutch, Portuguese, Spanish, Italian, and English. Within a few years they had been translated into more than a dozen languages and had won several European comic awards, including the Prix Alph'art Coup de Coeur, the Prix du Lion, and the Prix France Info. The books are an intensely personal memoir of one family's experience of the Iranian

THE END OF THE SHAH'S REIGN WAS NEAR.

revolution. In the book, the narrator, Satrapi herself, develops from a ten-year-old child to a divorced adult and shares her most intimate thoughts and feelings. These personal revelations give the books their immediacy and sweep the reader into the story.

The first book, *Persepolis: The Story of a Childhood*, describes Satrapis's hopes for the revolution and the terrible sense of betrayal and loss when the socialist democracy she had dreamed of was buried under religious fundamentalism. Told through the eyes of a child, the book is filled with humor and emotion, as when the young girls in Marji's school are given headscarves to wear; not knowing what they are, the students make them into a jump rope. Marji emerges as a very real girl, rebellious and clever, who asks her parents' friends to smuggle punk rock posters home from their European vacation. *Persepolis* ends with Marji bidding a painful farewell to her parents as she leaves to go to school in Vienna. Within a few years of its publication, work began on a French animated film version of *Persepolis*.

Persepolis 2 begins as the fourteen-year-old girl tries to adjust to her new surroundings. Satrapi is unflinchingly honest and detailed, describing her own faults and flaws as thoroughly as those of the prejudiced and insensitive Europeans she meets. The author describes every aspect of her path to adulthood, from the physical changes that seem to turn her into a different person to each mistake and experiment she makes on the way.

Living among Europeans proves to Marji that she is utterly Iranian, but returning to Iran only brings more contradictions.

Illustration of a symbolic show of the common people in a line pushing against the shah of Tehran for *Persepolis: The Story of a Childhood,* written and illustrated by Marjane Satrapi. *The Crown Publishing Group.*

Persepolis: Symbol of a Rich History

One of Marjane Satrapi's greatest frustrations with the Europeans she met while studying in Austria was how little they seemed to know about her homeland. Many confused Iran with its Arab neighbors and thought that Marji would speak Arabic. (Iran is not an Arab country, but a separate culture with its own proud history and language.)

The name Iran means "land of the Aryans." Aryans were an ancient people who settled a large area from Europe to India. During its long history, Iran has been invaded by Aryans, Greeks, Arabs, Mongols, and Turks, each contributing to the complex and vibrant culture of the country. The ancient Greeks called Iran "Persia" after one of its large southern provinces, Pars or Fars. The language spoken in Iran is called Farsi, after the same province.

The magnificent palaces of the ancient capital of Persepolis became a symbol of the rich history of the powerful Persian Empire, which ruled the world from the fifth to the second centuries BCE, stretching at its height from Greece to Pakistan. The Persian emperor Darius I built Persepolis around 500 BCE as a royal residence and ceremonial center, and its wealth and lavish architecture became legendary. When the Macedonian leader Alexander the Great (356–323 BCE) conquered the Persians in 330 BCE, he looted Persepolis and burned the city to the ground. The Greek writer Plutarch recorded that Alexander needed 5,000 camels and 20,000 mules to carry all the treasure he had taken from the great Persian capital.

Still feeling like an outsider, she finds herself crushed under the weight of hundreds of trivial rules. As she writes in *Persepolis 2*: "The regime had understood that one person leaving her house while asking herself: Are my trousers long enough? Is my veil in place? Can my makeup be seen? Are they going to whip me? No longer asks herself: Where is my freedom of thought? Where is my freedom of speech? What's going on in the political prisons? My life, is it livable?" *Persepolis 2* ends as a tearful Marji once again leaves her family and the homeland she loves for the freedom of expression she can find in the West.

Satrapi followed *Persepolis* and *Persepolis 2* with a tribute to her beloved grandmother, who died only a few years after Satrapi moved to Paris. *Embroideries* is another graphic novel drawn in Satrapi's starkly moving woodcut style. It conveys the story of a gathering of older Iranian women who share stories of life, love, and sex over tea one long afternoon. Like her first two books, *Embroideries* tells the story of secret lives, the small rebellions carried out by the powerless to make their lives sweeter under oppression. The women's sexy jokes and forbidden tales of affairs become a powerful statement of the ways in which the inner lives of people survive in spite of repression.

As of 2005, Satrapi was living in Paris and working on a graphic novel for young people titled *Chicken with Plums* (available in 2006) while writing commentary and drawing illustrations and comics for journals and newspapers around the world. In the United States, her works have been widely praised and often appear on lists of the top graphic novels.

For More Information

Books
Satrapi, Marjane. *Persepolis.* New York: Pantheon, 2003.

Satrapi, Marjane. *Persepolis 2.* New York: Pantheon, 2004.

Periodicals
Bloom, Amy. "*Persepolis* and *Persepolis 2*: Story of a Childhood, Story of a Return." *Yale Review* 93, no. 4 (October 2005): pp. 165–71.

Ripley, Amanda. "Beneath a Drawn Veil." *Time International* (June 2, 2003): pp. 58–61.

Satrapi, Marjane. "Tales from an Ordinary Iranian Girlhood." *Ms.* (Spring 2003): pp. 87–91.

Storace, Patricia. "A Double Life in Black and White." *The New York Review of Books* (April 7, 2005): pp. 40–44.

Zappaterra, Yolanda. "Persian Blues." *Design Week* (August 5, 2004): pp. 12–14.

Web Sites
Denn, Rebekah. "A Moment with . . . Author Marjane Satrapi." *Seattle Post-Intelligencer.* http://seattlepi.nwsource.com/books/123973_momentwith29.html (accessed on May 3, 2006).

Goldberg, Michelle. "Sexual Revolutionaries." *Salon.* http://www.salon.com/books/int/2005/04/24/satrapi/ (accessed on May 3, 2006).

"An Interview with Marjane Satrapi." *Bookslut.* http://www.bookslut.com/features/2004_10_003261.php (accessed on May 3, 2006).

"Persepolis: Ancient Capital of the Achaemenian Kings." *Iransaga: Persian History and Culture.* http://www.art-arena.com/persepolis.htm (accessed on May 3, 2006).

Shaikh, Nermeen. "Q and A: Marjane Satrapi." *AsiaSource.* http://www.asiasource.org/news/special_reports/satrapi.cfm (accessed on May 3, 2006).

Weich, Dave. "Marjane Satrapi Returns." *Powell's.com.* http://www.powells.com/authors/satrapi.html (accessed on May 3, 2006).

Jeff Smith. *Reproduced by permission of Jeff Smith.*

■ ■ ■
Jeff Smith

Born February 27, 1960 (McKees Rock, Pennsylvania)
American author, illustrator

"I just wanted to read a giant comic book that had all the elements that a book like Moby Dick *or* Le Morte D'Arthur *or the* Odyssey *had."*

For his 1,300-page epic *Bone,* Jeff Smith is considered among the greatest comics creators of all time. *Bone* follows three cousins on an adventure into the unknown. "It's a fish-out-of-water story," Smith told *Publishers Weekly.* Combining the flavor of J. R. R. Tolkien's *Lord of the Rings* trilogy with the universal appeal of Charles Schulz's *Peanuts* and Walter Kelly's *Pogo* comic strips, Smith engages readers with action-packed, humorous stories of friendship, compassion, and courage. Smith's ability to create an entertaining and smart tale for all-age readers truly distinguishes his work.

"Jeff Smith mixes humor and adventure perfectly," wrote Michael Arner on the *PopMatters* Web site, adding that "while story and art are certainly 'cartoony,' Bone is anything but childish." *Bone* has earned Smith dozens of the comics industry's top

Best-Known Works

Bone Graphic Novels

The Complete Bone Adventures (1993).

Bone Volume One: Out from Boneville (1995).

Bone Volume Two: The Great Cow Race (1996).

Bone Volume Three: Eyes of the Storm (1996).

Bone Volume Four: The Dragonslayer (1997).

Bone Volume Five: Rockjaw, Master of the Eastern Border (1998).

Bone Volume Six: Old Man's Cave (1999).

Bone Volume Seven: Ghost Circles (2001).

Bone Volume Eight: Treasure Hunters (2002).

Bone Volume Nine: Crown of Horns (2004).

Other Graphic Novels

(Illustrator) Sniegoski, Tom. *Stupid, Stupid Rat Tails: The Adventures of Big Johnson Bone, Frontier Hero* (2000).

Rose. Charles Vess, illustrator. (2002).

awards, including ten Eisner Awards, eight Harvey Awards, and recognition from the National Cartoonist Society.

Bones up on cartooning

Born on February 27, 1960, in McKees Rock, Pennsylvania, Jeff Alan Smith grew up in Columbus, Ohio. He loved storytelling from an early age. Some of his earliest memories are of drawing cartoon characters in crayon. By the time he reached kindergarten, he had created the basic characters for *Bone*. "I used to watch Saturday morning cartoons and draw these Bone characters, and have them go on little adventures—same stuff they do now," he told *Columbus Alive*. The characters were still with him by the time he reached college. At Ohio State University, he continued the characters' adventures in a comic strip called *Thorn*, which ran in the student newspaper *Lantern* between 1982 and 1984.

College did not hold as much interest for Smith as his comics. He left school in 1985 in order to fully devote himself to his work. *Thorn* had gained attention from newspaper syndicates, but the cartoonist quickly ended negotiations when it became clear that he would lose creative control and ownership of the comic strip. He shelved his strip and instead started the Character Builders animation studio with Jim Kammerud and Martin Fuller in Powell, Ohio. "[We] were all self-taught, learning everything we could from books like *Disney Animation: The Illusion of Life,*" Smith told Jeff Mason in an interview with *indy magazine.* The studio flourished, taking on several advertising, public announcements, and film projects.

For the next five years, Smith and his two partners were preoccupied with various projects. Despite the success of the animation studio (which continued to do well into 2006), Smith remained interested in his comic series. He left Character Builders in 1991 to launch Cartoon Books with his wife, Vijaya Iyer. The sole purpose of Cartoon Books was to publish *Bone* in comic book format.

Launches an epic adventure

Smith envisioned *Bone* as a sort of combination of Bugs Bunny and the *Lord of the Rings.* Though he wrote the story for his and his wife's entertainment, Smith remembered in an interview with *Ain't It Cool News* that he had "very low hopes" when he began to publish *Bone* "because the market is so dominated by superheroes, X-Men and stuff like that. But I thought we might find a small niche, because I was positive that more people liked Bugs Bunny than Wolverine." To Smith's pleasant surprise, the market welcomed *Bone,* and he reported having made money on *Bone* from its first publication in 1991.

Bone is the story of three cousins' adventures in new lands. Unlike many other epic adventure stories, the heroes of this story didn't boldly set out on an adventure; instead, they seemed lost. Chased out of their hometown, Boneville, by an angry mob, the cousins find themselves lost in a desert and simply want to go home. With their distinctly different temperaments, Fone Bone, Phoney Bone, and Smiley Bone adapt to their new surroundings in unique ways. Fone Bone's levelheadedness, Phoney Bone's cranky attitude, and Smiley Bone's happy-go-lucky way provide readers with a variety of insights into the culture of the valley in which the Bones find themselves. Filled with an assortment of good and evil characters who are engaged in a battle for control, the valley becomes a place where the Bones experience real tests to their character and grow, sometimes despite themselves.

Bone becomes a richer tale of good versus evil with the addition of Thorn, a girl whose royal blood thrusts her into the vortex of the valley's power struggles and who becomes the object of Fone Bone's affections. The Bones become enmeshed in the royal family's fight to win back its throne.

Bone has earned Smith dozens of the comics industry's top awards, including ten Eisner Awards, eight Harvey Awards, and recognition from the National Cartoonist Society. *Cartoon Books.*

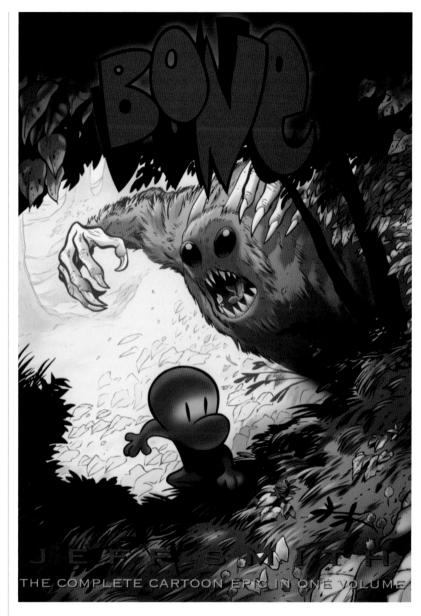

Smith had imagined *Bone* as an epic tale from the beginning, sketching out the story format in the late 1980s. "I had the long view, goals, places the characters needed to get to in order to move forward," Smith related to *Publishers Weekly*. The predetermined structure did not impede Smith from infusing his tale with spontaneity. While working toward his goals, he explained to *Publishers Weekly* that "I allowed myself to explore and let the story go where

Prequels to *Bone*

The *Bone* saga is a stand-alone tale, but the richness of the adventure offered Jeff Smith the opportunity to explore various aspects of the story's history, and he created two prequels to *Bone* with the help of writer Tom Sniegoski and artist Charles Vess.

Stupid, Stupid Rat Tails is about the Bone cousins' pioneering ancestor Big Johnson Bone, founder of their hometown, Boneville. For this prequel, Smith teamed with writer Tom Sniegoski. Smith described Sniegoski as "one of the funniest people I'd ever met in comics" to the *Comics Reporter.* Their resulting story had a slapstick comedy feel much like that of Saturday morning cartoons. Big Johnson Bone, a bold adventurer, battles through the unknown much like his modern-day relatives. Big Johnson Bone and his companions Blossom the mule and Mr. Pip the monkey ride a tornado into the same uncharted valley at the time when the rat creatures were overrunning it. The power-ful Big Johnson staves off the invasion for a while before he goes off to found Boneville. His adventures offer *Bone* readers insight into the early drama of the valley struggles and into the character of the Bones. It also reveals why the modern-day rat creatures bob their tails.

In *Rose,* the early story of the valley's royal family, Smith relates Thorn's ancestral history, starting when Gran'ma Ben, whose name is Rose, was in her teens. The tale chronicles the events that created the dynamics of the *Bone* story. Readers learn why Gran'ma Ben has such a strained relationship with her sister Briar and how the Lord of the Locusts came to dominate the valley. Unlike the cartoony style of the artwork in *Bone* and *Stupid, Stupid Rat Tails,* *Rose* looks more like a fantasy comic with realistic artwork by award-winning artist Charles Vess. While both prequels add to the *Bone* saga, they stand alone as interesting stories in their own right.

it would. That's the only way to write comedy. You can't really meticulously plot jokes—you have to let go, and when the characters get into trouble, you see what's interesting." Smith infused his saga with knee-slapping humor, but never lost his focus on the direction he wanted the story to go. "Overall, there were very few changes. I've pretty much told the story I wanted to tell. Somewhere I have the last page that I drew in 1989 before I started. It's very similar to the final version, with the exact same joke," Smith told *Publishers Weekly.*

Smith boosted the success of *Bone* when he began networking within the comics industry and at industry conventions. His creation really took off after Dave Sim featured a long segment of *Bone* #3 in his popular *Cerebus the Aardvark* #161 and the *Comic Buyer's*

Guide gave it a positive review. In 1993, Smith gathered the first six installments of *Bone* into *The Complete Bone Adventures,* with an introduction by leading comic book creator Neil Gaiman (1960–), and started raking in readers and awards. In 1993 alone, Smith sold tens of thousands of copies of his book and won an Eisner Award for Best Humor Publication, a Russ Manning Award for Most Promising Newcomer, and three Harvey Awards for Best Graphic Album, Special Award for Humor, and Best Cartoonist, among others.

Through the years, readers and awards continued to mount. In 1995, Smith republished *The Complete Bone Adventures* as *Bone Volume One: Out from Boneville* and created the rest of the saga as graphic novels until the series ended with volume nine. Smith published the entire *Bone* series in a massive single volume in 2004. Until that point, *Bone* was published in black and white; however, Scholastic had planned to print color editions of the series starting in 2006. *Bone* continued to sell in more than a dozen different languages throughout the world. With the completion of the series, Smith had yet to announce any new projects he might tackle.

For More Information

Periodicals

MacDonald, Heidi. "Jeff Smith on *Bone.*" *Publishers Weekly* (October 18, 2004): p. 34.

Mason, Jeff. "Interview with Jeff Smith." *indy magazine* (January 21, 1994). This article can also be found online at http://www.indyworld.com/comics/jeff.smith.

School Library Journal (October 2003): p. 31; (December 2004): p. 25.

Starker, Melissa. "A Letter to Boneville from Columbus Cartoonist Jeff Smith." *Columbus Alive* (October 27, 1999): 12.

Web Sites

Arner, Michael. *"Bone: One Volume Edition"* (book review). *PopMatters.* http://www.popmatters.com/comics/bone-one-volume-edition.shtml (accessed on May 3, 2006).

Boneville.com. http://boneville.com (accessed on May 3, 2006).

Dupont, Alexandra. "AICN Comics Exclusive! Alexandra DuPont Interviews *Bone* Creator Jeff Smith!!" *Ain't It Cool News.* http://www.aintitcool.com/display.cgi?id=15592 (accessed on May 3, 2006).

"Jeff Smith." *Mars Import.* http://www.marsimport.com/display_creator?ID=910 (accessed on May 3, 2006).

"A Short Interview with Jeff Smith." *The Comics Reporter.* http://www.comicsreporter.com/index.php/resources/interviews/2257/ (accessed on May 3, 2006).

Fuyumi Soryo

Born January 6, 1959 (Beppu, Oita, Japan)
Japanese author, illustrator

Fuyumi Soryo's manga series *Mars* is one of several series that introduced English-speaking readers to the innovative work being done in the shojo manga genre, a type of manga that is marketed especially to girls and focuses on romance and relationships. In fifteen volumes, this beautifully drawn series explores an unlikely romance between the dashing and rebellious Rei Kashino, a sixteen-year-old motorcycle racer who shows no fear of death, and his shy and studious classmate Kira Aso, whose beauty blossoms because of Rei's attentions. The fifteen volumes of *Mars,* as well as a prequel volume, *Mars: Horse with No Name,* offer English-speaking readers a taste of the intense emotions and sometimes raw language and sexuality that are so common and popular among Japanese shojo manga fans—yet the overriding message of the series is that a healthy, loving relationship has immense power to heal and bring true happiness.

"Going into high school is like the start of a new journey."

Early successes

In *Mars,* the hopes, dreams, and personal histories of the major characters are revealed in great detail, but English-speaking fans of the author must content themselves with very limited information about the creator. Fuyumi Soryo was born on January 6, 1959, and raised in the city of Beppu, in the Oita Prefecture on the southern Japanese island of Kyushu. Little is known about her education, but by the early 1980s she began to publish some shojo manga stories in the manga magazines that are so popular in Japan. Several of Soryo's early, shorter manga stories were published in Japan, including *Youdamari no Houmonsha, Love Styles, Taiyo no Ijiwaru,* and *Sole Maledetto.* By the mid-1980s, she had begun to create a longer series, titled *Boyfriend,* that was eventually collected

Best-Known Works

Graphic Novels (in English translation)

Mars 15 vols. (2002–04).

Mars: Horse with No Name (2004).

ES 8 vols. (2006–).

into ten *tankōbon* (the Japanese equivalent of the graphic novel). The series won the 1988 Shogakukan Manga Award, awarded to the best shojo manga of the year. As of 2005, it had not been translated into English.

In the mid-1990s, Soryo created a new series, *Doll,* that was published in the magazine *Betsu Friend KC.* The series was also translated into Italian and published in the Italian manga magazine *Amici. Doll* was short-lived, however. In 1996, Soryo turned her attention to creating a new series, titled *Mars. Mars* was first published in *Bessatsu Friend,* a monthly manga magazine offering positive stories to high school girls that is published by Kodansha, one of the biggest manga publishers in Japan. (*Bessatsu Friend* also published another popular shojo manga title with which *Mars* is often compared: *Peach Girl* by Miwa Ueda.) *Mars* became a huge success in Japan, where it was published continuously from 1996 to 2000. The magazine series was collected into fifteen volumes of tankoubon, or graphic novels, and the popularity of *Mars* made Soryo one of the leading shojo manga creators in Japan.

Mars travels

In the late 1990s and early 2000s, the popularity of Japanese manga began to spread around the world, both to the English-speaking markets in the United States, Canada, and Great Britain, but also to European countries like France, Italy, the Netherlands, and Germany, all of which experienced manga "crazes" as young readers sought out works that were decidedly different than the comic books and graphic novels with which they had grown up. In the United States, publishers began to introduce readers to new titles through magazines such as those read in Japan. *Smile* magazine, for example, was the first English-language magazine containing manga for girls, and it introduced the titles *Peach Girl* and *Mars* to American readers. But American readers were not inclined

Mysterious Manga-ka

American and other English-speaking manga fans are accustomed to the difficulties of getting to know more about their favorite manga authors, or manga-ka. American and British authors—who are frequently interviewed, reviewed, and profiled on various comics Web sites or who create their own Web sites and interact with fans—allow their readers to gain insight into their lives and their motivations for creating popular works. Readers feel that they form a relationship with these authors, and they develop loyalty to them. With Japanese authors, however, there are real barriers to understanding. Japanese culture prizes privacy, so authors typically release only very limited information about their lives. Even those authors who do disclose personal details often do so only on Japanese language Web sites, and these are very rarely translated into English. Often, the only clues a reader has to an author's life are the brief and sometimes cryptic or confusing notes that some authors include in the text of the manga. Fuyumi Soryo is an extreme example of a mysterious manga-ka. No personal information about her has been translated into English, she maintains no Web site, and she has written no notes to readers in the margins of her work.

In the mid-2000s, the popularity of Japanese manga in the United States is still a relatively new phenomenon, as concerted efforts to publish Japanese manga in the United States were only a few years old. Publishers have not made a great effort to introduce readers to their favorite authors. If the popularity of manga continues, however, it is likely that such publishers as TokyoPop, Viz, Del Rey, and others who publish translated versions of Japanese titles will do more to help fans connect with—and keep buying books by—their favorite authors.

to purchase magazines, and *Smile* magazine folded in 2003. American girls did buy graphic novels, however, and in 2002 Tokyopop began to release the *Mars* series in this form, finishing the fifteen-volume run in 2004.

Mars takes a very simple idea and develops it into an extremely complex and involving story. At the simple center of the series is the romance between two sixteen-year-old high school students, Rei Kashino and Kira Aso. What makes the series so complex is the way that Soryo slowly unfolds the complexities of her two main characters. Rei Kashino is introduced as a rough-edged playboy, hugely popular among the girls because of his good looks. He races motorcycles, plays basketball only to win money from his opponents, and brags that he is not afraid of death. Kira Aso is in many ways his exact opposite: intense and quiet, she devotes all attention to her artwork and prefers not to interact with her fellow students, who consider her weird anyway. When sparks fly between these two after a chance encounter, they begin a love affair that evolves throughout the series and pulls in a variety of interesting characters, including Tatsuya Kida, Rei's best friend, who puts aside his crush on Kira and gives the couple support through their troubles; Harumi, a female rival for Rei's attention who later becomes a friend to Kira; Akitaka, Rei's motorcycle racing coach and adult confidante; and several family members of the main characters, including Kira's cruel stepfather, who once raped her.

One of the elements of *Mars* that is especially noteworthy is Soryo's careful character development. Early in the series, Rei and Kira present themselves to the reader as mysteries or puzzles: in volume one, a character marvels at Rei's reckless lack of fear on a motorcycle and thinks, "He's only 16. How'd he get like that anyway?" Similarly, Kira is mute in the face of conflict and direct questioning, and characters wonder what secrets she has to hide. Over the course of the series, these questions and many others are revealed through the slowly growing relationship of trust between Rei and Kira—and through the way the supporting characters modify their own actions in response to the dignity that they see in Rei and Kira. For example, early in the series Harumi bullies Kira, trying to scare her away from Rei. Kira's reaction, though, convinces Harumi to change her ways. Perhaps most convincing and touching is the gradual development of a deep love relationship between Rei and Kira; by volume ten, they both show keen insight into understanding what is bothering each other and display a real sense of wholeness when they are in each other's company.

Initially, American readers may be somewhat surprised to read the frankness with which Soryo deals with sexuality; sex is common among her characters and discussed frequently. Readers also may be set back by the frequent use of expletives and occasional violence. Yet Soryo doesn't focus on sex, swearing, or violence. Instead, she explores how these things are not as important as the bonds of trust and friendship that develop between characters and that help the characters deal with the challenges in their lives. And those challenges are substantial: Kira doesn't trust men after she was raped by her stepfather, and Rei has been estranged from his father since the death of his twin brother. Through positive and supportive relationships, however, the characters help each other surmount their issues.

Soryo is more than a writer; she also provided the illustrations for this graphic novel series. Rei and Kira are both visually appealing people, especially the long-haired Adonis-like Rei. Their large eyes (in distinctive manga style) are used to express emotion when words are simply not adequate. Throughout the story Soryo experiments with techniques that break up the visual elements of the story: sometimes the frames of the story are neat and orderly, but during action-packed or emotionally intense moments the frames break down and Soryo becomes quite imaginative, breaking up the page both vertically and horizontally and layering images in engaging ways. Two other techniques are worthy of mention: for scenes depicting motorcycle races, homes, and cityscapes, Soryo brings in highly realistic, almost photolike backgrounds to add a sense of realism; and for scenes involving intense feelings of love—especially kissing scenes—Soryo splashes the page with dazzling starbursts to accentuate the powerful emotions felt by the characters.

English publication of *Mars* ended in 2004. By the series end, Rei and Kira are married, they have largely resolved the family troubles that plagued them throughout the book, and Rei is about to begin his career as a professional motorcycle racer. To round out the storyline, Soryo helped flesh out some of the holes in the series with a single-volume prequel called *Mars: Horse with No Name,* published in the United States in 2004. In all, the completed series remains a favorite among fans.

Soryo had finished work on *Mars* in Japan in 2000. In 2002, she began work on a new series, called *ES (Eternal Sabbath). ES* tells the story of a young female biomedical researcher, Kujo Mine, who develops a relationship with ES00, a human who has been genetically modified to live for up to 200 years or more. Part romance, part science fiction mystery, the series was published in the manga magazine *Morning* and in eight volumes of tankoubon. In Japan, *ES* was marketed to a slightly older audience, men and women in their twenties and thirties, and published between 2002 and 2004. As of late 2005, manga publisher Del Rey had announced plans to translate the series into English and introduce it in 2006. Thus, fans of Soryo's work with *Mars* looked forward to another interesting tale from this popular and talented manga author.

■ ■ ■

For More Information

Web Sites
"Fuyumi Soryo." *Anime News Network.* http://www.animenewsnetwork.com/encyclopedia/people.php?id=12764 accessed on May 3, 2006).

Humphries, Sam. "Book Review: *Mars*." *Artbomb*. http://www.artbomb. net/detail.jsp?idx=5&cid=363&tid=439 (accessed on May 3, 2006).

Kirei: A Mars Fan Site. http://www.tokyojupiter.com/manga/kirei/ (accessed on May 3, 2006).

Kodan Club. http://www.kodanclub.com/ (accessed on May 3, 2006).

"*Mars*." *TOKYOPOP*. http://www.tokyopop.com/dbpage.php?propertycode= MAR&categorycode=BMG (accessed on May 3, 2006).

Upatkoon, Ivevei. "*Mars*." *Ex: The Official World of Anime & Manga*. http:// www.ex.org/4.2/26-manga_mars.html (accessed on May 3, 2006).

Art Spiegelman. © *Henry Ray Abrams/Reuters/Corbis.*

Art Spiegelman

Born February 15, 1948 (Stockholm, Sweden)
American author, illustrator, editor

"What story do I have that's worth telling?... it seemed obvious to me that it had to be this story I got from my parents–Maus."

One of the best-known graphic novelists in the world, Art Spiegelman injected new energy into the comics genre with the creation of his intensely personal memoir of the Holocaust, *Maus, A Survivor's Tale: My Father Bleeds History* and *Maus II, A Survivor's Tale: Here My Troubles Began.* Spiegelman's contribution to comic book art began, however, long before the publication of *Maus.* As a central part of the underground comics scene since the 1960s and co-editor (with his wife Françoise Mouly) of the groundbreaking comics magazine *Raw,* Spiegelman has been a major influence in the modern comic book.

Raised on *Mad* and history

Art Spiegelman's parents were Jewish survivors of the Holocaust, the attempt by German Nazis to destroy Europe's Jewish

Best-Known Works

Graphic Novels

Maus, A Survivor's Tale: My Father Bleeds History (1986).

Maus II, A Survivor's Tale: Here My Troubles Began (1992).

(With Joseph Moncure March) *The Wild Party: The Lost Classic by Joseph Moncure March* (1999).

In the Shadow of No Towers (2004).

Children's Books

Open Me...I'm a Dog. (1997).

(Editor, with Françoise Mouly) *Little Lit.* 3 vols. (2000–03).

Comic Books and Magazines

Work and Turn (1979).

(Editor, with Françoise Mouly, and contributor) *Raw* (1980–91).

(With Robert Crumb, Robert Williams, Kim Deitch, and Tony Millionaire) *Legal Action Comics* 2 vols. (2005).

population during World War II (1939–45). This simple fact would deeply affect their son's life and art. When they regained their freedom after the end of World War II, Vladek and Anja Spiegelman emigrated to Sweden, where they lived for several years before leaving to make a new home in the United States. Their son Art was born in Stockholm, Sweden, on February 15, 1948, and raised in Rego Park in the New York City borough of Queens. He became fascinated with comics at the age of five or six, when he studied *Mad* magazines and *Batman* comic books for hours, teaching himself to read the word balloons. Before long he was copying the artists he liked, and creating his own comics.

Though Spiegelman's parents would have preferred that he become a doctor or dentist, young Art chose his career early. He studied cartooning at New York's High School of Art and Design. By the age of fifteen he had taken his first paying job at a weekly newspaper in Queens, and by the age of seventeen he had turned down an offer to draw a comic strip for syndication to various newspapers. He attended Harpur College (now the State University of New York at Binghamton) from 1965 to 1968, where he studied art and philosophy. He earned money to support his comics pursuits by working for the Topps Candy Company. Topps, a maker of baseball-card bubble gum packs and other novelty candies, employed many innovative young comics artists, and Spiegelman enjoyed his work there. Designing the decorative borders for baseball cards and creating the art for other Topps products, like *Wacky Packages* and *Garbage Pail Kids*, allowed him to do the kind of work he had admired in *Mad Magazine*, sly social satire concealed behind silliness.

Spiegelman's comic book art also helped him express the deep emotional pain he often felt. During the 1960s, Spiegelman had a nervous breakdown and spent time in a mental hospital. Shortly afterward, in 1968, his mother, Anja, killed herself, leaving no note or explanation. Her grieving son responded with a powerful comic titled "Prisoner on Hell Planet," which described the tortured pain and anger he felt over his mother's suicide.

Experiments in comix

The 1960s and 1970s were periods of radical social change and experimentation in the arts. Comic art was no exception, and a dynamic underground "comix" movement began to push the limits of acceptable content and style in comics. These new comix reflected the radical politics, outrageous behavior, and blatant sexuality that characterized the 1960s counterculture movement. Influenced by such underground artists as Robert Crumb (author of *Mr. Natural* and *Fritz the Cat*), Spiegelman began to draw for radical comix *Real Pulp, Young Lust,* and *Bizarre Sex.* He sometimes published using a pen name, like Joe Cutrate, Al Flooglebuckle, or Skeeter Grant. During the mid-1970s, he joined forces with friend and fellow comics artist Bill Griffith (*Zippy the Pinhead*) to produce a comic magazine titled *Arcade: The Comix Revue.*

In 1977, Spiegelman married Françoise Mouly, a French artist who had quit architecture school in Paris to come to New York and find a radical creative community. In 1979, Spiegelman began to teach history and the aesthetics of comics at New York's School for Visual Arts and, in 1980, he and Mouly began to edit their own avant-garde comic magazine, titled *Raw: Open Wounds from the Cutting Edge of Commix.* Printed in a large, *Life* magazine-sized format, *Raw* highlighted the work of important young comic book artists from all over the world. Its first edition of 4,500 copies sold out immediately.

It was in *Raw* that Spiegelman first published a comic strip that told the story of his parents' experiences during the Holocaust. In true comics style, he told his story through animal characters that dressed and walked like humans. Titled *Maus*, Spiegelman's strip depicted Jews as mice, Nazis as cats, Poles as pigs, and Americans as dogs. Other than having animal heads, however, the characters

Mad: Inspiration from the Usual Gang of Idiots

The humor magazine that sparked Art Spiegelman's interest in cartooning has been an inspiration to generations of other comics artists as well. Founded in 1952 by publisher Bill Gaines, *Mad* has provided social and political satire and outright goofiness to its readers for more than half a century.

Bill Gaines was the owner of EC Comics, publisher of a line of comic books that included *Tales of the Crypt, Weird Science* and *Shock SuspenStories.* The EC books were admired by readers and critics alike for the high quality of their writing and art and their unusual subject matter, which included a focus on controversial social issues such as racism. In 1952, with editor/cartoonist Harvey Kurtzman, Gaines added a humor comic to his catalog. This comic, titled *Tales Calculated to Drive You ... Mad,* was filled with social and political satire; parodies of popular movies,

radio, and television shows; and some of the best comics artwork around.

The work of cartoonists like Wally Wood, Will Elder, Jack Davis, Don Martin, and Dave Berg became regular features of the comic, which changed to a slick magazine format with its twenty-fourth issue in 1955. During the politically repressive 1950s and early 1960s, *Mad* was one of the few publications that offered readers a delightfully irreverent critical look at government policies. Though the magazine has a clear liberal slant, *Mad* skewers every part of popular culture with equal glee.

Through the decades, *Mad* has attracted a loyal reader base that revels in the publication's long-standing "in-jokes." These include the *Mad* mascot, a gap-toothed, grinning character named Alfred E. Neuman, whose motto, "What—me worry?" is found in every issue.

display a deep range of human emotion and behavior in a period of tremendous upheaval and tragedy.

Publishes *Maus*

Spiegelman had begun to draw *Maus* in 1978, and it took thirteen years to complete. The story is told from the point of view of his father, and Spiegelman taped hours of conversations with Vladek, who died in 1982. The completed work was published as a graphic novel in two parts: *Maus, a Survivor's Tale: My Father Bleeds History* (1986) and *Maus II, a Survivor's Tale: Here My Troubles Began* (1992).

One of the most powerful modern literary works of any genre, *Maus* not only describes the events of the Nazi attack on Jewish people in a deeply personal way, but also describes the profound

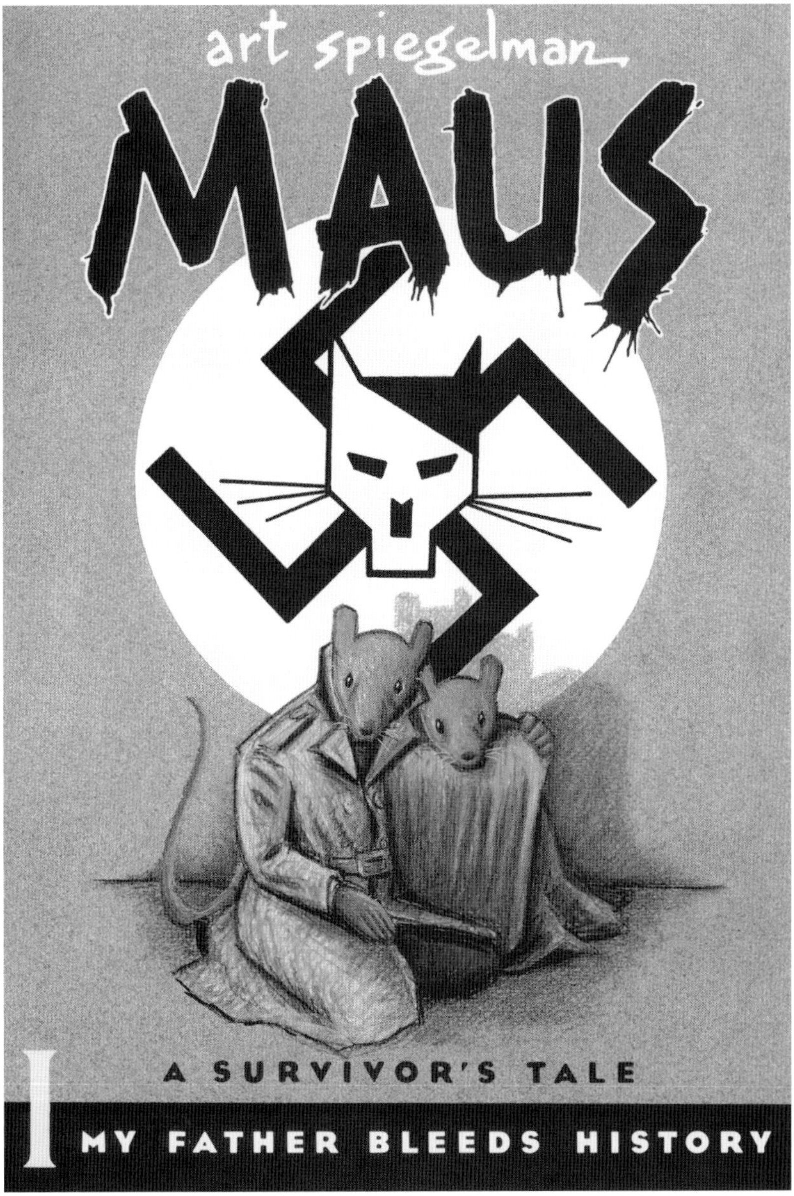
art spiegelman
MAUS
A SURVIVOR'S TALE
I
MY FATHER BLEEDS HISTORY

One of the most powerful modern literary works of any genre, *Maus* not only describes the events of the Nazi attack on Jewish people in a deeply personal way, but also describes the profound effect that these events have had on future generations. *Random House.*

effect that these events have had on future generations. While most of the story is told from Vladek's point of view, Spiegelman also explores his own complex feelings about his parents' terrible experiences. "I know this is insane," the "Art" character says to his wife, Françoise, "but I somehow wish I had been in Auschwitz with my parents so I could really know what they lived through! . . . I guess it's some kind of guilt about having had an easier life than they did."

Though not a comic in the "funny papers" sense of the word, *Maus* uses comic book techniques to give depth and complexity to the story. In his contributions to *Raw,* Spiegelman experimented with various styles of art and narrative, and he uses everything he has learned in the creation of *Maus.* The completed work is as visual as a film or stage play and as multi-layered as a novel. It is an intimate and detailed examination of a terrible period in history and its effect on the individuals who lived through it and their children who did not. No easy solutions or simple morals are given. Vladek is portrayed as both resourceful and petty, brave and bigoted, a survivor and a damaged soul. His son both longs for connection with his father and condemns his meanness. He feels both privileged not to have lived through what his parents have and deprived because he has parents who have been so negatively affected by the experience.

Critics and readers received *Maus* with a respect and admiration rarely given to a comic book. Along with dozens of comics awards, it won a special citation 1992 Pulitzer Prize, becoming the first comic book to win that prestigious award.

Life after *Maus*

In 1993, Spiegelman joined the staff of the *New Yorker* magazine as a regular artist and writer. His cover art, comics, and commentary fit well with the magazine's forward-thinking intellectual image, though they were often controversial. In 1997, he wrote and illustrated a children's book called *Open Me...I'm a Dog,* and he and Mouly began to edit a comics series for children called *Little Lit,* "trying to show," as he said in an interview with Christopher Monte Smith on *BookSense.com,* "that comics are not just for grown-ups anymore." Like much of his work for adults, Spiegelman's children's books are characterized by a combination of silliness and disturbing weirdness.

On September 11, 2001, Spiegelman was living with Mouly and their two children on the lower end of Manhattan when Islamic terrorists forced two commercial airliners to fly into the towers of the World Trade Center, New York's highest buildings. He watched in horror as the huge towers collapsed, then ran to find his children, one of whom attended school near the destroyed buildings. Like most New Yorkers, Spiegelman was devastated by the sudden attack on the city, and, like other political leftists, he was almost equally appalled by the U.S. government's response, which he saw as weakening civil liberties and rushing to war.

When Spiegelman drew the cover for that week's *New Yorker*, he expressed the inexpressible pain of many by simply drawing the silhouettes of the two towers in varying shades of deep gray and black. That cover would become the cover of his next book.

Spiegelman found release for his complex mixture of feelings by starting work on his next graphic novel, *In the Shadow of No Towers*. Unlike *Maus,* which had been a traditional narrative, *In the Shadow of No Towers* was more like "a fragment of a diary," as Spiegelman called it in an interview with Nina Siegel in *The Progressive*. In the book, which begins with the line "Synopsis: In our last episode, as you might remember, the world ended," the artist uses a variety of drawing styles to explore his shattered state of mind. He even uses old characters from classic comics to portray various aspects of himself: sometimes the narrator is the Jewish mouse Art from *Maus,* sometimes he is a character from classic strips *Happy Hooligan* or *Bringing Up Father.* Though some critics find the work too unfocused, many feel it is a powerful depiction of what it is like to live through a devastating moment in history.

Spiegelman left his job with the *New Yorker* in 2003. He remained in New York City and continued to work on expanding the boundaries of the comic book. One of his latest projects was a comics opera, titled *Drawn to Death: A Three-Panel Opera.*

For More Information

Books

Forget, Thomas. *Art Spiegelman.* New York: Rosen Publishing Group, 2004.

Witek, Joseph. *Comic Books as History: The Narrative Art of Jack Jackson, Art Spiegelman, and Harvey Pekar.* Jackson: University Press of Mississippi, 1990.

Periodicals

Bolhafner, J. Stephen. "Art for Art's Sake: Spiegelman Speaks on *RAW*'s Past, Present and Future." *Comics Journal* no. 145 (October 1991): pp. 96–100.

Doherty, Thomas. "Art Spiegelman's *Maus*: Graphic Art and the Holocaust." *American Literature* 68, no. 1 (March 1996): pp. 69–85.

Dreifus, Claudia. "Art Spiegelman: 'If There Can Be No Art about the Holocaust, There May at Least Be Comic Strips.'" *The Progressive* (November 1989): pp. 34–38.

Mason, Wyatt. "The Holes in His Head." *The New Republic* (September 27, 2004): pp. 30–41.

Patterson, Troy. "Graphic Violence: Supercartoonist Art Spiegelman Draws a Bead on 9/11 with *In the Shadow of No Towers.*" *Entertainment Weekly* (September 17, 2004): p. 44.

"Shadows and Light: Art Spiegelman on 9/11." *Miami Herald* (November 10, 2004).

Siegal, Nina. "Art Spiegelman." *The Progressive* (January 2005): pp. 35–40.

Stone, Laurie. "*Maus II: A Survivor's Tale:* And Here My Troubles Began." *The Nation* (January 6, 1992): pp. 28–31.

Van Biema, David H. "Art Spiegelman Battles the Holocaust's Demons—and His Own—in an Epic Cat-and-Mouse Comic Book." *People Weekly* (October 27, 1986): pp. 98–102.

Weschler, Lawrence. "Mighty *Maus.*" *Rolling Stone* (November 20, 1986): pp. 103–109.

Web Sites

"Art Spiegelman." *Pantheon Graphic Novels.* http://www.randomhouse.com/pantheon/graphicnovels/spiegelman.html (accessed on May 3, 2006).

Little Lit. http://www.little-lit.com/ (accessed on May 3, 2006).

"New York Voices: Art Spiegelman." *Thirteen: WNET New York.* http://www.thirteen.org/nyvoices/transcripts/spiegelman.html (accessed on May 3, 2006).

Smith, Christopher Monte. "Very Interesting People: Art Spiegelman." *BookSense.com.* http://www.booksense.com/people/archive/spiegelmanart.jsp (accessed on May 3, 2006).

Yukiru Sugisaki

(Japan)
Japanese author, illustrator

Manga is the Japanese word for comic book, and a manga-ka is the creative mind behind the dynamic artwork and complex storytelling of the Japanese comic. Romance, world-shaking adventure, and exotic robots—these features power much of classic manga, and they are at the center of the wildly creative works of manga-ka Yukiru Sugisaki. Versatile and productive, Sugisaki has produced several popular manga series that include both the subtle emotional development of shojo, or girl manga, and the rollicking science fiction adventure featured in shonen, or boy manga.

Unlike graphic novelists in the Western world, who often welcome celebrity, Japanese manga-ka are frequently shy of personal publicity, perhaps preferring to be identified with the fantastic characters they create. Yukiru Sugisaki has never even publicly identified herself as a woman, though fans who have seen her at book signings have publicized that information. She often draws herself as a man, an adolescent boy in a baseball cap, or a male bunny rabbit, and the only personal information she releases are her birthday (never the year), her astrological sign (Capricorn), and her blood type (O). Many in Japan believe that blood type reveals information about one's character in the same way that some Westerners believe in astrological signs. Sugisaki has also revealed that she is interested in video games, theatrical plays, and collecting anything to do with rabbits.

Creates *dojinshi*

Sugisaki began her public career as a comic artist by drawing *dojinshi,* or comics created by fans. (Dojinshi, often interpreted to mean "underground comic," can also be translated as "same substance, different people.") Though most dojinshi are privately

"When it comes to Sugisaki-sensei, I'm always on my toes!"

PAUL MORRISSEY,
SUGISAKI'S U.S. EDITOR

Best-Known Works

Graphic Novels (in English translation)

(With Yoshiyuki Tomino) *Brain Powered.* 4 vols. (2003–04).

The Candidate for Goddess 5 vols. (2004).

D.N. Angel 10 vols. (2004–05).

Rizelmine (2005).

Lagoon Engine 3 vols. (2005).

Lagoon Engine Einsatz. Forthcoming as of press time.

photocopied and passed around among friends, some are published and widely distributed. One of Sugisaki's most popular dojinshi was *Escaflowne,* which was published in book form in 1996 by the Japanese publisher Kadokawa. *Escaflowne* is the story of a teenage girl whose interest in the occult results in her being magically transported to the distant planet Gaia, where she must help a mysterious prince revive the sleeping god, Escaflowne. The original Escaflowne story had been created by HajimeYadate and Shoji Kawamori, and Katsu-Aki had drawn a serialized version of the comic. The romantic adventure story appealed to both boys and girls and became one of few manga stories that were published in both shonen manga and shojo manga magazines.

Another important Sugisaki dojinshi is *Sotsugyo M* (*Graduation M*), which has its roots in a popular Japanese CD-Rom game called *Sotsugyo.* The game centers on five graduating high school girls, and it has inspired many dojinshi. One of these, *Sotsugyo M,* changes the lead characters to five high school boys. Sugisaki's *Sotsugyu M* stories were published in serial form in *Asuka,* a popular girls' manga magazine.

Achieves U.S. success with shonen manga

After this point, Sugisaki began to publish more original stories, and many have been translated into several languages. One of the earliest was a science fiction story based on a popular anime, or animated cartoon show, called *Brain Powered,* which aired on Japanese television in 1998. Teaming with writer Yoshiyuki Tomino (1941–), Sugisaki provided artwork for manga stories that expand on the anime, which concerns an epic battle to save the planet from destruction. The competing forces in *Brain Powered* are mecha warriors (*mecha* is a Japanese word derived from the English word "mechanical"). While mecha can refer to any kind of mechanical creation, it is most often used in manga to mean giant robots or people wearing body armor who are part human, part machine.

Brain Powered describes an earth overwhelmed by severe climate changes, natural disasters, and unwise human choices. Out of this chaos, two forces emerge: Orphan, a group of evil scientists who use living machines called Antibodies to gain control of Earth; and Brain Powereds, mechas who oppose Orphan. Sugisaki's black-and-white artwork in *Brain Powered* is intricate and explosive, and the panels are packed with up-close detail that increases the impression of fast-paced action. *Brain Powered* was originally published as a serial by Kadokawa in *Shonen Ace,* a boy's manga magazine. In the United States, it was collected into four volumes of graphic novels and published by TokyoPop in 2003 and 2004. Located in Los Angeles, California, TokyoPop is one of the few American publishers of authentic Japanese manga, which mean that they read right to left in the original Japanese style, rather than left to right in the Western style.

Sugisaki followed up *Brain Powered* with another science fiction mecha adventure, titled *The Candidate for Goddess* (in Japanese, *Megami Kouhosei*). Set in the year 4088, *The Candidate for Goddess* relates the story of another embattled universe, where humans face a new enemy named Victim. Victim has destroyed planet after planet until only the planet Zion and its colonies are left. To combat Victim, people have created a defense force of giant robots called Goddesses. These mecha are controlled by human pilots, who train at Goddess Operation Academy. Five volumes of manga tell the stories of the brave young men who are the candidates for Goddess.

Like *Brain Powered, The Candidate for Goddess* is a boy-oriented action story, and the artwork reflects the intensity of the story. Word balloons leap outside of panels, and close-ups reveal the characters' emotions with impact. Though action and adventure are primary, the boys' relationships with each other are also at the center of the stories, which explore friendship, trust, and betrayal.

Returns to shojo manga

Sugisaki's next series would take her back into the territory of shojo, or girl manga, with a wildly popular ten-volume series

Japanese Manga: Something for Everyone

American comics received a severe blow in the 1950s, when social "experts" denounced comic books as a bad influence on young people. Dr. Frederick Wertham's 1954 book *Seduction of the Innocent* claimed that reading comic books led to juvenile delinquency. However, in Japan, comics never suffered this criticism, and comic books there have been a part of mainstream culture for decades. Not only do Japanese people of all ages enjoy comics, but creating dojinshi, or fan comics, is a popular hobby for many comic readers.

There are many different types of Japanese comics, designed to appeal to every age, gender, and interest. Small children who are learning to read begin with kodomo manga, or children's comics. As they grow older, they begin to read shonen manga and shojo manga, boys' and girls' comics. Shonen manga feature stories of action and adventure or sports, but can include romance as well. Shojo manga often revolve around romance, but can also be dramatic adventure stories with female heroes.

There are also manga for gay audiences. Shonen-ai manga tell stories of love between boys and shojo-ai manga describe girl-girl romances. Many non-gay readers also like to read these stories, and, indeed, gender changes and same-sex romances are also frequent features of regular manga.

Adult Japanese comic readers have a variety of manga to choose from. Seijin manga for men and redikomi manga for women deal with adult subject matter, including romance and sexuality. There are even pornographic manga, called hentai. Other manga deal with practical aspects of daily life, such as how to win at mah-jong and other gambling games, how to succeed in business, and how to be a good housewife.

called *D.N. Angel*. The hero of *D.N. Angel* is Daisuke Niwa, a sweet and sensitive fourteen-year-old boy who is experiencing his first crush on a girl named Risa. Daisuke is a member of an unusual family. For one thing, he has been trained by his parents to be an expert thief, an occupation that makes the kind and honest Daisuke very uncomfortable. In addition to this, he discovers a remarkable family curse: when the boys of the Niwa family turn fourteen, they are occasionally possessed by Dark Mousey, a dashing, mysterious, and ghostly thief.

When Daisuke approaches Risa to tell her that he likes her, he turns into Dark for the first time. Dark is not only three years older than Daisuke and skilled at the art of stealing, but he is also a handsome, ruthless ladies' man, while Daisuke is, as Risa crushingly tells him, the kind of boy girls only want to be friends with. To complicate matters further, Risa is a twin, and Dark loves her sister Riku. When Daisuke sees Risa, he transforms into Dark, and when Dark sees Riku, he transforms into Daisuke. Supporting characters include a bunny named With who can transform into either Dark or Daisuke, and Krad (Dark spelled backwards), who is Daisuke's enemy.

All of these transformations, combined with the Niwa family business of thievery, lead to many humorous romantic adventures. The plot devices of mistaken identity, twins, and confused lovers can be found throughout classic literature from Greek drama to the works of English playwright William Shakespeare (1564–1616). Sugisaki adapts them perfectly to the manga tradition, with cute big-eyed characters and magically transforming animals.

The volumes of *D.N. Angel* include plenty of lighthearted adventure, but there is a real message about adolescence to be found in the stories. The gentle Daisuke must transform into to the handsomer but much more hardhearted Dark to appeal to the girl he likes. However, Risa is a shallow, competitive girl who is drawn to superficial qualities, like Dark's good looks. Riku is independent and smart, a genuinely good person who hates Dark and appreciates Daisuke. Hidden behind the romance and silliness are deeper messages about the value of being true to oneself and the cost of growing up. *D.N. Angel* not only became a monthly serial in the shojo magazine *Asuka,* but it became a popular anime and has been translated into several languages. The English version was published by TokyoPop.

In 2002, Sugisaki followed up *D.N. Angel* with another shojo manga called *Rizelmine. Rizelmine* is a madcap comic boy-meets-robot romance, that, like *D.N. Angel,* has a more serious underlying theme. In *Rizelmine,* fifteen-year-old Iwaki Tomonori finds himself married to twelve-year-old Rizel, a mecha girl made up of tiny robotic parts called nanobots. Rizel's makers find that she needs to learn to love before she can become fully human, so they force a marriage with Iwaki. Iwaki is not happy with the arrangement and tries to avoid Rizel's advances. However, he must take care, because Rizel is primarily a weapon, and her bodily fluids are pure nitroglycerin, a volatile explosive. It is not uncommon for boys to make girls cry, but when Rizel cries, her tears are dangerous.

Rizelmine is another dark parable of adolescence. Feeling trapped by choices he never made for himself, Iwaki is often cruel to Rizel, whose pain can destroy buildings. This creates an interesting twist on some typical shojo manga themes, such as how girls can attract a boy and the relationship between a typical boy and a girl with superpowers. Though the stories in which Rizel chases Iwaki to an explosive end are comic, they are also disturbing. The story was published in the United States by TokyoPop in 2005.

Bridges manga worlds

Continuing her unusual career of drawing both boys' and girls' comics, Sugisaki's next work was *Lagoon Engine*, a science fiction action adventure about Yen and Jin, the Ragun brothers. Yen and Jin are part of a family whose destiny is to fight the Maga, evil ghosts who stalk their neighborhood. The ghost-story adventures involve a cast of boy adventurers and explores yet another facet of adolescence when some of the boys get crushes on each other. Three volumes of *Lagoon Engine* were followed by *Lagoon Engine Einsatz*, which returns to the favorite Sugisaki theme of transformation with Sakis, a girl whose destiny is to transform into a man and become king of Lagoonaria. Though TokyoPop published *Lagoon Engine*, *Lagoon Engine Einsatz* was published by AD Vision, a Houston, Texas-based producer of Japanese manga for North American audiences. In early 2005, *Lagoon Engine Einsatz* was serialized in the American manga journal *NewType*, becoming the first Japanese comic to be published in English before being released in Japan.

Sugisaki carefully oversees the production of both the Japanese and Western publications of her work. She is meticulous about the quality of the reproductions, translations, and cover art, leading Paul Morrissey, one of her TokyoPop editors, to say on the publisher's Web site, "When it comes to Sugisaki-sensei, I'm always on my toes!" (*Sensei* means teacher and is a term of respect.)

■ ■ ■

For More Information

Books
Clements, Jonathan, and Helen McCarthy. *The Anime Encyclopedia: A Guide to Japanese Animation since 1917.* Berkeley, CA: Stone Bridge Press, 2001.

Periodicals
Galuschak, George. "*D.N. Angel,* Vol. 1." *Kliatt* (November 2004): p. 28.

Galuschak, George. "Yukiru Sugisaki: *Rizelmine.*" *Kliatt* (November 2005): p. 25.

"*Lagoon Engine,* Vol. 1: Review." *Publishers Weekly* (February 21, 2005).

Lipinski, Andrea. "Yukiru Sugisaki: *Rizelmine.*" *School Library Journal* (November 2005): p. 177.

"*Rizelmine*: Review." *Publishers Weekly* (September 19, 2005).

Web Sites

Boudreau, Chad. "Manga for Beginners." *Comicreaders.com.* http://www.comicreaders.com/modules.php?name=News&file=article&sid=96 (accessed on May 3, 2006).

Deppey, Dirk. "She's Got Her Own Thing Now." *The Comics Journal.* http://www.tcj.com/269/e_own1.html (accessed on May 3, 2006).

Morrissey, Paul. "*Lagoon Engine*: The Editor Speaks!" *TokyoPop.* http://www.tokyopop.com/dbpage.php?propertycode=LGE&categorycode=BMG&page=article (accessed on May 3, 2006).

"NewType to Publish New Manga from Yukiru Sugisaki." *Animetique.* http://www.animetique.com/pressview.asp?pID=103 (accessed on May 3, 2006).

Sato, Kumiko. *The World of Shôjo Manga.* http://www.personal.psu.edu/staff/k/x/kxs334/shojomanga/index.html (accessed on May 3, 2006).

"Yukiru Sugisaki." *Anime News Network.* http://www.animenewsnetwork.com/encyclopedia/people.php?id=5959 (accessed on May 3, 2006).

"Yukiru Sugisaki." *Prisms: The Ultimate Manga Guide.* http://users.skynet.be/mangaguide/au1793.html (accessed on May 3, 2006).

Rumiko Takahashi

Born October 10, 1957 (Niigata, Japan)
Japanese author, illustrator

A runaway success in Japanese manga comics and reputedly one of the wealthiest women in Japan, Rumiko Takahashi has also gained popularity among readers of comics in the United States. Most of her major works have been successfully translated into English despite their strong reliance on Japanese puns and word-play, and the animated episodes of one of her longest-lasting series, *Ranma 1/2*, was a major contributor to the explosion in popularity that Japanese animation, or anime, enjoyed abroad in the 1980s and early 1990s. Takahashi has been surprised by the international success of her work; she was quoted on the *Maison Ikkoku* Web site as saying that "if it's really true, then I'm truly happy. But I must also confess as to being rather puzzled as to why my work should be so well received. It's my intention to be putting in a lot of Japanese references, Japanese lifestyle and feelings...even concepts such as a subtle awareness of the four seasons. I really have to wonder if foreign readers can understand all this, and if so, how?"

The answer to that question may lie at the heart of Takahashi's success. It is true that many aspects of her work are specifically Japanese. Her romantic manga, the Japanese version of comic books, such as *Maison Ikkoku* rely on situations such as living in a boardinghouse, which most young North Americans would not be familiar with. Her fantasy- and horror-oriented work draws on Japanese history and mythology. Yet other features of Takahashi's work are universal in their appeal. Her manga, no matter what their genre, are strongly character-driven, with sympathetic char-acters (often female) driving the story along in such a way as to keep readers coming back for more—a necessity in Japan's weekly magazine-oriented manga scene. And Japanese readers as well as foreign fans value manga for its sense of surprise and its ability to

"I wanted to write slap-stick comedy because it is a great way to get the readers to react quickly.... I guess I'm really just a kid at heart!"

cross genre boundaries. Takahashi is masterful in exploiting both of these qualities of manga. Her works brim with plot twists, always logically worked out, and with lively mixtures of elements. *Ranma 1/2*, for example, has a fantasy/action theme—a young male martial arts student begins to veer between genders after falling into a magic hot spring—but the theme is developed into a multitude of comic situations. Takahashi also has a finely honed knack for slapstick humor involving horseplay and ridiculous behavior.

Organizes manga club

Rumiko Takahashi was born in Niigata, Japan, on October 10, 1957. Her enthusiasm for manga was even stronger than that of most other Japanese young people, and she founded a manga appreciation society at Niigata's Chuo High School. At first she made drawings in the margins of manga she would bring to class, but soon began to publish works of her own in the club's newsletter. By the time she had finished high school, she was thinking about making art a career, but she had also become a good enough student to survive Japan's tough college entrance exams, and her parents pushed her toward the idea of a more conventional profession.

In college at Nihon Joseidai (Japan Women's University), Takahashi managed to balance her various objectives, taking classes during the day and attending the Gekiga Sonjuku, a manga training course run by veteran comics artist **Kazuo Koike** (1932–; see entry; famous for *Lone Wolf and Cub*) in the evening. The dual course of study did not trouble Takahashi, who was becoming more and more interested in manga. "Sonjuku was an evening course, about two hours long," she was quoted as saying on *Maison Ikkoku*. "It didn't really feel like school to me, more like participating in a club." Koike emphasized the importance of character and character development in comics, which fit together with Takahashi's life experiences at the time—living in a cramped, crowded building that later provided inspiration for some of the story lines in *Maison Ikkoku*. She paid close attention to her surroundings and observed the comings and goings of the other people who lived in the building. Koike also had Takahashi draw hundreds of pages of comic art, building a foundation of craftsmanship and a work ethic that never left her: she is very creative and is always trying something new as an artist.

Takahashi's parents wanted her to take a professional job after graduation, a key moment in the highly structured pattern of the traditional Japanese career. But there were influences in the other direction as well. Koike's course was a key training ground for Japanese creative talent, and classmates such as fantasy writer Reiki Hikawa recalled Takahashi as an artist with distinctive gifts. The scales began to tip as Takahashi took a job as an assistant to horror manga artist Kazuo Umezu and began to publish manga of her own, first in a university magazine and then in commercial settings. Finally, Takahashi accepted an offer from the publisher Shogakukan to contribute a story to its widely read weekly, *Shonen Sunday*. After several freestanding short stories, she launched her first well-known series, *Urusei Yatsura* (the title is a hard-to-translate pun meaning "Those Obnoxious Aliens"), in 1978.

That series would last until 1987, but Takahashi's life was basic at first. Living in an extremely small apartment that at times housed one or more of her assistants (which forced Takahashi to use a closet as a bedroom), she sometimes questioned the wisdom of her choice. But the manga field in Japan is large enough that standout talents can make a good living from their work in time— according to some estimates, a quarter of all books sold in Japan are manga. As Takahashi's popularity grew, she said in a "100 Questions" segment quoted on the *Rumiko Takahaski: Princess of Manga* Web site that the first thing she bought after profits started to roll in was a laundry service, and that "all the food I can buy now, that is pretty exciting. I can buy really good yakisoba (fried noodles with meat and vegetables) and oden (fish cake stew) at a place called 'Nobori.' Now I seem to be quite popular there."

InuYasha is an action adventure with elements of romance and horror, drawing heavily on Japanese mythology. *InuYashu © 1997 Rumiko Takahashi/ Shogakukan, Inc. Viz, LLC.*

Admires *Spider-Man* comics

Urusei Yatsura is a mixture of science fiction and high school romance, centering on a volatile relationship between a male high school student and a sexy female alien who chase each other around—with the stipulation that only if Ataru Moroboshi, the high school student, wins the game of tag will the alien race call off its invasion of Earth. Takahashi had been thinking about the story since she was very young. Although not much influenced by American comics, Takahashi has said that she admired the excitement of *Spider-Man* and tried to bring something similar to Japanese manga. The flexible science-fiction format allowed Takahashi to introduce a host of secondary characters, some of them drawn from Japanese and Chinese mythology. One minor character was Ryunosuke, a cross-dressing woman whose story lines eventually evolved into those of *Ranma 1/2*.

While *Urusei Yatsura* was aimed primarily at boys and young men, Takahashi's next series, *Maison Ikkoku*, attracts adult and young adult readers of both sexes. Maison Ikkoku is a boarding house where cash-poor college student Yusaku Godai lives. He hopes to leave, but the building's new manager, beautiful widow Kyoko Otonashi, changes his way of thinking. Once again, Takahashi's subplots flow naturally from the main narrative, and her minor characters, based on Takahashi's own apartment-mates from her post-college years, are fully developed. *Maison Ikkoku* began its successful run in Japan in 1982; when it was translated and published in the United States in 2004, it provided enough material for a fifteen-volume series. Reviewer Steve Raiteri, writing in *Library Journal*, called *Maison Ikkoku* "arguably manga's premiere romantic comedy: funny, touching, heartfelt, and genuinely human."

Both *Urusei Yatsura* and *Maison Ikkoku* were wrapped up in 1987, and Takahashi launched three new series that year; her ongoing success was due in part to her ability to repeatedly strike off in new directions. The most successful of the three was the gender-bending, genre-bending *Ranma 1/2*, whose protagonist could change from male to female and back again after being splashed with hot or cold water. (Ranma's father, also a martial-arts practitioner, is afflicted by a similar curse but changes into a giant panda instead of a woman.) The comic was made into a television series in Japan in 1989, and increases in the quality and consistency of Japanese animation in general contributed to an increase in popularity in the United States and other Western countries. *Ranma 1/2* became a staple of anime film showings on U.S. college campuses, and the likeable Ranma, with his/her unique set of romantic dilemmas, gained thousands of fans who previously had little exposure to manga. In all, thirty-eight volumes of *Ranma 1/2* manga graphic novels were published, and they circulated all over the world.

Wins Inkpot Award

Takahashi's other new series were not as popular as *Ranma 1/2*, but they illustrated the range of her imagination and enjoyed long runs of their own. The *Mermaid Saga* veered away from Takahashi's trademark humor in favor of graphic horror stories, and *One-Pound Gospel* was a satirical romance centering on a novice nun and a boxer to whom she is attracted. Takahashi continued to create new kinds of stories and to cultivate the surprising twists of story and theme that are integral to manga as an art form. Her earlier series were made into animated films, and as her publications continued to find new audiences she topped the 100 million sales mark in the mid-1990s. Takahashi's growing popularity in the United States was recognized with an Inkpot Award for outstanding achievement in the comic arts at the annual San Diego Comic-Con convention in 1994.

Although she has a shy personality and rarely gives interviews, Takahashi effectively cultivated an unusual public image that complemented her art. She often contributed short commentaries to accompany her work in *Shonen Sunday*, discussing popular music, professional wrestling, and other topics in an offbeat, deliberately obscure style and riffing off her fans' involvement with her richly drawn characters by answering questions about the characters themselves. One of her favorite topics was the Hanshin Tigers, a baseball team of which she remained a steadfast fan.

Takahashi launched another new series, *InuYasha*, at the end of 1996; more serious than *Ranma 1/2*, it is an action adventure with elements of romance and horror, drawing heavily on Japanese mythology. *InuYasha* spawned Japanese films and television shows, and began appearing in translation in the United States in 1998. The shorter, single-installment horror and fantasy manga Takahashi consistently turned out were brought together in collections under the title *Rumic World*. By the early 2000s, Takahashi was at the head of a large comics empire. *Ranma 1/2* began appearing in a widely distributed U.S. edition in 2003, and by that time Takahashi could claim credit for having made manga a part of mainstream U.S. entertainment. A new U.S. edition of *Maison Ikkoku* followed in 2004, and a steady stream of new Japanese projects based on her various creations commanded her time. She was the best-selling female comics artist of all time, and one of Japan's central cultural figures.

For More Information

Books

Masaki, Enomoto. *Noda Hideki to Takahashi Rumiko.* Tokyo: Sairyusha, 1992.

Takahashi, Rumiko. *The Art of InuYasha: Collection of Original Illustrations.* San Francisco, CA: Viz, 2003.

Periodicals

Raiteri, Steve. "Takahashi, Rumiko. *Maison Ikkoku*: Vol. 1" (book review). *Library Journal* (January 2004).

Raiteri, Steve. "Takahashi, Rumiko. *Ranma 1/2*: Vol. 1: Action Edition" (book review). *Library Journal* (September 1, 2003).

Web Sites

"Rumiko Takahashi." *Anime News Network.* http://www. animenewsnetwork.com/encyclopedia/people.php?id=149 (accessed on May 3, 2006).

"Rumiko Takahashi: The Princess of Manga." *Rumic World.* http:// furinkan.com/takahashi/ accessed on May 3, 2006).

Smith, Toren. "Rumiko Takahashi." *Maison Ikkoku.* http://www.csua. berkeley.edu/~leon/mi/html/rumiko.html (accessed on May 3, 2006).

Hiroyuki Takei

Born May 15, 1972 (Yomogita, Aomori Prefecture, Japan)
Japanese author, illustrator

Japanese manga artist Hiroyuki Takei is one of several younger manga creators whose works have become a big hit outside Japan thanks to the international publication of magazines linked to *Weekly Shonen Jump*, the most popular manga magazine in Japan. Takei's breakthrough hit is *Shaman King*, the tale of a thirteen-year-old shaman—someone with the power to communicate with spirits and ghosts—who hopes to win the great Shaman Fight and become the Shaman King, a religious visionary with close links to God. The series ran in thirty-two *tankoubon* (graphic novel) volumes in Japan between 1998 and 2004, where it sold more than sixteen million copies. Viz began publication of the series in English in 2003, reaching volume seven in the series by 2005.

"I want to have a bigger perspective on things. I want to broaden my mind."

Achieves early success

Like so many Japanese manga-ka (manga creators), Takei has kept many of the details of his life private. He was born on May 15, 1972, in Yomogita, in the Aomori Prefecture, which lies on the northern end of the main Japanese island of Honshu. His first success in creating manga came when he published a short series called *SD Hyakkaten* for a fanzine, an amateur magazine created by manga fans. Takei then created the story *Itako no Anna,* which introduced the character of Anna, a young female shaman who would go on to play a large role in Takei's later works. *Itako no Anna* also helped Takei win the Osamu Tezuka Award, which is named for Japan's most famous manga artist, and the Hop Step Award, given to new manga artists. For a time in the early to mid-1990s, Takei worked as an assistant for established manga artists Nobuhiro Watsuki (1970–) and Tamakichi Sakura.

Best-Known Works

Graphic Novels (in English translation)
Shaman King, 7 vols. (2003–).

In 1997, Takei broke into the upper ranks of Japanese manga when his series *Butsu Zone* debuted in *Weekly Shonen Jump,* Japan's leading weekly manga magazine, which is read by millions of Japanese, young and old. *Butsu Zone* is an action-packed story that follows the efforts of a young boy named Senju who must find and protect someone believed to be a reincarnation of a sacred Buddhist religious figure, the Buddha Miroku. Like many shonen manga (action-oriented manga most popular with teenage boys), *Butsu Zone* favors action scenes and monsters over plot and character development. The series ended abruptly after being collected into three tankoubon and has not been translated into English.

The reign of *Shaman King*

When Takei quit work on *Butsu Zone* and began drawing a new series called *Shaman King* for *Weekly Shonen Jump* in 1998, it quickly became clear that he had created a storyline and a set of characters suited to a long-running series. The story begins when Yoh Asakura, is enrolled as a new student at the Shinra Private Academy, a middle school in Tokyo. Yoh Asakura is no ordinary student, in a number of ways: first, he's a slacker who walks around in a slouch, listening to music on his headphones and avoiding schoolwork; second, he's a shaman, which means that he can communicate with all the spirits of the underworld—ghosts, forest spirits, wandering souls of the dead, and ancient gods. In the ongoing series, Takei follows Asakura as he makes friends and battles enemies in both the mortal world of school and the immortal world of ghosts and demons.

The driving force behind *Shaman King* is Asakura's quest to become the Shaman King, a figure who will become the savior of the world by communicating directly with God, or the Great Spirit. But Asakura is not the only one who wants to become the Shaman King; in fact, as the story goes on shaman from throughout the world converge on Tokyo to battle against each other to see who will attain the title. Asakura is aided by Amidamaru, a samurai

Puzzling Evidence

Manga fans wishing to know more about the creators of their favorite stories must often rely on the small comments that authors insert in the text of the manga, or in introductory notes published in graphic novel compilations of ongoing series. Thanks to the Japanese tendency toward privacy, however, these brief notes can sometimes prove very puzzling and mysterious.

Shaman King author Hiroyuki Takei occasionally adds brief notes and pictures to his graphic novels, but anyone hoping to learn deep secrets about the author will be dissatisfied. For example, in the endnote to the U.S. version of *Shaman King,* Vol. 1: *A Shaman in Tokyo,* Takei writes: "It's difficult to go through love and a manga series a second time because I think about it too much. Mainly because I am afraid of being hurt again. But this needs to be overcome, or you can never get involved with manga or marriage. Anyways, I'll try my best." Is Takei speaking about stopping work on his first manga series, *Butsu Zone,* and starting work on *Shaman King*? Is he referring to events in his own personal life that we know nothing about? It is very hard to tell. Later, he wonders whether his son will be embarrassed by the manga he has drawn, and—in his most obscure comment—he writes: "I love deer. When I'm around them, all my thoughts stop and my mind is at peace." Perhaps this comment offers a key to understanding the deeper meaning of *Shaman King . . .* or not!

warrior who has been dead for 600 years but whose powers Asakura can access when he communes with Amidamaru's spirit. On a more pragmatic level, Asakura is also helped by his school friend, Manta Oyamanda; by his fiancée, Anna Kyoyama (who also appeared in Takei's earlier works); and by several others.

Throughout the series, Asakura battles against a range of enemies, typically pitting Asakura and his "ghost companion" Amidamaru against another Shaman and his or her otherwordly counterpart, each of whom has different powers and skills. As with most shonen manga, the action scenes are a very important component of the series and have become the basis for the video games and card games developed from the story. But action isn't everything. Takei depicts the slow growth in sensitivity and seriousness of young Yoh Asakura, who learns important moral and religious lessons from the battles that he fights. For example, in *Shaman King,* Vol. 3: *The Lizard Man,* Asakura saves his rival Ryu from death by placing himself in great personal danger; and as a result, he learns the importance of trust. Amidamaru relates this lesson learned when he says: "Hatred fosters only hatred. Salvation for a self-sufficient man like you required that someone place trust in you, and that you entrust yourself to them." Such moral lessons, as well as musings about the environment, the meaning of religion, friendship, and other issues, give *Shaman King* an underlying seriousness that is not immediately apparent.

Shaman King soared in popularity in Japan soon after its introduction in 1998, becoming one of the most popular manga series in that country. The series producers introduced a 64-episode anime (animated cartoon) series in 2001. As with other popular titles like *Yu-Gi-Oh, Shaman King* was also made into trading card games and action-packed video games. The cross-marketing of the series made *Shaman King* a natural transfer to English-speaking markets, which began experiencing their own manga craze in the early 2000s. The series began appearing in *Shonen Jump* magazine when that magazine was introduced in the United States and Britain in 2003, and the graphic novels began to be published that same year, reaching volume seven by the fall of 2005. The anime version of *Shaman King* was also prepared for release in English-speaking countries in 2005. (The series is also published in France, Germany, Italy, Norway, and Sweden, among other European countries.)

The future of *Shaman King,* both in Japan and overseas, remains unclear, however. In late 2004, *Weekly Shonen Jump* announced the end of the *Shaman King* run at 285 episodes and 32 graphic novels, but suggested that the series could continue if 50,000 fans wrote in. In the United States, more translated versions of the graphic novels still needed to be published before the series reached the existing Japanese conclusion. For his part, Hiroyuki Takei has written several smaller tales in Japan that relate to characters he developed for *Shaman King,* including the stories *Funbari no Uta* and *Mappa-Douji.* It is not certain, however, if Takei will continue to work on *Shaman King* or if he planned to turn his talents to other manga series.

■ ■ ■

For More Information

Books
Takei, Hiroyuki. *Shaman King.* 7 vols. San Francisco, CA: Viz, 2003–05.

Web Sites
"Hiroyuki Takei." *Shonen Jump.* http://www.shonenjump.com/ mangatitles/sk/manga_sk-artist.php(accessed on May 3, 2006).

"Hiroyuki Takei (Manga Artist)." *Anime News Network.* http://www.animenewsnetwork.com/encyclopedia/people.php?id=5932 (accessed on May 3, 2006).

"Products: Shaman King." *Viz Media.* http://www.viz.com/products/products.php?series_id=164 (accessed on May 3, 2006).

Shaman King. http://www.tv-tokyo.co.jp/anime/shaman/ (accessed on May 3, 2006).

Shaman King Anime. http://www.shamankinganime.com/sk/series.asp (accessed on May 3, 2006).

"Takei Hiroyuki." *Prisms.* http://users.skynet.be/mangaguide/au1870.html (accessed on May 3, 2006).

Naoko Takeuchi. *Courtesy of Kurt Busiek.*

Naoko Takeuchi

Born March 15, 1967 (Kofu, Japan)
Japanese author, illustrator

"For [Sailor Moon] and its characters to have special meaning to many people, I think tenacity and twinkles in the eyes are essential for the creator as well."

Naoko Takeuchi has become a public celebrity, an unusual phenomenon in the world of Japanese manga. "Manga" is the Japanese word for comic books, and most manga-ka, or Japanese comic artists, are reserved, private people. However, Takeuchi is the creator of one of the most popular manga concepts in the world, and she has been unusually willing to allow her fans to get to know her. Her best-known work, the girl-power story called *Sailor Moon,* not only became a much-watched animated cartoon show, or anime, but its characters have been reproduced on a wide variety of merchandise from dolls to shoes. In 1999, Takeuchi married another well-known manga-ka, Yoshihiro Togashi (1966–), and the two have become a sort of "supercouple" of the manga world, working together and even creating comics about their married life.

Best-Known Works

Graphic Novels (in English translation)

Sailor Moon 18 vols. (1998–2001).

Takeuchi has published many more manga in Japan, including *Chocolate Christmas* (1987–88), *Maria* (1989–90), *The Cherry Project* (3 vols., 1990–91), *Codename: Sailor V* (3 vols., 1991–97), and *Princess Naoko Takeuchi's Return-to-Society Punch!* (1998–2004).

Begins career as pharmacist

Takeuchi was born on March 15, 1967, in the city of Kofu in the Yamanashi Prefecture of Japan, well known in that country as the home of the venerated Mt. Fuji, the nation's largest mountain. Takeuchi began to draw and dream of becoming a manga artist when she was still a young child, and in high school she joined the drawing club. After graduating from high school, she went to Kyoritsu Chemical University. At the age of eighteen, while studying to be a pharmacist, she created her first published manga, a romance titled *Love Call,* which won the new artist award from *Nakayoshi,* a well-known magazine for young girls.

After graduating from college in 1986 with a degree in chemistry, Takeuchi went to work as a pharmacist at Keio Hospital in Tokyo. However, the encouragement of a supportive editor and her own devotion to her art inspired her to keep working on manga. *Chocolate Christmas,* introduced in 1987, and *Maria,* first published in 1989, were two of her first successful manga. Both comics were stories of the emotional worlds of adolescent girls, a theme that would remain important in Takeuchi's work. *Chocolate Christmas* contains an engaging twist in its name, telling the story of the lonely Ryon, who at Christmastime develops a crush on a suave radio disc jockey named Choco-San. *Maria* is a comic version of the 1912 Jean Webster novel, *Daddy Long Legs,* about an isolated young girl in boarding school who has a mysterious benefactor.

Takeuchi's first widely popular series was *The Cherry Project,* a love story set in the world of figure skating. *The Cherry Project* was first printed in *Nakayoshi* in 1990. Though Takeuchi enjoyed exploring the romantic and vulnerable side of her teenaged girl characters, she developed their strengths as well. For her next comic, she chose another popular manga theme: the girl with superpowers. *Codename: Sailor V* tells the story of Minako, who transforms into the Sailor V, powerful fighter for justice against evil. *Codename: Sailor V* made its debut in *Run-Run,* another well-known manga magazine.

Sails to success

The success of *Sailor V* prompted Takeuchi to expand on its basic idea. She gave the traditional "magical girl" theme a twist by adding another familiar Japanese theme: the group of heroes. Many Japanese adventure stories feature a "team" of five heroes who fight together. In the early 1990s, Takeuchi began work on *Pretty Soldier Sailor Moon,* tales of the adventures of five schoolgirls who transform into a team of superheroes with the help of the magical cat, Luna. Usagi, Rei, Ami, Minako, and Makota are the supergirls, and their fighter alter egos are Sailor Moon, Sailor Mars, Sailor, Mercury, Sailor Venus (Sailor V from the previous manga), and Sailor Jupiter. In English translations, the girls' names become Serena, Raye, Amy, Mina, and Lita. The dashing and mysterious boy Tuxedo Mask provides romantic interest, though in later episodes two female characters named Sailor Uranus and Sailor Neptune also become romantically involved.

Takeuchi chose the sailor theme because the sailor suit, worn by many schoolgirls as a uniform, symbolizes girlhood innocence. When activated by Serena's magical locket and the cry "Silver moon crystal power!" the five normal girls not only become super-powerful, but also become beautiful and sexy. Their demure sailor suits transform into skimpy skirts, tight tunics, and high-heeled boots. This sexualized image has caused some critics to question *Sailor Moon's* message to its young audience.

However, that audience was devoted to *Sailor Moon,* and the team of superheroines became an international phenomenon. Millions watched the *Sailor Moon* anime series on television and bought *Sailor Moon* products, while Takeuchi continued to create new *Sailor Moon* manga. Underlying the action and adventure, she always concentrates on the emotional lives of her characters as they struggle with growing up as well as protecting the world.

In 1998, the success of *Sailor Moon* led the popular *Young You* magazine to offer Takeuchi a regular feature, which she has called a "private essay comic." The strip, titled *Princess Naoko's Return to Society Punch!* depicts the artist's life and career, detailing

Sailor Moon Is Everywhere

In an interview with Charles McCarter on *EX: The Online World of Anime and Manga*, Naoko Takeuchi said, "In Japan, there is a lot of anime targeted specifically at girls. I would like to see this trend continue throughout the world." With the creation of her wildly popular *Sailor Moon* series, Takeuchi herself made a significant contribution to the spread of girls' manga.

Sailor Moon captivated Japanese girls from its first installment, published in *Nakayoshi* in 1992. Almost immediately an anime version was released, first on Japanese television, then around the world, and it was translated into Spanish, French, English, and other languages. The animated show ran for five seasons, with 200 episodes. The anime was followed by three *Sailor Moon* animated films, a live-action television show, and a long-running stage musical called *Sera-My,* in which actors performed a different episode in each performance.

Fans not only avidly read the manga and watched the anime, but they also bought hundreds of officially licensed *Sailor Moon* products. Several different manufacturing companies were licensed to make *Sailor Moon* shoes, key chains, purses, dolls, and craft kits. Some industry analysts predicted that the perky blonde Sailor Moon/ Serena doll would surpass the famous Barbie doll's popularity in the world market.

problems with publishers as well as personal hopes, dreams, and relationships.

On January 6, 1999, Takeuchi married respected manga-ka, Yoshihiro Togashi, author of *Yu Yu Hakusho* and *Hunter x Hunter.* The two have one son and have worked together producing *dojinshi,* or independently published Japanese comics. Some of these, such as *Prince Yoshihiro and Princess Naoko* and *Togashi Kingdom,* give a whimsical picture of their family life, with Takeuchi portrayed as a rabbit and Togashi as a dog.

■ ■ ■

For More Information

Periodicals

Dolan, Kerry A., and Gale Eisenstodt. "Watch Out, Barbie." *Forbes* (January 2, 1995): pp. 58–61.

Grigsby, Mary. "*Sailormoon*: Manga (Comics) and Anime (Cartoon) Superheroine Meets Barbie." *Journal of Popular Culture,* vol. 32 (Summer 1998): pp. 59–61.

Kingwell, Mark. "Babes in Toyland." *Saturday Night* (February 1997): pp. 83–85.

"Moon Power." *Video Business* (September 9, 2002): p. S24.

Raugust, Karen. "Smooth Sailing." *Publishers Weekly* (October 25, 1999): p. 28.

"Sailor Moon Targets Mass Market." *Playthings* (June 2000): p. 75.

Web Sites

Ashley, Angel. "Naoko Takeuchi." *Moonlit Dreams.* http://www.geocities.com/moonlitdreams50/naoko.html (accessed on May 3, 2006).

Hime No Oheya (Japanese Sailor Moon site). http://sailormoon.channel.or.jp/home.html (accessed on May 3, 2006).

"The Manga of Takeuchi Naoko." *Kurozuki.com.* http://www.kurozuki.com/takeuchi/ (accessed on May 3, 2006).

McCarter, Charles. "She Is the One Named Takeuchi Naoko." *EX: The Online World of Anime and Manga.* http://www.ex.org/3.6/13-feature_takeuchi.html (accessed on May 3, 2006).

Takeuchi Naoko. http://sensei.takeuchi-naoko.com/ (accessed on May 3, 2006).

"Takeuchi Naoko." *Manga Style.* http://mangastyle.net/takeuchinaoko.htm (accessed on May 3, 2006).

Vallen, Mark, "Naoko Takeuchi." *The Black Moon: Art, Anime, and Japanese Culture.* http://www.theblackmoon.com/Naoko/take.html (accessed on May 3, 2006).

Bryan Talbot. *Copyright 2006 Bryan Talbot.*

Bryan Talbot

Born February 24, 1952 (Wigan, England)
British author, illustrator

"Writing's the easy bit . . . it's nothing compared to the sheer volume of work that the artist has to do."

British comics creator Bryan Talbot's *The Tale of One Bad Rat* is often held up as an example of what can be accomplished by the graphic novel. With carefully drawn characters, a heart-rending storyline, and breathtaking art, Talbot's 1994 story about a homeless young girl haunted by memories of sexual abuse was widely celebrated as one of those rare works—along with **Art Spiegelman's** (see entry) *Maus: A Survivor's Tale*—that illustrates the artistic possibilities in a medium often criticized for dealing primarily in superheroes and mechanized robots. Though *The Tale of One Bad Rat* is Talbot's best-known work, the writer/illustrator has been creating comics since 1978 and is credited with creating the first British graphic novel, *The Adventures of Luther Arkwright,* in the late 1980s. Many of the most popular British comics creators of the late twentieth and early twenty-first century—including **Alan Moore, Neil Gaiman, Grant Morrison, Warren Ellis, and Garth Ennis**

Best-Known Works

Graphic Novels

The Adventures of Luther Arkwright. 3 vols. (U.K.) 1987–89; 1 vol. (U.S.) (1997).

A Tale of One Bad Rat (1995).

Heart of Empire (1999; on CD-ROM, 2001).

Alice in Sunderland. Forthcoming.

(see entries)—credit Talbot with inspiring their careers. Talbot has worked in a variety of areas, including authoring mainstream superhero stories, and in the 2000s producing a CD-ROM version of his *Hearts of Empire*, a sweeping adventure story set in the English past.

Roots in the underground

Bryan Talbot was born on February 24, 1952, in Wigan, a midsized town in northern England with a reputation for a grim industrial past. Looking back on his upbringing, Talbot has often commented that it makes perfect sense that he became a comic book artist: "I've always read comics," he told an interviewer for the *Pro File* Web site, "and always drawn." He recalled making his own comic books while he was in elementary school, carefully folding pages, stapling them together, and creating his own stories. "I never realised I could make a living doing comics," he continued, "though I knew I wanted to work in art somehow."

Though Talbot loved comics, he couldn't imagine creating them as a career, so he studied art instead. Talbot passed his college entrance exams (required for admission to higher education in England) and decided to take courses at the local Wigan School of Art. Instead of studying illustration, which would have trained him in the kinds of skills he would need to be a comics creator, he took classes from teachers who emphasized abstract art, or art that shied away from realistic depictions of the world. His abstract works weren't very good, he acknowledged, and his lack of enthusiasm for them contributed to his failure to gain entrance into the other art schools to which he applied. In the end, according to the *Pro File* Web site, Talbot felt he learned little from his art education.

Dropped out of school, and with a wife and the first of his two children to support, Talbot opened a head shop, a retail store that offered goods to members of the then-thriving counterculture (a subculture whose values and practices are different from the mainstream, and typically included drug use). Though discouraged by his art education, Talbot still drew comics. In the early 1970s, he drew one series called the "Chester B. Hackenbush Trilogy" that was published by a friend who owned a small press, and soon wrote and drew other small comics. It was the beginning of his long apprenticeship in the underground comics scene, a movement of comics artists in the United States and England that focused on publishing experimental comics with adult themes. In an interview on the *Cult/BBC* Web site, Talbot joked that this involvement with alternative comics in the mid-1970s was the first time drawing comics had made him feel cool: "At the time, to write and draw an underground comic was the next coolest thing to playing bass in a rock band."

Pens first British graphic novel

After writing and illustrating several smaller comics works in the mid-1970s, Talbot began to work on the much longer, more complicated work that would become *The Adventures of Luther Arkwright.* Part science-fiction, part historical novel, the story told the tale of a man who had the ability to travel between the parallel universes that exist in the novel: the present day and seventeenth-century England. *Luther Arkwright,* Talbot told *Pro File,* "was an attempt to do an intelligent adventure story for adults that was every bit as rich as a text novel and was drawn in illustration-quality artwork." Talbot published the first episodes of the story in 1978 in *Near Myths* magazine, and he continued the work in *pssst!* magazine until 1982; after a five-year hiatus, Talbot completed the book in two years in comics published by Valkyrie Press. (The story was finally brought together in three volumes in Britain in the late 1980s, and was published in a single volume in the United States by Dark Horse in 1997.)

With *Luther Arkwright,* Talbot became the first British comics creator to produce a graphic novel—a sustained narrative in comics form. He won immediate acclaim among the British comics community. Comics creator Warren Ellis (1968–), who reviewed the book on the *artbomb* Web site, later wrote that "*Luther Arkwright* is probably the single most influential graphic novel to have come out of Britain to date" and "will always be one of the most explosive creative experiences comics have yet undergone." The book's explicit treatment of drug use and sexuality meant that it would never be appropriate for a mainstream audience but, on the strength of the recognition he earned for the book, Talbot began to get a variety of other work that allowed him to give up his job managing the head shop in order to become a full-time comic book artist.

Through the 1980s and early 1990s, Talbot published a wide variety of comic books, both as writer and writer/artist. He co-created several stories for the British comics magazine *2000AD,* including stories for *Nemesis the Warlock* and *Judge Dredd,* two popular ongoing British series. He also broke into the American market, writing and illustrating works in the *Hellblazer* and *Sandman* series. His biggest successes came when providing the art for Tom Veitch's *The Nazz* and, in 1992, when he authored a two-part Batman story called *Mask* for the *Legends of the Dark Knight* series published by DC Comics. During these years, Talbot grew more adept at both his storytelling and his art.

Stumbles onto a bad rat

Ever since he had traveled to the Lake District in northern England as a child, Talbot had had a great affection for this famous region of lakes, valleys, and mountains, crisscrossed by trails. He had always wanted to set a story there, and in the early 1990s he began to write the tale of a runaway teenage girl from London who escapes with her pet rat to a new life in the Lake District. Then, he had an inspiration: the girl's motive for fleeing the city was the sexual abuse she had endured at the hands of her father. Talbot thus embarked on a tale that would become one of the most arresting graphic novels ever written. The story begins with Helen, the young girl, wandering through London, suffering the indignities and dangers of the homeless, including being hassled by the police and solicited by prostitutes. Longing to escape the city and her memories of being abused, she heads north to the Lake District, once home to the author of her favorite childhood stories, Beatrix Potter. In the Lake District, she finds peace working and boarding at a small inn. She eventually comes to terms with the abuse she has suffered, resolves to quit hating herself and blaming herself, and confronts her father. By the book's end, Helen has a smile on her face as she paints the lovely scenery of the Lake District.

The Tale of One Bad Rat is a striking example of what can be accomplished in a graphic novel. At the heart of the book's success

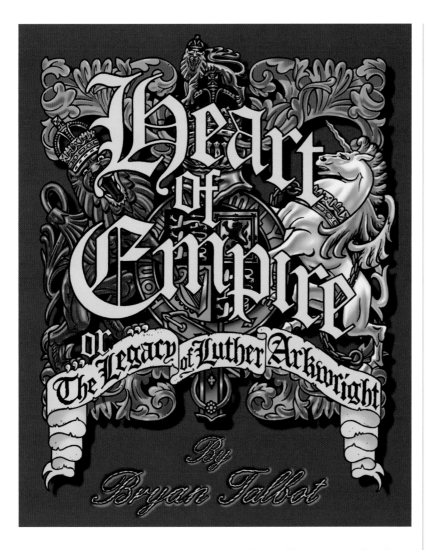

The graphic novel *Heart of Empire, or The Legacy of Luther Arkwright.* Copyright 2006 Bryan Talbot.

is the heart-rending story, which Talbot tells without flinching from the bare emotions of a tortured girl struggling with a terrible past. The story is complicated and multilayered, with numerous references to elements from Beatrix Potter's work. Talbot uses the visual elements of the comic book to enhance the story: Helen's memories of her past are cast in dark, angry tones, and Talbot masterfully draws a father who can look benign one moment and evil the next. The darkness and violence of the early scenes is contrasted with the pastoral beauty of the Lake District scenes, which Talbot renders with loving care. The result is a masterful combination of images and words. *The Tale of One Bad Rat*, published by Dark Horse in 1994, was widely reviewed and praised in the comics community. It won multiple awards around the world, including an Eisner Award, and is frequently named to lists of top graphic novels. Perhaps most telling, the book is frequently used by counselors to help young people who have suffered abuse see that they are not to blame for the things that were done to them.

In 1999, Talbot returned to producing comics for adults with his *Heart of Empire*. Though *Heart of Empire* is a sequel to the *Adventures of Luther Arkwright,* set twenty-three years after the events in that story, it is a very different work. Talbot told *Mars Import* Web site interviewer John Anderson that, unlike the experimental and complicated earlier story, with his new Arkwright comic, "I just wanted to create an exciting adventure story for adults that was an enjoyable ride for the reader. Its plot is totally linear and the storytelling clear and straightforward." *Heart of Empire* is presented in full color, unlike the earlier *Arkwright* story. The work continues the historical science fiction approach, as it follows Arkwright's daughter, Victoria, who comes to oppose the evil dictatorship of Queen Anne and brings about the downfall of the British Empire. True fans of Talbot's were thrilled when the author/artist released a full CD-ROM version of *Heart of Empire* that contained all of his sketches for the work, along with detailed commentary about the extensive historical research used to write the story. Perhaps most interesting to comics fans is the ability to see the unfolding creative process in penciled, inked, and colored versions of every page.

In the 2000s, Talbot has alternated between authoring or drawing single stories for other comics and working on his next full-length project. That work, *Alice in Sunderland,* is described on the *Official Bryan Talbot Fanpage* as an "approximately 300 page long graphic novel with the themes of storytelling, history and myth" centered around the history of the English town of Sunderland and its most famous inhabitant, Lewis Carroll (1832–1898), author of the story *Alice in Wonderland.* A perfectionist in creating his artwork, Talbot carefully labored over the work; it was described as nearly complete in late 2005.

■ ■ ■

For More Information

Books
Talbot, Bryan. *The Tale of One Bad Rat.* Milwaukie, OR: Dark Horse, 1995.

Periodicals

Booklist (September 15, 1995): p. 127.

Web Sites

Anderson, John. "An Interview with Bryan Talbot." *Mars Import.* http://www.marsimport.com/feature.php?ID=2&type=1 (accessed on May 3, 2006).

"Bryan Talbot." *Read Yourself Raw.* http://www.readyourselfraw.com/profiles/talbot/profile_talbot.htm (accessed on May 3, 2006).

"Bryan Talbot." *BBC: Cult TV, DVD & Lovely Stuff.* http://www.bbc.co.uk/cult/news/cult/2005/05/03/19072.shtml (accessed on May 3, 2006).

"Bryan Talbot, the Best Kept Secret in Comics." *Pro File.* http://www.popimage.com/nov99/profile/talbotinterview.html (accessed on May 3, 2006).

Gilman, Michael. "Interviews: Bryan Talbot." *Dark Horse Comics.* http://www.darkhorse.com/news/interviews.php?id=605 (accessed on May 3, 2006).

The Official Bryan Talbot Fanpage. http://www.bryan-talbot.com (accessed on May 3, 2006).

Tomoko Taniguchi

(Hokkaido, Japan)
Japanese author, illustrator

Manga creator Tomoko Taniguchi has made a name for herself, both in Japan and in the United States, with all-ages stories bearing positive, upbeat messages about family, friendship, love, and loneliness. Though her works are similar to many in the booming Japanese market for shojo manga (manga for girls), Taniguchi stands out for her desire to publish her work beyond the shores of her island nation. Even before she published her first work in Japan, Taniguchi dreamed of publishing in America. She persisted in her dream even when friends in America and Canada assured her that "no one would read shojo manga in their countries, because girls are different," she related to *Graphic Novelists* (*GN*). Her patience was rewarded with the successful publication of her books in English translation more than a decade after her first publication in Japan. Taniguchi happily told *GN* that the "time has come!"

Tomoko Taniguchi was born in Hokkaido, Japan. Taniguchi told *GN* that in her culture authors do not usually share the year of their birth because "sometimes age bothers us in this field." Little is known about her youth, though the *Animefringe* Web site indicated that she longed to be a manga creator from an early age. Rather than taking formal art lessons, Taniguchi developed her storytelling and artistic skills through diligent independent practice. Her formal education focused on language.

When Taniguchi saw *Star Wars* in Japan in the late 1970s, she knew she had to learn English. "*Star Wars* changed my life!" she told *GN*. "If George Lucas had not made *Star Wars*, I would not have studied English so hard." In college, Taniguchi studied the language at the University of Michigan in Ann Arbor, where she also absorbed American culture, falling in love with science fiction

"This has always been one of my big dreams—having one of my manga published abroad, because I have many friends in many countries. . . ."

Best-Known Works

Graphic Novels (in English translation)

Call Me Princess (1999).

Aquarium (2000).

Spellbound (2001).

Princess Prince (2002).

Just a Girl 2 vols. (2003).

Let's Stay Together Forever (2003).

Miss Me? (2003).

Popcorn Romance (2003).

movies, especially those about Spider-Man and the X-Men. While in America, Taniguchi explored the possibility of publishing her manga, even though her friends told her that "Western girls prefer actually dating than reading such shojo manga," she told *GN*. Unable to secure an American publisher, she returned to Japan.

Taniguchi's career as a professional manga creator began in the mid-1980s when she submitted a forty-page story to a contest in a monthly Japanese horror magazine. The story won first prize and was published in the magazine. When the horror magazine stopped publication, she submitted her work to shojo manga magazine *Omajinai Comics*. Her story "An-Pan-Balance" was a winning submission and marked her debut as a shojo manga creator.

Taniguchi told *GN* that winning magazine contests was a common way for manga creators to get started. "Almost every magazine has a contest, monthly or annually. So we have many chances," she said. "I always explain to both Japanese readers and American readers that there are lots of chances for you to enter the manga field, but staying in this field is more difficult. Every month somebody wins, but many of them have a difficult time two years later." Taniguchi worked hard to continue success in her career. She spent a year drawing for *Omajinai Comics* before publishing her first fully developed manga in 1989 in Japan, *Let's Stay Together Forever*. (This title would be translated and published in the United States in 2003.) She told *GN* that "I was really lucky. Many of my friends, who debuted at the same magazine in the same year, had not published any graphic novels by the time I had published nine books."

With *Let's Stay Together Forever,* Taniguchi set a tone of emotional sensitivity that would permeate her later work. Telling about a high school romance fraught with troubles, Taniguchi navigates the relationship between two people, heavy metal rocker Leo and shy girl Ayami, who belong to sharply divided social groups. Her characters approach each other cautiously, getting to know one another while learning to deal with the social pressures of their different social cliques. Taniguchi handles the emotional struggles and growth of her characters with great care. In *Let's Stay Together Forever,* she composes her artwork to reveal the emotional strain Ayami and Leo experience when they are first seen in public at an ice cream shop. Taniguchi creates a sense of social pressure by filling the pages with negative opinions and gossip of onlookers staring at them. Taniguchi's technique builds a sense of the panic felt by Ayami and Leo. In the end, Taniguchi reveals the benefits of respecting your own true desires without giving in to social pressure.

Taniguchi's approach to storytelling differs from that of many shojo manga artists. Most shojo stories involve a long-running, soap-opera-like story for a steady set of characters, but Taniguchi creates shorter stories with a shifting ensemble of characters. While most of her stories involve some sort of romance, she also tackles issues such as starting school without friends and dealing with the impending loss of family property, with suicidal feelings, and with a person whose affections you don't share. She also approaches such unusual circumstances as living as a practicing witch and growing up as a girl when you are really a boy. *Aquarium,* first published in Japan in 1990 (translated and published in the United States in 2000) offers insight into a teenage girl's suicidal feelings after failing an important high school placement test. *Call Me Princess,* first published in Japan in 1992, is a teenage romance about a girl's hopes of finding a boy who will treat her like a princess.

A decade after starting what turned into a successful career as a manga creator in Japan, Taniguchi still harbored dreams of publishing in the United States. Her dream started to turn into reality when she met **Colleen Doran** (1963–; see entry), creator of *A Distant Soil.* Taniguchi related to *GN* that she had long admired Doran's artistic ability and was happy when one of her best friends in America introduced her to Doran and the pair became friends. Doran published a drawing of Taniguchi's in one of her comics with a

Central Park Media Manga

Central Park Media became a pioneer of Japanese anime and manga in the United States in the 1990s. Started by John and Masumi O'Donnell in Manhattan in 1990, Central Park Media translated a wide variety of Japanese cartoons and comics for the American market. Confident that Japanese popular culture would be of interest to Americans, Central Park Media tried to be as true to the original products as possible, not changing scenes or dialogue to better suit American expectations. While Central Park Media has become one of the leading Japanese anime (animated cartoon) and live-action film suppliers in the United States, it also continues to publish translated manga.

Tomoko Taniguchi's graphic novels, and those of many other manga creators, are available through the Central Park Media Press Web site. The site presents a preview of manga in a unique format: the look of a real book. Users can actually turn the pages of Taniguchi's Let's Stay Together Forever, clicking and dragging to turn each page, the graphics seeming to peel back like the pages of a paper book.

caption noting Taniguchi's wish to be published in America. When Central Park Media editor C. B. Cebulski noticed the drawing, he contacted Taniguchi to offer her a publishing contract. Starting with Call Me Princess, Taniguchi's fifth manga title in Japan, Central Park Media offered Taniguchi's work to English-language readers in 1999. Eventually all of her previous work was translated into English. Despite the outdated hairstyles and fashions in some of her early stories, Taniguchi's stories became best-sellers for Central Park Media. For all Doran's help making her dream come true, Taniguchi told GN: "I owe her a lot!"

The enormous growth of the manga market in the United States during the late 1990s and the popularity of Taniguchi's work prompted Cebulski to try something new. He started up his own comics publishing firm, Fanboy Entertainment, and persuaded Taniguchi to do something no other Japanese manga creator had done before: write a manga specifically for an American audience. Taniguchi's Spellbound, published in 2001, tells the story of Ami, a teenage girl dealing with all the everyday highs and lows of adolescence while also living as a practicing witch. Her magical skills enable her to save her friends and learn more about true love. This manga has not crossed back to Japan: it is only available in English.

In the early 2000s, Taniguchi remained focused on producing new manga. She experimented with her new work, stepping away from the pattern of writing "all ages" stories to write tales that would appeal to older readers (though not "sexy stories," she explained to *GN*). She described her early work as "happy stories to encourage girls," but her work for older readers would be "a little cynical." Her new stories were for women who "have problems at work, at life, or at love." Taniguchi thought about publishing these new types of stories under a pseudonym. "Maybe this sounds strange to American people," Taniguchi said to *GN*. "In Japan manga artists often use a pseudonym. We hide name, age, address. Many of us want to stay mysterious in order to let our work stand on its own."

Taniguchi related that another "big step" for her career would come in 2006: She would publish her first work for Marvel Comics, one of America's largest comic book publishers. Taniguchi worked with Cebulski (another person to whom she "owes a lot") to produce a story for *I (HEART) Marvel: Marvel AI*. "Ai" means "love" in Japanese. The story about the Scarlet witch's romance with a robot is very short, but meant a great deal to Taniguchi because "working for Marvel is one of my biggest dreams," she told *GN*.

With new publications forthcoming and editions of her work in print in Japan, Korea, Mexico, Taiwan, and the United States, Taniguchi seemed well on her way to fulfilling the dream she described in her first English translated manga: to have her friends be able to find her work "anywhere on Earth."

For More Information

Web Sites

"*Aquarium* Manga Review." *Tokidoki Entertainment Journal.* http://www.tokidokijournal.com/manga/aquarium/ (accessed on May 3, 2006).

Central Park Media Press. http://www.centralparkmedia.com/cpmpress (accessed on May 3, 2006).

Font, Dillon. "True-Blue Dreams Coming True: The Shojo of Tomoko Taniguchi." *Animefringe.* http://www.animefringe.com/magazine/2003/10/feature/01/ (accessed on May 3, 2006).

Tomoko Taniguchi Official Site. http://www.h6.dion.ne.jp/~tomoko-t/index.html (accessed on May 3, 2006).

Other

Additional information for this article was obtained through email correspondence with Tomoko Taniguchi in December 2005 and January 2006.

Osamu Tezuka

Born November 3, 1928 (Toyonaka, Osaka, Japan)
Died February 9, 1989 (Tokyo, Japan)
Japanese author, illustrator, filmmaker

Osamu Tezuka virtually created the modern genre of manga, the Japanese version of comic books, by drastically rethinking a range of existing Japanese graphic art forms. One of the most influential artists in the entire graphic tradition, Tezuka helped shape both the look and the thematic content of contemporary Japanese comics. The cinematic grace of manga, accomplished by an artist who manipulates the ebb and flow of action in graphic frames as a film director might manipulate frames of film, was largely Tezuka's creation, as were the large, dark eyes conventionally associated with female characters in Japanese comics. Tezuka also inspired Japanese artists to tackle serious themes in the graphic medium, creating complex works that were hundreds of pages long. The Japanese often refer to Tezuka as the Father of Manga or even the God of Manga, and the *History of Manga* Web site summed up his influence with the opinion that "Manga today is flourishing on the foundations laid by Tezuka Osamu."

"I felt that existing comics were limiting....I also believed that comics were capable of more than just making people laugh."

Fascinated by insects

Born on November 3, 1928, in Toyonaka, Japan, near Osaka, Tezuka grew up in Takarazuka, in Japan's Hyogo Prefecture. Quite a variety of artistic influences marked his childhood. His family encouraged his artistic skills, often leaving a sketch pad by his bed. Tezuka turned his talent toward his love for insects, producing precise entomological drawings while he was still very young. Sometimes he organized his school friends to search for insects in the woods, and he later incorporated the written Japanese character meaning "insect" into his signature. He also entertained his classmates with small comic strips. Tezuka's parents owned a

Best-Known Works

Graphic Novels (in English translation)

Black Jack 16 vols. (1993–2000).

Adolf 5 vols. (1995–96).

Phoenix: A Tale of the Future 5 vols. (2002–04).

Astro Boy 23 vols. (2002–04).

Metropolis (2003).

Lost World (2003).

Nextworld 2 vols. (2003).

Buddha 8 vols. (2003–05).

movie projector and enjoyed showing Western films, including early examples of animation, as well as Japanese cinema in their home.

Tezuka's high school years coincided with the upheaval of World War II (1939–45; war in which Great Britain, France, the Soviet Union, the United States, and their allied forces defeated Germany, Italy, and Japan). He thought about studying to become an entomologist but instead decided to take medical classes at Osaka University, partly because of a childhood episode in which an infection threatened him with the loss of both arms but was cured by the energetic intervention of a devoted doctor. In spite of this motivation, the artistic side of Tezuka's personality kept resurfacing. He kept making drawings during classes, and in 1946 he published a comic strip called "Diary of Ma-chan" in a student newspaper. The newspaper soon hired Tezuka to draw a regular strip, but he never gave up on his medical studies. In 1951, he earned a degree from the Osaka University College of Medicine, and ten years later he received a second medical license at Nara Medical University.

Though he finished his education, it was during school that Tezuka created the work that permanently changed his career. *Shin Takarajima* or *New Treasure Island*, published in 1947, was based on the Robert Louis Stevenson (1850–1894) classic novel *Treasure Island*. Tezuka's version diverged sharply from the comics Japanese readers were familiar with. Adapting a work of classical

Astro Boy, or *Tetsuwan Atom* in Japanese, made its debut in 1952 and lasted for an impressive 193 episodes. *Dark Horse Comics.*

literature was not unusual; Japanese graphic narratives, unlike those in the United States, had a long history that involved works aimed at all age groups and sectors of society. Rather, it was Tezuka's visual style that caught readers' eyes. Tezuka devoted an unusual amount of space to depicting the unfolding of events in pictures only. An opening scene in which the story's young protagonist hurries to get on a ship that is about to sail occupied 8 of the book's 180 pages, with close-ups of the boy, shots of a car zooming along the seashore, and so on. Tezuka clearly signaled that the pictures were as important as the words.

Tezuka's innovations had various sources of inspiration. A lover of serious European films, he tried to replicate the visual styles of their directors in the graphic medium. Although he later deplored the direction taken by the Disney Studios in the United States, he greatly admired the work of Walt Disney himself and absorbed the American master's classic animated films one by one as they appeared in the 1940s. He watched an average of one film a day over the course of a year, and it was reputed that he saw the film *Bambi* eighty times and *Snow White* fifty times. Finally, Tezuka was inspired by a more general desire to create something new and positive out of the ruins of postwar Japan. *New Treasure Island* sold a reported 400,000 copies, all without the benefit of any significant marketing effort in Japan' struggling post-war economy.

Lion character may have inspired Disney

The 1949 manga publication *Metropolis*, probably based on Fritz Lang's classic German science-fiction film but given a distinct Japanese twist, was Tezuka's next major success; it was adapted into an animated film by *Akira* creator Katsuhiro Otomo (and directed by Tezuka protege Rintaro) in 2002. Tezuka's 1950 creation *Jungulu Taitei*, also known as *Jungle Emperor Leo* or *Kimba the White Lion*, also may have inspired a later cinematic effort; when Disney Studios' *The Lion King* was released in Japan in 1994, a group of Tezuka's proteges alleged that its story had been based in large part on Tezuka's *Kimba* stories and urged the studio to add a note to prints of the film crediting Tezuka for his ideas. The Disney studio, however, maintained that the ultimate source of its film was William Shakespeare's play *Hamlet*.

Tezuka's wife eventually declined to pursue legal action against Disney, pointing to the numerous instances in which Tezuka had borrowed Disney techniques in his own work. One example was his use of large, dark eyes in his characters in the female-oriented shojo manga genre; based ultimately on such characters as Bambi and Mickey Mouse, the technique became so widespread as to become stereotypical for youthful manga characters. Tezuka felt that drawing oversized eyes made it easier for him to depict fine shades of emotion, and works such as Tezuka's *Princess Knight* series (1953–56) became extraordinarily popular among young

Japanese readers. *Princess Knight* featured the adventures of Princess Sapphire, a girl who grows up pretending to be a boy; it drew inspiration from the Takarazuka Revue of Tezuka's childhood and spawned a host of other androgynous (having the characteristics of both male and female) manga protagonists.

The postwar Japanese orientation toward the future formed a backdrop for Tezuka's first international success. "In 1951, there were still ruins in Japan," Tezuka's associate Yoshihiro Shimuzu told James Brooke of the *New York Times*. "People made efforts to create a bright future and better Japan. Astro Boy became the symbol of their dream." *Astro Boy,* or *Tetsuwan Atom* in Japanese, made its debut in 1952 and lasted for an impressive 193 episodes. The series was a sequel to an even earlier Tezuka comic called *Captain Atom.* The initial run of *Astro Boy* was just the beginning of its success. Made into an anime series, it began airing on Tokyo television in 1957. In 1963, Tezuka visited the United States to finalize a deal for the broadcast of *Astro Boy* cartoons on American television; it became the first Japanese anime shown in the country, but the NBC network deemphasized its Japanese origins in promoting the show. *Kimba the White Lion* and *Princess Knight* were later shown on NBC as well.

In 1961, Tezuka had started his own production company, Mushi Productions and revolutionized Japanese animation nearly to the degree to which he had remade the world of Japanese comics. In place of the expensive American technique by which individual animation cels (frames) were handpainted, Tezuka pioneered the use of a set of cels showing typical emotions and poses for characters featured in a film or series of films. This technique became standard in Japan and lowered the costs associated with animated films.

Maintained business and creative roles

Nevertheless, Tezuka's business insight was inferior to his skill as an artist, and Mushi Productions, despite a successful animated series adaptation of *Astro Boy,* failed to prosper. Even while discharging his responsibilities as president of the company, Tezuka continued to write new material of his own and suffered from overwork. Mushi Productions filed for bankruptcy in 1973. The positive side of these developments, from the viewpoint of manga historians, was that Tezuka continued to come up with fresh ideas. Such new Tezuka series as *Amazing Three* (1965–66) continued to find favor with the Japanese public.

Tezuka also began to unleash his ambition to create manga works on a grand literary scale. He was not the only manga artist to hold serious aspirations for the graphic medium, but Tezuka's writings such as *The Phoenix,* a massive series begun in 1954 and continued intermittently until his death, were unusual in their breadth and complexity. *The Phoenix,* taking the mythical bird of ancient Greece as its central motif, veered between Japan and the West, and between past and future. *Buddha,* which also took shape over many years, was a lengthy graphic biography of Buddhism's founder. Tezuka's work did not treat the Buddha with the reverence of a god, but rather made him a wise and important figure at the center of a rowdy comic tale. For all the book's humor, it was impeccably researched. The *Buddha* was translated into English and published in the United States in the early 2000s. Owing partly to the graphic difficulties in translating Japanese comics (Japanese is read from right to left), many of Tezuka's works have remained available only in Japanese, however.

Nevertheless, in the later part of his life, Tezuka gradually became known in the West. In 1967, he won a Silver Lion Award at the Venice International Film Festival, and in 1984, he won the grand prize at the Zagreb Animation Festival. His reputation was enhanced by several ambitious late works that took up themes from world history; *Tell Adolf,* which first appeared in 1983, was set in pre-World War II Germany and featured three characters named Adolf: one Jewish, one a non-Jewish German, and the third Adolf Hitler himself. Tezuka also created lighter films such as *Legend of the Forest,* an homage to Walt Disney's treatments of classical music set to a passage from Tchaikovsky's Symphony No. 4, and *The Manga Introduction to the Japanese Economy,* which became known in the United States under the title *Japan Inc.* Throughout his career, Tezuka remained a versatile artist who created comics out of almost any conceivable subject matter. Many of his works, however, shared an aversion to war and a consciousness of the preciousness of life.

After his death from stomach cancer in Tokyo on February 9, 1989, Tezuka was acclaimed for his role in making manga perhaps Japan's most visible and popular art form, with an estimated one in every four books sold in Japan falling under the manga classification. An Osamu Tezuka Museum of Comic Art opened in Takarazuka in 1994, and a set of Tezuka postage stamps was issued by the Japanese government three years later. New Tezuka projects continued to appear in English translation, and there remained much to learn about the products of one of the most creative figures ever to work in the graphic medium.

For More Information

Books

Schodt, Fredrik L. *Manga! Manga!: The World of Japanese Comics.* New York: Kodansha International, 1983.

Periodicals

Brooke, James. "Heart of Japanese Animation Beats in a Robot Boy." *New York Times* (April 7, 2003).

"Eclectic: Japanese Manga." *The Economist* (December 16, 1995).

Gustines, George Gene. "An Icon of Animation and His Atomic-Powered Adventures." *New York Times* (February 8, 2004).

Heer, Jeet. "Buddha Comes to America: New Translation of Osamu Tezuka's Comic-Strip Tale of the Enlightened One." *National Post* (Canada) (May 20, 2004).

Rosen, Judith. "Buddha Comes to America." *Publishers Weekly* (December 22, 2003).

Web Sites

"A History of Manga Part 3: Tezuka Osamu and the Expressive Techniques of Contemporary Manga." *A History of Manga.* http://www.dnp.co.jp/museum/nmp/nmp_i/articles/manga/manga3-1.html (accessed on May 3, 2006).

Osamu Tezuka: The Father of Manga. http://tezukasite.tripod.com (accessed on May 3, 2006).

"Osamu Tezuka (The God of Manga)." *Anime News Network.* http://www.animenewsnetwork.com/encyclopedia/people.php?id=883 (accessed on May 3, 2006).

Tezuka: God of Comics. http://www.hanabatake.com/research/tezuka.htm (accessed on May 3, 2006).

Tezuka Osamu World. http://en.tezuka.co.jp (accessed on May 3, 2006).

Roy Thomas

Born November 22, 1940 (Missouri)
American author, editor

Many comic book fans dream of becoming part of the world of comics, creating the superheroes and dramatic adventure stories that fill the pages of the comic books that they love to read. This dream began for Roy Thomas during his boyhood in the 1940s, an era that is often called the "Golden Age" of comics because of the massive popularity of comics created by DC and Marvel Comics. When Thomas grew up, he turned his dream into reality, starting as co-editor of a fan magazine and going on to become editor-in-chief of Marvel Comics. Throughout his career, Thomas has overseen the creation of hundreds of comics, writing many himself, and leading comics into a new and more literary direction.

Thomas was born on November 22, 1940. He was still in college in 1961 when he began to work on a fan magazine called *Alter Ego*, started by comics fan and historian Jerry Banks. By 1964, Thomas had risen from contributor to co-editor of *Alter Ego*, which focused on the history of popular comic superheroes as well as profiles of the artists who created them.

While working on *Alter Ego*, Thomas began to correspond with Mort Weisinger, who edited the *Superman* series for DC Comics. In 1965, with Weisinger's encouragement, Thomas left a teaching job in the Midwest to move to New York to take a job as Weisinger's assistant. However, Thomas was an independent and creative worker, and did not get along with his new boss. Within weeks, he left DC to take a job as a staff writer for Marvel Comics.

At Marvel, Thomas began to write stories for such classic Marvel titles as *The Avengers* and *X-Men*, both superhero team comics, a genre that Thomas would continue to develop throughout his career. It was during these first years at Marvel that Thomas met

"To me, the authentic comics are the original ones."

Best-Known Works

Graphic Novels

(With others) *Star Wars: A Long Time Ago...* 1977–86 (comics series); 7 volumes. (2002).

The Dragonlance Saga. 3 volumes. (1988–89).

(With Gerry Conway) *Conan the Barbarian: The Horn of Azoth.* (1990).

(With Tim Conrad) *Amuric.* (1991).

Richard Wagner's The Ring of the Nibelung. (1991).

(With John Buscema) *Conan, the Rogue.* (1991).

The Many Armors of Iron Man. (1992).

(With Esteban Maroto) *Dracula: Vlad, the Impaler.* (1993).

(With Randy Lofficier and Ted McKeever) *Superman's Metropolis.* (1996).

(With Michael Lark) *Superman: War of the Worlds.* (1999).

(With others) *The Song of Red Sonja and Other Stories.* (2004).

(With others) *The Monster of the Monoliths and Other Stories.* (2004).

The Chronicles of Conan. 10 volumes. (2003–06).

Collections

(Editor, with Bill Schelly) *Alter Ego: The Best of the Legendary Comics Fanzine.* (1997).

(Editor, with Murphy Anderson) *All Star Companion.* (2004).

(With others) *Marvel Visionaries: Roy Thomas.* (2006).

Stan Lee (1922–), editor-in-chief and creator of such famous Marvel heroes as Spiderman. Lee became a friend and mentor to Thomas during the early development of his comics career.

By the late 1960s, Thomas had begun to tire of comics' focus on superheroes. He thought it would help to elevate the status of the comic book if comics were based on historical or literary characters. For his first effort, he chose a character from a series of pulp novels written by Robert E. Howard (1906–1936) in the 1930s. Howard's stories describe an imaginary ancient past that includes the lost continent of Atlantis and a variety of mythical tribes and kingdoms. One of his most memorable heroes is a burly barbarian warrior named Conan the Cimmerian, who first appears in a 1932 novel called *The Phoenix on the Sword.*

Howard's novels were re-released during the 1960s, and they inspired Thomas to buy the rights to turn Conan into a comic book hero. His lengthy *Conan the Barbarian* series introduced a new genre to comic books, the "sword-and-sorcery" comic. By the mid-1970s, *Conan* had become one of Marvel's best-selling titles, and several of its characters, such as Red Sonja, a spirited warrior queen, had spun off into their own comic series.

In 1972, Stan Lee became president and publisher of Marvel, and Roy Thomas was promoted to editor-in-chief. For the next two years, Thomas attempted to lead Marvel in new directions but became discouraged and resigned the position, preferring to return to writing and editing comics. He continued to develop the sword-and-sorcery line, adding titles like *The Iron Hand of Almuric,* about an ancient warrior transported into outer space to battle alien monsters on a strange planet, and *Kings of the Night,* about northern barbarian tribes battling the Roman empire. In 1977, he capitalized on the enormous popularity of the *Star Wars* movies by creating twenty volumes of *Star Wars* comics that received praise from both fans and critics.

While working at Marvel, Thomas supervised the creation of dozens of books each month, and continually pushed the company to try new approaches in order to attract more readers. For example, he oversaw the production of a line of comics designed to draw in female readers, even taking the unusual step of hiring women writers to increase the realism of the female heroes. These comics, such as *The Cat, Night Nurse,* and *Shanna, Queen of the Jungle,* were fairly successful, as were the two humor comics, *Crazy* and *Spoof,* that Thomas developed in an effort to lure the readers of *Mad* magazine over to Marvel.

Finally, in 1981, Thomas could no longer work out his disagreements with the administration at Marvel. He left the company and went to work for DC Comics. There he returned to his first love, the classic comics of the Golden Age of the 1940s. He brought back the original Justice Society of America (JSA), another comic superhero team. Though dozens of DC superheroes had been members of the JSA through the years, fans were especially loyal to the original Golden Age members, such as the Atom, Green Lantern, Hawkman, and Hourman. Thomas brought them all back and actually set the story in the Golden Age, telling stories of the All-Star Squadron battling Nazis during World War II (1939–45). Thomas also created a new team that he called Infinity, Inc., made up of the children of the original JSA members.

In the late 1980s, Thomas returned to Marvel, where he continued to reach beyond the superhero format for comic ideas. From Norse mythology, he got the inspiration for *Thor,* who was not only a superhero, but the god of thunder. *Dr. Strange* told the supernatural adventures of a sorcerer battling the demons and monsters who serve the forces of evil.

During the 1990s, Thomas ventured into the world of independent comic publishers, where he continued his efforts to broaden

Comics: Gold, Silver, and Bronze

Throughout his career, Roy Thomas has had a respectful fascination with the comics of the Golden Age. The production of comic books began in 1933 with a collection of Sunday comic strips put together by a salesman named Max Gaines. The Golden Age of comics began five years later when DC Comics released a book called *Action Comics No.1,* which introduced a new hero called Superman. Throughout the next few decades, larger-than-life heroes like the Phantom, Sandman, and Daredevil fought villains like Deathbolt, Nuclear, and Night and Fog, to the delight of readers.

A period of political and social repression during the 1950s dealt a severe blow to the comics industry, but in the 1960s sales began to pick up and the Silver Age of comics began. Some comic historians place the beginning of the Silver Age of Comics in 1961, with the publication of *The Fantastic Four,* created by Marvel Comics' Stan Lee and Jack Kirby. This comic marked a new rise in reader interest in superheroes, and a new breed of hero, with superpowers and also very human insecurities and worries.

The Bronze Age of comics began in the early 1970s with the introduction of a new type of non-super hero, such as the barbarian warriors pioneered by Roy Thomas. Bronze Age comics also began to develop grittier plots that dealt with social issues like racism and drug addiction.

the appeal of comic books by adapting serious classics to comic form, such as his comic version of Richard Wagner's operas. Though considerably more highbrow than *Conan* or *Thor,* Thomas's *Ring of the Nibelung* also tells the dramatic adventures of ancient warriors. The Victorian gothic novel *Dracula* by Bram Stoker was also perfect for Thomas's comic book adaptation, with its dark occult setting and blood-drinking villain.

Always willing to work wherever he could have the most freedom to develop his original ideas, Thomas returned to DC to produce a pair of unique classic adaptations, this time based on Fritz Lang's futuristic melodrama film *Metropolis* (1927) and H. G. Wells's chilling novel *War of the Worlds* (1898). In a clever twist, Thomas brings the comics right inside the classics with *Superman's Metropolis* and *Superman: War of the Worlds,* both of which place the famous DC hero in a central role in both stories.

The modern wave of underground comics, with its grim heroes and bleak points of view, has little appeal to Thomas. As he told

Mike Robinson in an interview on *Heroes and Dragons,* "To me, comics were optimistic, bright, and cheerful. People had troubles, but we were still dealing with heroes. I see that missing now." Thomas himself created many memorable heroes who have earned a permanent place in comic history.

For More Information

Periodicals

Flagg, Gordon. "*The Song of Red Sonja and Other Stories.*" *Booklist* (May 15, 2004): p. 1606.

Mohr, Rick. "*The All-Star Companion.*" *Reviewer's Bookwatch* (November 2004).

Raiteri, Steve. "*Star Wars: A Long Time Ago . . .: Vol. 1: Doomworld.*" *Library Journal* (November 1, 2002): p. 67.

Raiteri, Steve. "*The Chronicles of Conan Vol. 1: Tower of the Elephant and Other Stories.*" *Library Journal* (January 2004): p. 80.

Web Sites

Amash, Jim. "Roy Thomas Interview." *Two Morrows.* http://www.twomorrows.com/kirby/articles/18thomas.html (accessed on May 3, 2006).

Conan: Official Website. http://www.conan.com/index.shtml (accessed on May 3, 2006).

Offenberger, Rik. "Retrospectively Roy: A Look Back at the Career of Roy Thomas." *Silver Bullet Comic Books* http://www.silverbulletcomicbooks.com/features/110551511457953.htm (accessed on May 3, 2006).

Robinson, Mike. "A Conversation with Roy Thomas." *Heroes and Dragons.* http://www.heroesanddragons.com/Archive/Interviews/RoyThomas/DEFAULT.htm (accessed on May 3, 2006).

Craig Thompson. *AP Images.*

Craig Thompson

Born 1975 (Traverse City, Michigan)
American author, illustrator

"I want each book to be its own entity, with its own sound and texture, like Beck albums! I'm not going to become an 'autobiographical cartoonist' or anything."

For many people the emotional turmoil of life, with its ups and downs, is something to keep to themselves, or even to run away from. Not Craig Thompson. In his graphic novels, Thompson tackles big, emotionally charged topics such as the complications of growing up, missing friends, first love, family ties, and coming to terms with religious belief. His most celebrated work is the autobiographical *Blankets*, which tells the story of his teenage romance and coming to terms with his strict fundamentalist religious upbringing. His honest depictions of raw emotions quickly won fans, and his books have been honored with Harvey Awards, Eisner Awards, and Ignatz Awards.

Grows up in fundamentalist family

Born in 1975 in Traverse City, Michigan, Thompson was raised with his brother and sister in rural Marathon, Wisconsin. Devout Christians, Thompson's parents brought up their children according to strict ideas about family and faith. The Bible formed a firm foundation for his early life and learning. He was homeschooled for a year with materials from the Christian Liberty Academy, using the Bible as the main textbook. But even during his public school years, Thompson remembered reading the Bible for an hour each day. Generally, as a young boy, Thompson shunned ideas and books that did not accord with the Bible. Thompson shared with John Anderson in an interview for *Mars Import* that "I believed—as I was told—that it was the ONLY book one needed to read."

Thompson's upbringing in rural Wisconsin kept him isolated from much of the broader world, but it did bring his family closer together. Thompson related in several interviews that his family did not communicate well with one another. From an early age, Thompson turned to drawing to express his feelings and thoughts. And as he grew, he developed his own sense of the world, one that contrasted with his parents'. One of the most dramatic differences was his eventual abandonment of Christianity in favor of a more personal spiritual life. Thompson would eloquently and forthrightly address his emotional and intellectual struggles in his books, but speaking with his parents remained difficult. Thompson made the difficulties clear to Anderson. Noting that his second book, *Blankets*, "did indeed spark the first real conversation post-faith with his parents," he said that "It was exhausting, and yet nourishing to finally get all those cards out on the table, in a family with stunted communication." He told Daniel Robert Epstein in an interview for *Suicide Girls* that his parents were at first "pretty upset," adding that they said his book "bared witness for the devil."

Thompson related to *Graphic Novelists* (*GN*) that his parents have "an awkward blend of pride and shame in the success of the book."

Throughout his school years, Thompson pondered how to make a living through his art. While he had read comic strips from an early age and some of his close school friends had loved comic books, Thompson did not develop a strong interest in comics in his first (and only) year at community college. His first ideas for a career were as an artist or animator. But when he came across comics such as Mike Allred's *Madman* and Jeff Smith's *Bone,* he started to consider comics as a career. He began to draw a comic strip for his college newspaper and loved it. "It filled all my needs," Thompson told Karin L. Kross of *Bookslut.* "I was able to draw cartoons, to tell a story; but I also had total control, and I wasn't just a cog in some machine somewhere."

Although Thompson attended one semester of art school, he was ultimately "disappointed by the reality of art school," Thompson told *GN.* "I found my previous year of community college much more academically fulfilling." By 1997, Thompson had dropped out of college for financial reasons and committed himself to pursuing his art. He moved to Portland, Oregon, and took a variety of illustration and graphic art jobs to make ends meet while he worked on his comics. He completed a few minicomics and started many projects that he never finished before creating *Goodbye, Chunky Rice,* which would become his debut graphic novel.

Goodbye, Chunky Rice

Goodbye, Chunky Rice is a tale about two close friends from a small town and their emotional reaction to one's leaving to explore the wider world. (Writing the story coincided with Thompson's own move to the unknown of the big city, leaving behind close friends.) Chunky Rice is an adorable turtle who journeys out to sea, leaving his friend, the lovely mouse Dandel, behind. While the main story revolves around these friends, other characters round out the tale, offering varying perspectives on the loss of loved ones and being distant from friends. In *Shotgun Review,* Troy Brownfield called the book "an amazing creative feat," adding that "it's honestly accessible to all ages, and it works with a complex layering of themes and ideas. At times the air of wistfulness and the cute creatures (wonderfully depicted in Thompson's fanciful art) prod your memory of exceptional children's literature." Published in 1999, the novel won a Harvey Award and nominations for other top comics industry awards and has since gone into a sixth printing.

Goodbye, Chunky Rice is a tale about two close friends from a small town and their emotional reaction to one's leaving to explore the wider world. *Top Shelf Productions.*

Despite the media attention and accolades *Goodbye, Chunky Rice* brought Thompson, he did not perceive himself to be limited to the comic style of his debut book. He did, however, conceive of another project that would explore deeply felt emotions. For his next book, Thompson told the story of his first love and his decision to abandon Christianity.

Blankets

Thompson freely admits that *Blankets* is an autobiography. But he edited the truth a bit to make a compelling story. The character in *Blankets*, for example, has only one brother; Thompson has a brother and a sister. Thompson's coming-of-age story is full of life. He eloquently depicts the troubles of sharing a bedroom with his brother, the changing Midwest seasons, church camp, molestation, the strictness of his parents, falling in love with a girl from another town, and questioning his faith. The result was described by James Poniewozik of *Time* as "a bittersweet meditation on family, faith, loss and memory." The depth and detail Thompson poured into *Blankets* totaled nearly 600 pages, making it the longest comic book in history that was not originally published in installments over time.

Thomson drew and lettered each page with care over a three-and-a-half-year span. His work process resembled that used by writers of prose. First he worked out the story, then drew thumbnail sketches of the entire book, then created the final inked pages. The entire book was drawn by hand in black ink on white vellum Bristol board. Thompson related his preference for black-and-white to Joseph Gallivan in the *Portland Tribune*. "I don't like color for comics, something about keeping it calligraphic," he noted. "Chris Ware (who appears in *Raw* magazine and drew *Jimmy Corrigan* for Pantheon Graphic Novels) said comics are drawings that are written. I can work in color, but black and white is instant; it's expressive like the writing experience. Color slows down both the creator and the reader."

The resulting book grabbed the attention of the comic book industry, as well as the general reading public. "*Blankets* is one of the top ten most significant works within the comic book medium ever," wrote David Hopkins in *Fanboy Radio Newsletter*. *Library Journal* hailed it as a "triumph." *Blankets* won three Harvey Awards, two Eisner Awards, and two Ignatz Awards, the top three awards in the comics industry.

In between graphic novels

While traveling in Europe for several months to promote *Blankets* and research his next project, an Arabian fairytale, Thompson kept a journal. His sketches and notes from his trip were published in *Carnet de Voyage*. The resulting book offers readers insight into Thompson's obsession with drawing: he draws everything that catches his eye, from pretty girls, to exotic food, to bustling markets, to snowy woodlands. He draws so much that his hand hurts at the end of each day. What *Carnet de Voyage* also does is provide a glimpse of Thompson as a maturing adult, the next logical step after his coming-of-age story in *Blankets*. Thompson,

Varying Artistic Styles

Craig Thompson's artistic ability has enabled him to express himself in a number of different styles. Although he described himself to *GN* as "a simple brush-and-ink guy" who "drew both *Chunky Rice* and *Blankets* with the same variety of cheap water color brush," Thompson coaxed very different looks from his brush for his various projects. About how he decided what approach to take on a particular project, Thompson explained to *GN* that "the content informs the drawing style."

Drawing inspiration from the Muppets, Thompson's cute, cartoony style for *Goodbye, Chunky Rice* lent an innocence to his characters. His characters' big eyes and rounded features gave them a look of tenderness that exaggerated their emotions.

After *Goodbye, Chunky Rice,* Thompson related his desire for artistic change to Epstein: "I was sick of cutesy little cartoon animals and the real slick brush line I was using. So right away I knew I was going to break away from both of those conventions and have a loose expressive brush line and work with humans." For *Blankets,* Thompson drew humans more realistically, depicting himself as an awkward, gangly teen, his father as a burly, gruff man, and his love, Raina, as an angelic beauty. For his ongoing work on *Habibi,* Thompson told *GN* that he had been "fueling up on Islamic art and architecture and calligraphy and geometric design, and I need that to be present in the pages." In his future work, he said that he would continue to explore new artistic styles.

however, did not predict that his work would remain autobiographical. He related to *Suicide Girls* that "I definitely want to move on from myself as a writer and when you're younger you have to focus more on yourself. Hopefully 20 years from now I will be doing more broad work. The next project I want to do is something with a more social conscience."

Indeed, he described his project titled *Habibi* as his "world music" album, with an "ethnically diverse cast against more exotic/epic backdrops." He explained that inspiration for infusing this project with social and political relevancy came from his neighbor, **Joe Sacco** (1960–; see entry), creator of such works as *Palestine* and *War's End: Profiles from Bosnia.* Thompson told *GN* that his next project, after *Habibi,* would be geared toward younger readers because "suddenly the medium isn't for them anymore, and we need to start converting the future generations!"

Each publication of his new work revealed more depth to Thompson's storytelling and artistic talent. As his friend Hillevi remarks of Thompson in *Carnet de Voyage*: "You have so many layers that you can peel away a few, and everyone's so shocked or impressed that you're baring your soul, while to you it's nothing, because you know you've twenty more layers to go." With so much more to reveal, Thompson seemed poised for a long career in comics.

For More Information

Periodicals
Library Journal (January 2004): p. 48; (March 15, 2005): p. 67.

Poniewozik, James. "*Blankets.*" *Time* (August 25, 2003): p. 57.

Web Sites
Anderson, John. "Craig Thompson: The Mars Import Interview." *Mars Import.* http://www.marsimport.com/feature.php?ID=4&type=1 (accessed on May 3, 2006).

Brownfield, Troy. "Comics Convention: An Instant Classic: *Goodbye Chunky Rice.*" *Shotgun Reviews.* http://www.shotgunreviews.com/comics/chunky.html (accessed on May 3, 2006).

Collins, Sean. "*Carnet de Voyage.*" *Comic Book Galaxy.* http://www.comicbookgalaxy.com/072604_sc_review.html (accessed on May 3, 2006).

Doane, Alan David. "*Blankets.*" *Comic Book Galaxy.* http://www.comicbookgalaxy.com/blankets_review.html (accessed on May 3, 2006).

Doot Doot Garden: The Artwork of Craig Thompson. http://www.dootdootgarden.com (accessed on May 3, 2006).

Heneley, Rebecca. "*Blankets.*" *Sequential Tart.* http://www.sequentialtart.com/reports.php?ID=3557&issue=2004-11-01 (accessed on May 3, 2006).

Hopkins, David. "*Blankets*: It Is Just Good." *Fanboy Radio Newsletter.* Vol. 1, No. 1, October 2003. Available online at: http://www.fanboyradio.com/newsletters/FBR1.pdf (accessed on May 3, 2006).

Kross, Karin L. "An Interview with Craig Thompson." *Bookslut.* http://www.bookslut.com/features/2004_02_001502.php (accessed on May 3, 2006).

Peckham, Matthew. "Sequential Art: *Carnet de Voyage.*" *SF Site.* http://www.sfsite.com/columns/matt015.htm (accessed on May 3, 2006).

Smith, Zack. "The Friday Review: *Goodbye Chunky Rice.*" *Ninth Art.* http://www.ninthart.com/display.php?article=515 (accessed on May 3, 2006).

Other
Additional information for this profile was obtained through e-mail correspondence with Craig Thompson in December of 2005.

Yoshihiro Togashi

Born April 26, 1966 (Yamagata Prefecture, Japan)
Japanese author, illustrator

"I lived only to elude the letter of the law, and to come up with ways to goof off without getting caught by the teachers."

Thanks to the success of his manga series *YuYu Hakusho* and *Hunter x Hunter,* Yoshihiro Togashi is one of the most popular manga-ka (manga creators) in Japan. Both series have been released in the United States by Viz Media, one of the biggest publishers of Japanese manga for the English-speaking market. Both of Togashi's stories are shonen manga, a form of manga that is especially popular among teenage boys because of its high levels of action and adventure, humor, and the rowdy behavior of the major characters. As with many popular manga series, *YuYu Hakusho* and *Hunter x Hunter* have been made into anime series (animated cartoons), card games, DVDs, and video games.

Wins manga prize

Yoshihiro Togashi was born on April 26 (some sources say 27), 1966, in the Yamagata Prefecture of Japan, which is located in the northwestern portion of the main island of Japan. He has an older sister and a younger brother who also became a cartoonist. Little is known about the details of Togashi's early years and family life; this is probably due to the respect that the Japanese pay to the private lives of famous people. Togashi broke into the highly competitive world of manga publishing when he was just twenty years old. In 1986, he won an award sponsored by *Weekly Shonen Jump,* the most popular shonen manga magazine in Japan. The Tezuka Award, named after the famous Japanese manga creator Osamu Tezuka (1928–1989), allowed Togashi to publish a short work called "Tonda Birthday Present" in the magazine. In Japan, most manga are first published in the hugely popular magazines; then, if they are extended into a series and embraced by fans, they are collected into tankoubon, or graphic novels.

Togashi began publishing his first series, *Tende Showaru Cupid (An Ill-Tempered Cupid in Heaven)*, in 1989. Originally appearing in

Weekly Shonen Jump, it was later collected into three tankoubon volumes in Japan, though never published in the United States. Also in 1989, Togashi published the series *Okami Nante Kowakunai! (I'm Not Afraid of Wolves),* which was collected into a single volume in Japanese only. These series allowed Togashi to expand his skills as both a storyteller and an artist, and he would soon use his talents to create one of the most popular manga series ever: *YuYu Hakusho.*

Publishes fan favorite

YuYu Hakusho began appearing in *Weekly Shonen Jump* in 1990 and soon became one of the most popular series in the magazine. (The title is literally translated as "The Playful Ghost White Paper," but is taken to mean "Ghost Files" or "Poltergeist Report.") *YuYu Hakusho* tells the story of Yusuke Urameshi, a fourteen-year-old student at Sarayashiki Junior High School. In the early part of the series, Yusuke is revealed as a terrible student, more interested in fighting and combating authority figures than in attending classes. The only one who sees his good side is his longtime friend Keiko Yukimura, who later develops into his girlfriend. In an uncharacteristically selfless action, Yusuke saves the life of a young child by jumping into traffic, but he himself is killed. Now a ghost, Yusuke journeys to the underworld, where he finds out that they are not ready for him. The leaders of the underworld send him back to the world of the living, where he is looked after by Botan, a pretty young spirit from the underworld. Yusuke returns to school, but he is now charged with being an underworld detective, assigned with bringing back demons who have escaped from hell.

During the course of the series, which ran in the weekly magazine from 1990 to 1994, Yusuke had a variety of adventures: first, he fights and defeats three demons who have stolen three powerful artifacts from the underworld; next he participates in a contest to become a disciple (student) of a powerful warrior named Genkai. With each battle, Yusuke grows more skilled and powerful, but so do his opponents. Eventually Yusuke gains so much power that the king of the underworld questions whether he should be allowed to remain among the living. As the series ends, Yusuke helps contribute to ridding the world of demons and is united with Keiko in a mysterious ending that sees them both washed out to sea.

Though *YuYu Hakusho* is full of action—with nearly every chapter containing some kind of fight scene—the engaging plots and insightful characterization keep readers coming back for more. All of the characters grow and change in interesting ways through the series. Yusuke, for example, begins the series as a rowdy, disruptive character who claims in *YuYu Hakusho* Volume 3: *In the Flesh*, "My only mission in life is to get my kicks while I can." But he grows more responsible as he becomes an agent of good and gains power. An interesting subplot in the series involves the rivalry between Yusuke and Kuwabara, a student who wants to challenge Yusuke's stature as the toughest kid in school. At first, the two are bitter enemies, but they slowly learn to appreciate each other and become friends. These developing characters and their relationships make *YuYu Hakusho* more than just an action story.

Another interesting element of the series is the way that Togashi inserts himself into the story from time to time. In Volume 6: *The Four Beasts,* for example, he teaches readers how to play a game he calls "Dice Roshamboxing," which he invented while he was in school. Togashi explains to readers that he wasn't a rebel like Yusuke: "I lived only to elude the letter of the law, and to come up with ways to goof off without getting caught by the teachers." In Volume 7: *Hiei and Kurama: A Tale of Friendship,* Togashi adds a number of pages of sketches that explain strange dreams that he has had, or pranks that he pulled when he was young. These additions to the series help readers relate to the author, imagining that he was once a young boy attending school.

YuYu Hakusho was published as nineteen tankoubon volumes in Japan and sold 40 million copies, a huge number even in a country crazed for its manga. Beginning in 2003, Viz Media gained the rights to publish *YuYu Hakusho* in English translation. As of late 2005, Viz published eight volumes of the series, and English-speaking fans could follow the continuing series in *Shonen Jump,* the English-language equivalent of the Japanese magazine. *YuYu Hakusho* was also made into an anime series; in Japan, there were 112 episodes of the television series and two feature-length movies. American fans could see the series on the Cartoon Network, though it has not been aired consistently and—because of its violence and occasional harsh language—is considered too mature for young audiences.

High-Profile Manga Marriage

Manga artists, like many Japanese celebrities, are known to be quite vague about their private lives, rarely releasing information about their families or their personal hopes and aspirations. This penchant for privacy made the very public announcement of the marriage of manga superstars Yoshihiro Togashi and Naoko Takeuchi (1967–) all the more notable. Togashi, creator of *YuYu Hakusho* and *Hunter x Hunter,* and Takeuchi, creator of the hugely popular *Sailor Moon* series, announced their romance at a popular comics convention in Tokyo by issuing a self-published comic book that they created together. Their fame and wealth were well known to manga fans, and collectors quickly snatched up the limited-edition book. Just before their January 6, 1999, wedding, the couple appeared at another comics convention and sold limited-edition postcards and calendars commemorating their upcoming wedding.

Innovates with *Hunter x Hunter*

In 1998, Togashi proved that he was not a one-hit wonder when he began publishing the action-adventure tale *Hunter x Hunter,* which features twelve-year-old Gon Freaks and his desire to follow family tradition and become a Hunter, an elite class of fighter licensed to hunt for treasures and magical beasts—and to fight other warriors. Gon must undergo a challenging licensing exam that involves extreme feats of strength and fighting skill, and then he is teamed with other Hunters in a series of physical and mental challenges. Gon is joined in his adventures by several friends, Kurapika, Killua, and Leorio, and episodes in the ongoing series focus on the motivations and actions of the various characters.

Like *YuYu Hakusho, Hunter x Hunter* is first and foremost an action series, and there are frequent violent fight scenes. Sometimes the violence is quite graphic, with hearts ripped from chests and heads lopped off with swords. Yet Togashi also focuses on character development and, notably, on the complex code of conduct that rules the behavior of the Hunters. The Hunters are frequently involved in contests or games, and they must work together as a team to attain victory. Togashi sometimes steps away from the action to explore just how groups make decisions; in *Hunter x Hunter* Volume 3: *Resolution,* for example, he uses several pages to explore how a majority rule vote can destroy a group's unity, writing "If group conflict keeps arising, with one side always on the outs...the group's cohesion, never very strong to begin with, will eventually collapse!!" Such material adds a seriousness that is in contrast to the violent action.

Hunter x Hunter has been published in *Weekly Shonen Jump* in Japan since 1998, and also in the English version, *Shonen Jump*. However, ill health forced Togashi to take a break in publication in 2005. As of that year, sixteen volumes of *Hunter x Hunter* had been published in Japan, with sales numbering twenty million copies. English translations were released beginning in 2005, with the sixth volume expected to be published in 2006. In the United States, *Hunter x Hunter* is released as part of Viz Media's Shonen Jump Advanced series, a category not appropriate for younger teen readers. *Hunter x Hunter* has also been released in a Japanese anime version, numbering sixty-two episodes, and in various card games, video games, and DVD movies. While production of new *Hunter x Hunter* episodes were delayed because of Togashi's illness, expectations remained that he would begin publication again in 2006.

■ ■ ■

For More Information

Books

Togashi, Yoshihiro. *YuYu Hakusho.* Vol. 3: *In the Flesh.* San Francisco: Viz, 2004.

Togashi, Yoshihiro. *YuYu Hakusho.* Vol. 6: *The Four Beasts.* San Francisco: Viz, 2005.

Togashi, Yoshihiro. *Hunter x Hunter.* Vol. 3: *Resolution.* San Francisco: Viz, 2005.

Periodicals

Publishers Weekly (April 11, 2005): p. 36.

Web Sites

The Official YuYu Hakusho Web Site. http://www.yuyuhakusho.com/index.cfm (accessed on May 3, 2006).

Viz Media. http://www.viz.com (accessed on May 3, 2006).

"Yoshihiro Togashi." *Anime News Network.* http://www.animenewsnetwork.com/encyclopedia/people.php?id=1608 (accessed on May 3, 2006).

"YuYu Hakusho." *Shonen Jump.* http://www.shonenjump.com/mangatitles/yyh/manga_yyh-artist.php (accessed on May 3, 2006).

Akira Toriyama

Born April 5, 1955 (Kiyosu, Aichi Prefecture, Japan)
Japanese author, illustrator, game designer

Akira Toriyama is one of Japan's most celebrated manga artists and writers. His stories, which primarily appeal to children, usually spotlight classic struggles between good and evil. His characters are classic heroes and villains, with no middle ground between them, and are endowed with tremendous superpowers. Additionally, Toriyama places his characters in expertly devised fantasy worlds, with storylines that blend action and comedy.

Toriyama's artwork is appealingly goofy and exaggerated, and is characterized by crisp, clean lines and a strong design style. His male characters are generally small, but are muscular and resilient; his female characters are cute and charming. In reviewing the 2005 release of *Dr. Slump, Vol. 1* on *The Comics Reporter* Web site, Tom Spurgeon observed that "most of the charm (of the series) bubbles up from Toriyama's art, the large heads atop squat, solid bodies, rounded lines communicating a happy-to-be-right-here vibrancy broken only occasionally by exaggeration of expression or motion. Everything is adorable, and everything is sort of *dependable,* if that makes sense."

An attraction to drawing

Akira Toriyama was born on April 5, 1955, in Kiyosu, located in Japan's Aichi region. His interest in art dates from his early childhood. "I've always liked to draw," he explained in an interview on the Stormpages Web site. "When I was little, we didn't have many forms of entertainment like we do today, so we were all drawing pictures. In elementary school, we were all drawing manga or animation characters and showing them to each other."

Unlike other children, for whom art is a temporary pastime, Toriyama found that he loved creating images on paper. He began

"I have always drawn my manga ... with the desire to create something unique to comics, something that can only be expressed in the form of comics."

drawing portraits of schoolmates and attended a neighborhood drawing class. His favorite animated television program was *Tetsuwan Atom* (known in English as *Astro Boy*), which was popular among Japanese youngsters during the early 1960s, and he was fascinated with horror films, action-adventure television shows, and various Walt Disney animated features. In his drawing class, he earned a prize for copying images from one of his favorite childhood films: Disney's *101 Dalmatians,* released in 1961.

Early manga

Toriyama studied graphic design at the Prefectural Industrial High School and began his career working for a graphic design company. Initially, he resented having to sketch and re-sketch everyday objects, as per the order of his superiors. "Ugghh... Why do I have to draw one hundred pairs of socks?!,' I would complain," he recalled, in an interview on the *Buu's Dragon Ball Pages* Web site. "In retrospect, those things may have helped me."

In 1977, Toriyama entered a contest for amateur artists sponsored by *Shonen Jump,* a weekly magazine put out by Shueisha, a major manga publisher. The story he submitted grabbed the attention of Kazuhiko Torishima, one of the editors, who hired him as a cartoonist. Previously, while in school or in his spare time, Toriyama only had sketched characters; now, he began drawing manga with plotlines.

The following year, Toriyama created his first manga for *Shonen Jump*: *Wonder Island*, set in an outlandish universe inhabited by airborne fish and skateboarding monkeys. *Wonder Island* was only modestly successful, but it did not deter Toriyama from conjuring up other manga. Next, he created *Highlight Island*, which debuted in 1979 and charted the antics of a young schoolboy named Kanta. Another early credit was *Tomato Girl Detective,* which was unusual for its time in that its hero was a girl, instead of a brawny, courageous male.

As he came of age, manga artist Akira Toriyama realized that artists, in order to be successful, must constantly observe and ponder their surroundings. "It's been a habit of mine since childhood to always be looking around," he noted, in the Stormpages interview. "When I go shopping, I have more fun observing the town than shopping. For my work, the town scenery, small things, and people's clothes all are useful."

Toriyama, meanwhile, acknowledged the advantages of inventing or creatively distorting objects, rather than attempting to duplicate reality. "I probably have the most fun thinking up

Several of Toriyama's DragonBall mangas, or comic books. © *Amet Jean Pierre/ Corbis Sygma.*

original vehicles," he added. "I usually consider details such as how to get into them and where their engines are. When you draw a real-world car, you have to obtain some references. I'd hate to have someone point out that I'm wrong. But if it's something I invented, I can have it my way . . . . My manga is in the slapstick style, so if the characters are caricatured humans, then it'd be strange for everything else not to be caricatured."

As he creates his characters, Toriyama first envisions their personas. He matches the nature of their personalities first with faces, and then with body types. Once this is accomplished, he decides upon costumes that are appropriate for the environments they inhabit. If the characters are to be depicted in combat, he devises outfits that would be realistically comfortable while they battle their enemies.

Initial achievement

Toriyama's first great success was *Dr. Slump*, which debuted in 1980. *Dr. Slump* is the cheery, comic tale of Dr. Senbei Norimaki (whose name translates to "little rice cracker"), a zany scientist who constructs Arale ("even littler cracker"), a robot that resembles a young adolescent girl. Arale is a less-than-perfect creation—she is nearsighted and must wear glasses—but she also has superhuman strength.

Originally, *Dr. Slump* was published in *Shonen Jump*, where it was serialized weekly for five years. It also was adapted into an animated television series, or anime. In 2005, *Publishers Weekly* described the series as "Toriyama's twisted *Sesame Street*, a slapstick romp with an endearingly oddball cast of characters . . . . Toriyama has created his own demented sitcom, and his fantastic imagination and comic invention never let up. Simple ideas—Arale trying to rescue a bear from the zoo, Slump inventing a 'Future camera'—spin off into unexpected comic directions, and Toriyama never stints on visual humor."

Searching for a new project

Once *Dr. Slump* became an established hit in Japan, Toriyama began pondering the subject of his next *Shonen Jump* serial. He was a fan of actor and martial artist Jackie Chan's *Jui kuen* (*Drunken Master*), a 1978 feature film about a playfully bratty boy who learns discipline when his uncle, a kung fu master, teaches him the complex "drunken monkey" or "drunken boxing" fighting style. *Jui kuen* became the inspiration for *Dragon Boy*, a character who debuted in *Shonen Jump* in 1983. *Dragon Boy* was a precursor to Toriyama's most successful manga—and what become one of the most famous manga ever—*Dragon Ball* (also spelled *Dragonball*), which debuted in 1985.

Dragon Ball is a fantasy-adventure centering on Son Gokû, a character based on the mythological Chinese "Monkey King," a popular children's fable that is the model of the adventure story in which a hero sets out on a perilous mission. The tale details the struggle of Son Gokû and his allies against the Saiyans, a dishonorable band who are racing across and destroying the universe and wishing to take over Earth. In order to stay alive, Son Gokû and his pals must search for the Seven Dragon Balls. Anyone who holds them may conjure up a great dragon, who will grant any request.

Originally, Toriyama planned to draw his main character as an ape. "That would have been the Monkey King exactly," he explained on the Stormpages Web site. "That wouldn't show any creativity, so I decided to make the main character human. I wanted a normal human boy . . . ." However, Toriyama chose to endow Son Gokû with a tail. "That way, he could hide behind a rock, but if his tail showed, the readers could tell he's right there." In keeping with the spirit of the "Monkey King" fable, Toriyama added an array of colorful supporting characters to accompany Son Gokû on his quest.

Unparalleled accomplishment

Dragon Ball was a major international phenomenon. Foreign editions were published across Asia and Europe. It became a highly rated 153-episode animated television series, which aired from 1986 through 1989; in the United States, the show was broadcast on the Cartoon Network. It was the basis for a video game series, and spawned several made-for-television movies and a toy franchise. In 2001, Lycos, the Internet search engine, released a list of names and words that were most frequently looked for on its site. "Dragon Ball" ranked number two, just behind Britney Spears and ahead of Pokemon.

Toriyama created his final *Dragon Ball* manga in 1989. He immediately followed up with a sequel: *Dragon Ball Z* (for Zen). Here, the adult Gokû links up with his friends, from whom he has been separated for several years. With him is Gohan, his four-year-old son. *Dragon Ball Z,* which includes less comedy and more combat and action than its predecessor, features martial artists who hail from assorted worlds and possess astonishing superpowers.

A model poses next to a figure of Songoku, from the popular Japanese animated show *Dragonball Z.* © *Yuriko Nakao/Reuters/Corbis.*

As they vie for control of the Dragon Balls, they become airborne, toss energy blasts, and alter themselves to increase their abilities.

More success

Like its predecessor, *Dragon Ball Z* became a highly rated animated TV series, which premiered in Japan in 1989. During the next seven years, 291 episodes were produced. The series also spawned a string of successful made-for-television movies and video games. *Dragon Ball Z* episodes began running in the United States on the Cartoon Network in 1998 and eventually became the channel's most popular show.

Despite creating the characters who inspired and populated the *Dragon Ball* and *Dragon Ball Z* animes, Toriyama maintained a creative distance from the artists who produced the series. "I don't tend to interfere with the animators' process," he explained on the Stormpages Web site. "I wanted a fantastic story, so I did tell them that, but the basic production was all up to them. I might put in a small word where I thought it'd really matter." Ultimately, the animes impacted Toriyama's creative process as he wrote and drew his manga. "When I talked to the animation director, Toyo'o Ashida, and saw his drawings, I thought that it was more effective to depict fights with sharper lines," he added. "Until then, I had tended to use subtler colorings, but I changed to more defined colors, like in the animation. I learned that you can get the same effects as gradated colors if the coloring is done right. So I was able to do sharp colors, which were more suitable for a boys' magazine, and learned an easier way of coloring at the same time."

The *Dragon Ball* animes also impacted the manner in which Toriyama viewed his creations. "I thought, 'So, this what Gokū sounds like'," he recalled in an interview on *Buu's Dragon Ball Pages*. "Thereafter, every time I sat down to draw the manga, his voice would come to mind." He expressed his admiration for animators by adding, "They have to draw the steps between one movement and another, so I'm impressed that they can get the timing down so well. That's something that I can't imitate. Also, I am jealous of the way anime can render sudden movement so well....I am very envious of the fact that they can use 'light.' In anime, a scene with an explosion can be rendered with a brilliant flash of light and sound, but with manga, the only thing I can do is to put in an onomatopoeia (a word, such as purr, hiss, hush, clang, or kerplunk that sounds like a sound) for an explosion."

Easing up

Despite his respect for animators, Toriyama has no interest in joining their ranks. "The method of producing comics in Japan is very hectic, but it's also rewarding because it's possible to do both the story and art all by yourself," he explained in a 2003 interview published in *Shonen Jump*. "In this way, it's possible to bring out one's individuality." Nonetheless, Toriyama abruptly ceased producing his *Dragon Ball* manga in 1995, reportedly because he wanted to work at a more unhurried pace and wished to spend more time with his wife and two children. During their decade-plus run, he turned out 519 separate *Dragon Ball* and *Dragon Ball Z* stories on a weekly basis, totaling just less than nine thousand pages.

After he left *Dragon Ball Z* in 1995, Toriyama signed with TOEI Animation to oversee the development of an anime series titled *Dragon Ball GT* (Grand Tour). This series spotlights the further adventures of Son Gokū, who is portrayed as a child. Here, he sets out in search of a new set of Dragon Balls. The anime of *Dragon Ball GT*, consisting of sixty-four episodes, was broadcast on Japanese television in 1996–97, but was not as popular as its predecessors. As *Dragon Ball GT* premiered, Toriyama undertook the writing of a new TV series, based on *Dr. Slump.* Seventy-four episodes eventually were produced.

Multifaceted, multitalented

In addition to creating characters and devising storylines, Toriyama designed costumes for and served as art director on Japanese television series, starting in 1989 with *Dragon Quest* (known as *Dragon Warrior* in the United States). His art direction-costume designer credits through the 1990s and 2000s include various *Dragon Quest, Torneko,* and *Tobal* video games. Toriyama's character designs have been featured in the *Dragon Quest* and *Tobal* video game series, and in *Chrono Trigger.*

Dr. Slump and the *Dragon Ball* series are not Toriyama's only manga creations. Others include *Sand Land*, the futuristic chronicle of Rao, a sheriff, and Beelzebub and Thief, a pair of demons who search for water on a dry, treacherous desert; *Kajika*, the saga of a boy who is transformed into a fox-human; and *Cowa!*, the tale of two comical monster-creatures who reside in a fantastical world. However, only *Sand Land* has been translated into English as of 2005.

∎ ▨ ▢

For More Information

Periodicals

Akira Toriyama interview. *Shonen Jump* (January 2003).

"*Dr. Slump, Vol. 1.*" *Publishers Weekly* (May 9, 2005).

Gardner, Chris. "Fox Draws Deal for 'Dragonball' Live-action Pics." *Hollywood Reporter* (March 12, 2002).

Web Sites

Akira Toriyama Interview. http://www.stormpages.com/ssjsean/ati.htm (interview with Toriyama) (accessed on May 3, 2006).

"Da Man." *Buu's Dragon Ball Pages.* http://www.geocities.com/Tokyo/Towers/8583/dbAuthor.html (accessed on May 3, 2006).

"*Dr. Slump, Volume 1.*" *Comics Reporter.* http://www.comicsreporter.com/index.php/briefings/cr_reviews/2820/ (accessed on May 3, 2006).

Toriyama's World. http://www.toriyamaworld.com/ (accessed on May 3, 2006).

J. Torres

Born October 12, 1969 (Manila, Philippines)
Canadian author

J. Torres is the rare comics author who has succeeded in both independent and mainstream comics. In his independent works, such as *Sidekicks, Days Like This,* and *Alison Dare,* Torres explores issues such as friendship and teenage life with real sensitivity to the emotional complexities of growing up; in his mainstream stories for the *Teen Titans Go!* series, Torres shows a sure hand with fast-paced action, yet he never loses touch with the relations between the teen superheroes. What unites his work in these different realms of the comics publishing industry is Torres's deep interest in family dynamics and the emotional state of young people. In a column he penned for the Web site *Comic Book Resources,* Torres stated: "It seems most of the stuff I write, regardless of genre or concept or format, involves some kind of family theme or dynamic. If it's not about a character trying to keep their family together (*Alison Dare*) or someone searching for a lost family member (*Siren*), it's about someone finding a kind of surrogate family to help them accomplish something (*Sidekicks*)." What makes Torres's work so distinctive is that he has been able to treat these themes in ways that are appropriate for readers of all ages, using both humor and sentiment. His skills have earned him several comics industry awards, and promise a bright future.

"[Teen Titans Go! is] *sort of like a dream gig....It's almost like I've been preparing for this project my whole life.*"

Works his way into comics business

Joseph Torres was born on October 12, 1969, in Manila, the capital city of the Philippines. When he was four years old his parents, Renato (an engineer) and Guia (an accountant), fled the political instability in the Philippines and settled—in the dead of winter—in Montreal, Quebec, Canada, where Torres later became a Canadian citizen. After finishing high school, he attended McGill

Best-Known Works

Graphic Novels

Sidekicks: The Transfer Student. (2003).

Copybook Tales. (2003).

Days Like This. (2003).

Jason and the Argobots. 2 vols. (2003).

Alison Dare: Little Miss Adventures. 2 Vols. (2003, 2005).

Love as a Foreign Language. 4 vols. (2004–05).

Scandalous. (2005).

Teen Titans Go! 3 vols. (2004–05).

Degrassi: Extra Credit. Forthcoming.

University in Montreal, where he earned a bachelor's degree in communications in 1993, followed by a post-graduate diploma in education in 1994. After college he gained a job as an elementary school teacher—but being a teacher was not what he had hoped to do for the rest of his life. "I think I've always wanted to be a writer," Torres told Ruel S. de Vera of the *Philippine Daily Inquirer*, "and comic books were my first love. So it made sense to get started there even though I had aspirations to write children's books or work in TV as well.... I wanted to work in comics really early on, I just didn't know how to do it."

Even before he graduated from college, Torres began working on a mini-comic with his friend, illustrator Tim Levins. The pair created *Copybook Tales,* a story about two young men growing up in the early 1990s and trying to make it as storytellers. The story was semi-autobiographical, with the characters loosely based on himself, Levins, family, and friends. At first, they self-published the comic book; by 1996, they had sold the series to SLG Publishing. Torres told *Graphic Novelists* (*GN*) that he worked on the story "whenever I had a chance," between teaching English as a second language and directing a summer camp. "Looking back, I sometimes cringe at some of the storytelling, the corny lines, bad jokes, etc.," Torres told de Vera, "but overall, I'm pretty proud of it." The comic helped Torres and Levin get their foot in the door, and they have both been working steadily in the comic book industry ever since. By 2000, Torres had gotten enough comics work that between creating the mini-series *Siren,* writing for *Nickelodeon Magazine,* and handling the *Rugrats* comic strip, he was able to quit teaching to write full time.

Succeeds in independent comics

Torres's first big success with an original comic came with *Sidekicks.* Introduced in 2000 and first published in comic book format by Fanboy Entertainment, *Sidekicks* is set in a high school for the gifted. Not the intellectually gifted, mind you—this is no school for super bright kids—but for those gifted with super-powers who need help in figuring out how to use those powers for good. Other than the fact that these kids have superpowers, the characters in *Sidekicks* are normal teens, with all their concerns about fitting in, finding love and friendship, and maintaining a good relationship with their parents. *Sidekicks* is illustrated by Takeshi Miyazawa (1978–), a Canadian illustrator whose work resembles the look of Japanese manga.

In 2003, Oni Press (which specializes in producing comics that don't fit into the standard superhero mold produced by DC Comics and Marvel Comics) bought *Sidekicks* and released it as a graphic novel called *Sidekicks: The Transfer Student.* A *Publishers Weekly* review noted that the book was "written in the universal language of youth trapped in high school hell." Both drawings and words teamed to capture the high school experience, and the book was unusual for its realistic and sensitive treatment of female characters. *Sidekicks* established Torres as someone to watch in the comics industry.

In the mid-2000s, Torres published a number of works that proved him to be a writer who brought a fresh sensibility to comics. His biggest success came with *Alison Dare: Little Miss Adventures,* a story about a twelve-year-old girl who is the daughter of an archaeologist and a masked superhero called the Blue Scarab. Though her parents hope that she will lead a normal life, Alison Dare craves adventure—and she finds it. Rebelling against the limits placed on her by parents and school, Alison leads her friends Wendy and Dot on a series of adventures that combine danger, humor, and adept explorations of friendship. Torres told *GN* that to invent this character, he "took a childhood favorite, Jonny Quest, made him a girl attending my sister's private Catholic girls' school, and gave her Lara Croft and Clark Kent for parents.

Basically, I created a pastiche out of cartoon, comics, video games, and movies that I like and hoped that the mix of genres, combined with some familial themes and personal experience, would result in something familiar yet fresh and fun for the whole family." Like *Sidekicks, Alison Dare* was focused primarily on girl characters and crafted to be appealing to kids of all ages; in fact, the book was nominated for an Eisner Award for "Best Title for Young Readers." The second volume of *Alison Dare* was published by Oni Press in 2005; both volumes were illustrated by J. Bone.

While *Alison Dare* and *Sidekicks* were suited for middle school and high school readers, Torres's *Days Like This* and *Scandalous* stretched the audience appeal to adults. *Days Like This* was set in the early 1960s and followed the rise to stardom of a group of talented young African American singers known as "Tina and the Tiaras." Based on Torres's research into the pop music industry of the time, the book resonated with the emotional thrills of teenage success. *Publishers Weekly* called *Days Like This* "a cheery little fable about girls on their way to the top." Torres followed *Days Like This* with *Scandalous*, a story set in 1950s-era Hollywood. Again well researched, *Scandalous* takes readers inside the world of two gossip columnists who are vying for supremacy in the competitive world of celebrity tabloid newspapers. The illustrator for both works was Scott Chantler.

Joins Teen Titans team

In the summer of 2003, the Cartoon Network began to air an animated television series based on the DC Comics series *The New Teen Titans,* which was an updated version of the comic series called *Teen Titans,* which began in 1964. The TV series immediately became a huge success for network and publisher alike. DC— ever open to an opportunity to hook young readers on a comics series—decided to launch a new comics series called *Teen Titans Go!,* designed to appeal to readers of all ages. One author they turned to was J. Torres.

Torres was thrilled to be invited, he explained to de Vera: "I've always had a special place in my heart for the Teen Titans. And sometimes I still can't believe that I'm working on a series based on characters who were favorites of mine in high school . . . . I see *Teen Titans Go!* as an opportunity of a lifetime." Torres leaped right into telling stories about the five Teen Titans—Robin, Starfire, Cyborg, Beast Boy, and Raven—and as project editors had hoped, he proved spectacularly adept at the combination of adventure and

Since the fall of 2003, Torres has written twenty-nine of the thirty individual *Teen Titans Go!* comics, which later became a successful television show. *Fernando Leon/Getty Images.*

humor. At first, Torres was slated to be part of a team of writers, but DC liked his work so much that he has been the writer for all but one issue in the entire series. Since the fall of 2003, Torres has written twenty-nine of the thirty individual *Teen Titans Go!* comics (Adam Beechen wrote #8), fifteen of which have been collected into three *Teen Titans Go!* graphic novels.

Coming from the world of independent comics, where he had nearly complete control over the characters and the content of his books, to an ongoing series with specific character demands and a specific target audience might have seemed like a challenge, but Torres greeted it as an opportunity. He has told several interviewers how important it is for comics creators to pass their love of comics on to a new generation of readers, and *Teen Titans Go!*

has been his way of doing that. Torres's work on *Teen Titans Go!* did not signal a move away from producing original works. In fact, among others, he continued to work on *Love as a Foreign Language,* an ongoing series published by Oni Press about an English teacher working in Seoul, Korea, who must overcome the difficulties of living in a foreign culture.

Torres has also branched out into a number of different areas. He has written several episodes for the *Hi Hi Puffy AmiYumi* animated television show, penned stories for the *X-Men, Batman: Legends of the Dark Knight,* and *Batman Strikes* series, and in 2005 began work on a graphic novel series called *Degrassi: Extra Credit,* based on the *Degrassi: The Next Generation* television show. Torres thrives on the variety. He told de Vera: "I think I'd go crazy if all I did was superhero stuff and I'd probably go broke if all I did was the vanity press, indy stuff." Or, as he told the *Teen Titans* Web site, "Life is a buffet, my friend. You have to try a little bit of everything and go back for more of what you like."

■ ■ ■

For More Information

Periodicals

Publishers Weekly (June 9, 2003): pp. 38–39; (September 29, 2003): p. 46.

Raiteri, Steve. Review of *Days Like This. Library Journal* (September 1, 2003): p. 143.

Web Sites

De Vera, Ruel S. "This Fil-Canadian Writes Comics about Teens and Titans." *Philippine Daily Inquirer* (Manila, Philippines). http://news.inq7.net/sunday/index.php?index=1&story_id=46830 (accessed on May 3, 2006).

Encarnacion, Jonathan. "Talkin' TCAF: J. Torres." *Silver Bullet Comics.* http://www.silverbulletcomics.com/news/story.php?a=451 (accessed on May 3, 2006).

Jozic, Mike. "J. Torres: Age Appropriate." *Silver Bullet Comic Books.* http://www.silverbulletcomicbooks.com/features/107535404816206.htm (accessed on May 3, 2006).

JTorresOnline. http://jtorresonline.com (accessed on May 3, 2006).

"Supernatural Lola." *Broken Frontier.* http://www.brokenfrontier.com/headlines/details.php?id=619 (accessed on May 3, 2006).

"Teen Titans Go!: J. Torres Interview." *Teen Titans.* http://teentitans. toonzone.net/index.php?content=ttgo/misc/torres (accessed on May 3, 2006).

Thompson, Greg. "Interview with J. Torres." *My Comic Shop.* http:// www.mycomicshop.com/subscriptionservice/communications?AID=95 (accessed on May 3, 2006).

Titans Go. http://www.titansgo.net/comic_guide.php (accessed on May 3, 2006).

Torres, J. "Open Your Mouth" (May 8, 2003). *Comic Book Resources.* http://www.comicbookresources.com/columns/index.cgi?column=oym& article=1641 (accessed on May 3, 2006).

Other

Additional information for this profile was obtained in an e-mail interview with J. Torres on December 2, 2005.

Miwa Ueda

(Hyogo, Japan)
Japanese author, illustrator

Miwa Ueda captures the trials and tribulations of teenage romance in her popular manga series titled *Peach Girl*. Likened to a soap opera for teenagers, *Peach Girl*—published first in Ueda's native Japan and later in the United States—explores the emotional well-being of high schoolers as they navigate the difficulties of love and friendship, self-acceptance, and self-esteem. Throughout the series, the discussion of sexuality is more explicit than typical Western stories for young people, so it is often recommended for readers over the age of thirteen.

"[O]f all the characters in the comics I've ever written, Momo is the one who's closest in real life to the way I was when I was young."

Who is Miwa Ueda?

Born in Hyogo, Japan, Miwa Ueda's life is a bit of a mystery to Western readers. Though she maintains a Japanese language Web site, only one interview and scattered reviews of her translated work appear in English. To know more about Ueda, English-language readers must consult the brief notes she inserts into the text of her stories. In one such note, Ueda confides with readers that, like the character Momo, she too had been on her high school swim team and had been teased when her skin turned bronze in the sun. Ueda's other notes to readers ranged from laments about her favorite radio station changing its musical format, to a description of her quest to see fireworks on her day off, to her thoughts about her characters.

Ueda published her first manga in Japan in 1985; called *Peach Colored Elixir,* it won the *Bessatsu Friend* Award. (*Bessatsu Friend* is a monthly manga magazine offering positive stories to high school girls; it is published by Kodansha, one of the biggest manga publishers in Japan.) But it is *Peach Girl* that has earned her the most popular attention and a huge fan base in the United States. *Peach*

Best-Known Works

Graphic Novels

Peach Girl 8 vols. (2001–03).

Peach Girl: Change of Heart 10 vols. (2003–04).

Girl debuted in Japan in 1997, winning the Kodansha Manga Award the following year.

With its success in Japan, *Peach Girl* soon came to the attention of U.S. publishers, who in the late 1990s began to realize the market for translated versions of Japanese manga. Wanting to offer female comic readers something new, in 2000 Mixx Entertainment started printing monthly English translations of *Peach Girl* in *Smile* magazine. The issue in which *Peach Girl* debuted was the first all shojo (girl) manga magazine printed in the United States. Although the magazine folded in 2003, shojo manga caught on in the American market, and *Peach Girl* developed a loyal fan base. By that time, shojo manga had gravitated from manga magazines and obscure, specialty comic book stores to the shelves of mainstream bookstores and the Internet. In 2003, TokyoPop, a subsidiary of Mixx, continued U.S. distribution of *Peach Girl* solely in graphic novel form.

The first *Peach Girl* graphic novels were published flipped, which meant they were converted to the left-to-right reading format familiar to Western readers. But as the popularity of manga soared in the United States, fans came to prefer the right-to-left reading format used in Japan because it was more authentic. After the eighth volume in the series, published in 2003, TokyoPop began printing *Peach Girl* in the un-flipped "100-percent authentic manga" format. The graphics looked just like the original Japanese format, and the sound effects were left untranslated. The popularity of these editions prompted TokyoPop to republish the original eight volumes in the traditional manga format as well.

Exploring more than teenage romance

The *Peach Girl* story centers around the experiences of high school classmates Momo Adachi, Sae Kasiwagi, Kiley Okayasu, and Toji Tojikamori; various family members and former girlfriends complicate the story and add intrigue. Starting school late due to illness, Momo, a perpetually tanned blonde girl, finds her physical appearance to be a social stigma. Though her skin is bronzed and her hair bleached from her hours spent at swim team practices, people mistake her for a "party" girl who spends her free time at the beach, and consequently she has a hard time making friends. Ueda related having similar feelings when she was young. "I also had a complex about people being scared or intimidated when they saw me," she said in *Peach: Miwa Ueda Illustrations*. Sae befriends Momo, but as the story progresses readers discover that Sae treats Momo more like an enemy than a friend. Jealous by nature, Sae schemes to steal everything from Momo, from her fashion accessories to her boyfriends. Kiley and Toji are Momo's two male love interests. And it is the shifting nature of the *Peach Girl* characters' love interests that forms the foundation of Ueda's stories.

On the surface, *Peach Girl* is an exploration of the natural attractions and jealousies of young love. The love triangles created by the characters' friendships reveal deeper issues of self-acceptance and socially appropriate behavior. Momo, for example, hates her dark skin and feels certain it is the reason she has so few friends. She slathers on lotion to keep from bronzing further. As the series progresses, it becomes clear that Ueda is using Momo's skin color as a device to help illustrate Momo's need to accept herself. As Momo struggles with her self-esteem she shows remarkable compassion and kindness for others' foibles and shortcomings, especially Sae's.

Sae is the character Ueda uses to display incorrect social behavior. Ueda described her intentions for the character in *Peach: Miwa Ueda Illustrations*: "When it comes to Sae's attitude and actions, there are certain people out there who can say really nice things in front of you, then turn around and say something totally different to someone else. Looks can be deceiving so I wanted to depict the characters as being blind-sided by Sae's true personality." Sae lies, connives, and schemes to ruin almost all Momo's desires: she tells Momo that she should not buy a particular purse only to purchase it herself later, and she uses trickery to convince Toji to stop dating Momo. Few people would tolerate Sae's behavior, but Momo remains a steadfast friend even as she tries to avoid Sae's tendency to hurt her.

Aimed at a female audience, *Peach Girl* focuses more on the emotional states of Momo and Sae than the male characters. The boys are more often used as props to expose the feelings of either Momo or Sae. This is not to say that Kiley's pining for an old

Art of Shojo Manga

Shojo manga, or manga for girls, was developed in the early 1950s by male comics creators as **Osamu Tezuka** (1928–1989; see entry) and Tetsuya Chiba (1939–). When female comic writers and artists came to dominate the creation of shojo manga in Japan in the 1970s, the genre began to distinguish itself with a unique artistic presentation.

The female creators gave shojo manga pages a more emotional look. Avoiding the rigid borders that male creators used to divide the book page into neat rows, female creators developed a more fluid, multilayered page layout. They used differently shaped borders around scenes to highlight various levels of importance. Sometimes smaller shapes were layered on top of larger areas. Sometimes characters were drawn so large that they overlapped the borders of several scenes. Even more striking, however, was the graphic depiction of emotion. While the characters' large eyes still welled up with tears to show sadness, depictions of anger and frustration could permeate an entire page. Like other shojo manga creators, Ueda uses backdrops of flowers or hearts to show her characters' happiness and lightning strikes or blurry black backgrounds to show anger or despair.

girlfriend or Toji's tortured longing for Momo are not revealed to the reader; they are just less important than the feelings of the female characters.

The series' focus on the female characters' emotional states is obvious in the differences between the way the female characters are drawn. In *Peach Girl*, as with many other shojo manga, the female characters are depicted with large, expressive eyes, while the male characters have more proportionately drawn eyes. Eyes are often considered windows to the soul, and *Peach Girl* offers much larger "windows" into the female characters.

Although Ueda had published a number of short-lived series, including *Angel Wars, Glass Hearts,* and *Oh My Darling* in Japan in the mid-1990s, *Peach Girl* remained her focus in the 2000s. With the series ongoing and published in the United States starting in 2003, Ueda related that she had "a lot of expectations" for the

Peach Girl story development, but had not decided on an ending for the series, according to an interview in *Peach: Miwa Ueda Illustrations*. Ueda receives a great deal of mail from *Peach Girl* fans, but she confesses that she does not listen to them when developing her stories. "I'm thinking about my readers, but I won't be compelled to follow exactly what they truly want," she said in *Peach*. Only time will tell how Momo and Sae will mature.

For More Information

Books

Peach: Miwa Ueda Illustrations. Los Angeles, CA: TokyoPop, 2000.

Web Sites

Arnold, Andrew. "Drawing in the Gals." *Time.* http://www.time.com/time/columnist/arnold/article/0,9565,589081,00.html (accessed on May 3, 2006).

Fletcher, Dani, and Jennifer Contino. "Oh Shoujo." *Sequential Tart.* http://www.sequentialtart.com/archive/feb02/ao_0202_1.shtml (accessed on May 3, 2006).

"Manga Reviews." *Sequential Tart.* http://www.sequentialtart.com/archive/june01/ao_0601_rev1.shtml (accessed on May 3, 2006).

Mark Waid. *Ira Hunter.*

■■■

Mark Waid

Born March 21, 1962 (Hueytown, Alabama)
American author

   Young readers coming to the superhero comics of the 1990s and 2000s could not have avoided the impact of author Mark Waid. Not only has Waid had his hand in writing an amazing number of superhero stories, from *Flash* to the *Fantastic Four, Superman* to *Batman,* and many more, he has infused his superhero tales with some of the magic of the early years of the genre. In story after story, Waid has updated the meaning of the superhero for contemporary readers, without turning toward the irony and cynicism that defined the comics of the late 1980s and early 1990s. His *Kingdom Come* (1997) was widely praised as an allegory (symbolic representation) for the continuing importance of the classic comic heroes, and his *Superman: Birthright* (2004) brought renewed complexity to the story of Superman's origins. With his engaging characterization and his fast-paced plots, Waid has more than accomplished his goal of making comics fun again.

Best-Known Works

Graphic Novels

The Flash 6 vols. (1992–2000).

Captain America 2 vols. (1996, 1998).

Kingdom Come (1997).

Impulse: Reckless Youth (1997).

(With others) *JLA* 7 vols. (1998–2002).

Kingdom (1999).

Ruse 2 vols. (2002–03).

Crux 2 vols. (2002).

(With others) *Edge* (2002).

Fantastic Four 6 vols. (2003–05).

Empire (2004).

Superman: Birthright: The Origin of the Man of Steel (2004).

Gravitates toward superheroes

Waid was born on March 21, 1962, in Hueytown, Alabama, on the outskirts of the city of Birmingham. His love for comics began at age four when he obtained a copy of *Batman* #180, the cover of which he later framed and kept above his desk to remind himself of his lifetime love of comics. He hasn't stopped collecting comics since. Waid was a solid student who finished high school and pushed on to college at the age of sixteen. At Virginia Commonwealth University he changed majors three times, from journalism to English to physics, but after three years he eventually dropped out to pursue his dream: to become a writer in the comic book industry.

Waid got his foot in the door writing freelance stories for the fanzines, or fan-created magazines, *Amazing Heroes* and *Comics Buyers's Guide*. An editor at *Amazing Heroes* liked his material, and in the mid-1980s he joined the staff of that magazine as a writer and editor. From there, Waid jumped to the big time, joining industry giant DC Comics as an editor in 1987. Waid served as editor for a variety of writers on such titles as *Legion of Superheroes, Secret Origins, Doom Patrol,* and a wide range of other works. He also had a hand in creating stories or suggesting plot lines, and thus gained a valuable apprenticeship in the craft of creating comics. By 1989, Waid decided that he was ready to become a full-time writer on his own and he left DC to pursue a freelance career. (Freelance writers have the freedom to write stories for a variety of publishers, rather than for a single employer.)

In his first years as a freelancer, Waid earned the reputation as being one of the hardest-working writers in the business. He wrote about major characters such as Superman and Batman, and he wrote about minor characters such as the Legionnaires and Ka-Zar. What characterized his work was the obvious passion he had for superhero stories. In an interview on the *Fanzing* Web site, Waid admitted that he was deeply invested in his stories: "I'm here to tell you that, like it or not, I would be absolutely incapable of producing the work I produce if I weren't personally attached to it. The up-side to the process is that I'm invested, that my work carries genuine emotion because it carries a small piece of me in it."

No *Flash* in the pan

In 1992, Waid was offered the opportunity to take a turn at writing stories for a long-established DC Comics character, the Flash, best known for his lightning-fast speed. The Flash that Waid inherited was the alter-ego of Wally West, and the third and most powerful character to bear the name. Waid retold Flash's origin story, introduced some new powers for the character (including the "speed force"), involved him in a long-term romance, and led him in a series of battles against villains Abra Kadabra, Savitar, and Cobalt Blue. Waid remained the main writer on the series for one hundred issues, from 1992 through 2000; he was joined over this time, however, by a number of artists and, for a time, by co-writer Brian Augustyn (1954–). In the midst of his run on *Flash,* Waid was wooed by DC's arch-rival in the superhero business, Marvel Comics, to write for one of its long-running series, *Captain America.* Waid worked on the series in two bursts of creativity, realized in the publication of two graphic novel collections in 1996 and 1998. Together, his work on *Flash* and *Captain America* proved Waid's skill at handling some of the biggest superheroes in publishing history.

In 1997, Waid penned the work that lifted him into the top tier of comic book authors. Teaming with celebrated comic book artist **Alex Ross** (1970–; see entry), Waid wrote a story, *Kingdom Come,* that proved to be one of the most imaginative alternate takes on the DC Comics superhero universe ever attempted. In the future imagined in *Kingdom Come,* Superman, Batman, and the other DC regulars have "retired" from the hero business, allowing a new generation of superheroes to keep the world safe. As this new generation battles with each other and with villains for control of the world, they create the very conditions that could destroy mankind. Superman and Wonder Woman re-form the Justice League and prove once again to be the champions that humanity needs.

Kingdom Come came at a time when the comics industry needed a reminder of the power that exists in superhero stories. In the late 1980s and 1990s, a number of comics writers had explored the "dark side" of superheroes, exposing their weaknesses and calling into question the very idea that such heroes were truly champions of good. Though these stories enjoyed a brief popularity, by the mid-1990s comics sales were way down, and industry observers felt that this was in part because readers no longer believed in the idealism of the characters they had once revered. *Kingdom Come* reversed this slide by showing that the classic superheroes still had something to offer: as Superman says to government representatives toward the end of the series, "The problems we face still exist. We're not going to solve them for you, we're going to solve them with you, not by ruling above you . . . but by living among you." With these words, Waid announced that superheroes were still relevant. (Sadly, however, the successor to *Kingdom Come,* titled *Kingdom,* was not nearly as successful.)

To independents and back

Though he had achieved some real success working with the major comics publishers, Waid was one of a number of comics creators who longed for the freedom to create characters and stories that fall outside the established rules of DC and Marvel. In 1999, he joined with several equally well-known peers to form a publishing venture called Gorilla Comics. At Gorilla, Waid began work on a new series called *Empire,* but the company's financing dried up so quickly that the series died after just two issues (it was later resurrected by DC Comics). Shortly after this failed venture, Waid joined the staff of CrossGen, another start-up publisher that hoped to offer writers and artists more creative freedom. Waid's most notable contribution to the new company was a series titled *Ruse,* a detective story set in nineteenth-century Britain (he also authored *Crux* and *Sigil*). Waid described the main characters in *Ruse* to Mike Allred of *Comic Book Resources* as: "Simon Archard, the world's greatest detective, [who] is by this point in his career so good at what he does that he's bored stiff and has begun to withdraw into himself because he sees no more challenges [and] Emma, his assistant (or partner, if you ask her), [who] sees that there is still some warmth and humor buried deep inside him and has charged herself with bringing that out come hell or high water." Despite gaining strong reviews, *Ruse* ceased publication

Publishing Upstart CrossGen

Mention comic books and most people think superheroes; mention superheroes and most people think Superman, Batman, Spider-Man, and other well-known characters. For comics creators, the absolute dominance of superheroes and the companies that control them, DC Comics and Marvel Comics, has long been perceived as a roadblock to innovation, barring the introduction of new non-superhero works. In the 1990s, soaring comic book sales encouraged a number of comics creators to establish new publishing ventures to try to expand the market. In the vast majority of cases, these startups were a disaster, but Cross-Generation Comics—better known as CrossGen—almost bucked the trend.

CrossGen was founded in 1998 by entrepreneur Mark Alessi. For nearly two years he put in place the building blocks that he hoped would lead to success: he hired both new and established writers (including Mark Waid) and offered them decent salaries; he worked with creative staff to develop a variety of distinct storylines, none of which involved superheroes; and he established solid production and distribution arrangements. The founding of the company—which was far better organized than most of the shoestring operations that came and went in the 1990s—was welcomed by comics industry magazines. Veteran writer Mark Waid told Mike Jozic on the *Silver Bullet Comic Books* Web site: "As a company, I think CrossGen is poised to be a major force in tackling the problems of being a niche market that plague comics today."

CrossGen enjoyed several strong years, thanks in part to series like Waid's *Ruse; Sigil,* created by Alessi and Gina Villa; and *Meridian,* written by Barbara Kesel. Cross-Gen was also an innovator, becoming one of the first publishers to deliver comics over the Internet. But its success soon came to an end, thanks to financial scandal, bookstores backing out of agreements to carry CrossGen graphic novels, and finally, in 2004, bankruptcy. Despite the strong beginnings, another small publisher proved unable to crack the near monopoly enjoyed by DC and Marvel.

in 2004 when CrossGen folded. Like it or not, Waid was forced back into the arms of the big publishers—and he made the best of it.

Waid's first big success following his days with CrossGen came with the *Fantastic Four.* Introduced in 1961 by Marvel Comics, the Fantastic Four were a group of four scientist/adventurers who gained superpowers after one of their experiments went awry. Genius Reed Richards can stretch his body to incredible lengths; conscientious Sue Storm Richards can become invisible and create force fields; Johnny Storm (Sue's younger brother) becomes the Human Torch; and Ben—who Waid has called the "least complex character in the Marvel Universe"—is made of stone and has amazing strength. In an essay called the "Fantastic Four Manifesto" published in the first graphic novel collection of his work on the series, Waid explained his real affection for the original characters and argued that "All they need is for someone like me to remember why I love them and then, applying that TLC, polishing them up until readers can't help but [see] why they were so damn attractive in the first place." Polish them he did: Waid began a three-year run on the series that boosted the popularity of the Fantastic Four to new heights, thanks largely to Waid's imaginative exploration of what it meant for the characters to live with their powers and to try to continue their work as scientists. Waid produced six volumes of graphic novels, and the success of his series led, in 2005, to the release of a popular live-action film and several video games.

Fresh off his revitalization of *Fantastic Four,* in 2003 Waid turned his attention to the greatest superhero of all: Superman. Despite Superman's status as the most written-about character in comic book history, DC Comics felt that it was time for a new generation of readers to be introduced to the story of Superman's origins, and they turned to a man with a solid reputation for breathing new life into old heroes. While keeping the basic story intact—Superman still comes from the planet Krypton as an infant; he is still raised by Martha and Jonathan Kent; he still falls for Lois Lane; and he still battles Lex Luthor—Waid looked deeply into the characters and their motivations and found a new story. In the afterword to his *Superman: Birthright: The Origin of the Man of Steel,* Waid explains that he let two questions guide his approach: "Why does he [Superman] do what he does?" and "How can I possibly identify with someone like that?"

The power of these two questions, teamed with Waid's virtuosity at getting inside the heads of his characters, led to some key new insights into the Man of Steel. Clark finds his motivation for heroism while working in violence-torn Africa, for example, and he consciously adapts his Clark Kent persona as a kind of disguise that frees him to exert his superpowers in the city of Metropolis. Waid digs deeper into the relationship between Superman and Lex Luthor, and he makes important adjustments to the characterization of Lois Lane and cub reporter Jimmy Olsen. These, and a handful of other adjustments and rethinkings, helped make *Birthright* a huge success both among longtime Superman fans and a new generation of readers.

Reflecting on the fact that writing about superheroes remains meaningful, Waid wrote on the *Newsarama* Web site: "Long past the point where I believed I had anything left to learn from a simple hero of my childhood, Superman stands revealed to me as a tool through which I can examine the balance of selflessness and self-interest in my own life, which is every bit as valuable a lesson as the ones he taught me years ago." Perhaps it was this sense of personal fulfillment and exploration that kept Waid attached to comics writing. In the early 2000s, Waid was one of a number of prominent writers who signed on to DC Comics's efforts to rethink its superhero line for the twenty-first century. If *Superman: Birthright* is any indication, Waid may be leading the way as superhero comics undergo one of their periodic revolutions that continue to make them one of the most popular forms of entertainment for young people.

For More Information

Books

Waid, Mark. *Fantastic Four*. Vol. 1: *Imaginauts*. New York: Marvel, 2003.

Waid, Mark. *Superman: Birthright: The Origin of the Man of Steel*. New York: DC Comics, 2004.

Periodicals

"Comics 101." *Entertainment Weekly* (December 17, 2004): p. 88.

Gustines, George Gene. "Recalibrating DC Heroes for a Grittier Century." *New York Times* (October 12, 2005): p. E3.

Publishers Weekly (August 12, 2002): p. 278.

Web Sites

Allred, Will. "Mark Waid Interview." *Comic Book Resources*. http://www.comicbookresources.com/news/newsitem.cgi?id=969 (accessed on May 3, 2006).

Contino, Jennifer. "CrossGen Comics: A New Kid on the Block." *Sequential Tart*. http://www.sequentialtart.com/archive/may00/art_0500_8.shtml (accessed on May 3, 2006).

Jozic, Mike. "Mark Waid: Getting to the Crux of the Matter." *Silver Bullet Comic Books*. http://www.silverbulletcomicbooks.com/features/98662205385005.htm (accessed on May 3, 2006).

Lien, Barb. "Comic Books Aren't about Rules, They're about Flying." *Sequential Tart*. http://www.sequentialtart.com/archive/june99/waid.shtml (accessed on May 3, 2006).

"Mark Waid." *Fanzing*. http://www.fanzing.com/mag/fanzing13/iview.shtml (accessed on May 3, 2006).

Waid, Mark. "The Real Truth about Superman: And the Rest of Us, Too." *Newsarama*. http://www.newsarama.com/general/SuperPhilCh1Pre.htm (accessed on May 3, 2006).

Chris Ware

Born December 28, 1967 (Omaha, Nebraska)
American author, illustrator

Comic book artist Chris Ware is sometimes compared to literary giants Raymond Carver, William Faulkner, Charles Dickens, and James Joyce. Poet J. D. McClatchey has called him the "Emily Dickinson of comics," referring to the nineteenth-century poet known for her sometimes obscure poems. Ware himself shies away from such comparisons, telling interviewers that he is a poor writer and generally playing down his talent and achievements. He told Beth Nissen of *CNN Book News*, for example, that "The pictures are ideograms—drawn words, if that makes any sense . . . the pictures tell the story—I'm a terrible writer." He is famous for his meticulously drawn images, tiny details, and careful colorings. *Jimmy Corrigan: The Smartest Kid on Earth*, Ware's first full-length graphic novel, took seven years to write, but it won him the prestigious *Guardian* First Book Award in 2001. A reviewer for *Book* magazine wrote that "Ware's are some of the most beautiful pictures ever seen in comic books."

"Drawing was the only way I had of distinguishing myself, of trying to impress people . . . with my one pathetic ability."

Raised in Nebraska

Franklin Christenson Ware was born in Omaha, Nebraska, on December 28, 1967, the only son of Doris Ann Ware, a single mother who was a reporter on the same newspaper as her father, the *Omaha World-Herald*. Ware did not know his father and grew up living with his mother and maternal grandparents. He often spent hours copying cartoons from back issues of the newspaper while his mother worked on the other side of the desk. For a while he studied art at the Joslyn Art Museum in Omaha, but he learned about comics primarily by studying and copying them. Known in school as "Albino" because of his pale complexion, Ware has said that he used drawing as a way to avoid being bullied. He told

Best-Known Works

Graphic Novels

Floyd Farland, Citizen of the Future 1987.

The ACME Novelty Library. 16 vols. (1993–2005); single volume collection, 2005.

Jimmy Corrigan: The Smartest Kid on Earth (2000).

Quimby the Mouse (2003).

(Editor) *McSweeney's Quarterly Concern Issue 13* (2004).

Also the creator of many comic strips, including "I Guess," "Quimby the Mouse," "Big Tex," "Rocket Sam," "Jimmy Corrigan: The Smartest Kid on Earth," "Blab!," and "Rusty Brown," published in periodicals such as *Raw, New York Times,* and *New City.*

Nissen, "Drawing was the only way I had of distinguishing myself, of trying to impress people—impress people with my one pathetic ability," he said, with a rueful laugh. "There's nothing less impressive than a scrawny kid with poofy hair, drawing superheroes."

Much of Ware's work depicts characters who are marginal figures, unable to join in with "normal" social life, and several interviewers have linked this with Ware's own childhood experience. He told Nissen, for example, that "Kids were threatening to kill me all the time. I ate lunch by myself. I had some friends I talked to on the weekends—but they wouldn't talk to me at school. And I wasn't good at games—I was about as physical as an inert gas." Besides his interest in comics, as a child Ware also developed an interest in music. In particular he became a fan of ragtime piano music and was so accomplished as a piano player that for a time he considered becoming a professional musician. Alongside his career as a comic book creator, Ware is also a collector of ragtime memorabilia and publishes *The Ragtime Ephemeralist*, a magazine devoted to the subject.

Discovered by Art Spiegelman

Ware's mother remarried and the family moved to San Antonio, Texas, where Ware attended the University of Texas, Austin, and studied fine art, specializing in painting. He graduated with a bachelor of fine arts degree in 1990. Although his art school teachers disapproved, Ware published his first comic strips in *The Daily Texan* in 1987, his sophomore year. Some of these were seen by **Art Spiegelman** (1948–; see entry), author and illustrator of the *Maus* comic books and publisher of *RAW,* one of the most popular magazines among fans of alternative comics, or comics that are more adult in content and style than typical superhero comic books. Spiegelman was so impressed with Ware's wit, style, and attention to detail that he contacted him directly. Ware told Chip Kidd in an interview for *Print* magazine, republished on the Pantheon Books Web site, that he almost choked when he realized who it was. Commenting on what he saw in Ware's work, Spiegelman said "It's uncanny that someone so young would have such an apparent recollection of the history of comics, and the talent to expand upon it."

What Spiegelman was referring to is the contrast between Ware's drawing style, which is reminiscent of comics and magazine advertisements from the 1940s or earlier, and the written content of the comics. Kidd explains his own "discovery" of Ware in similar terms, pointing out the contrast in "Thrilling Adventure Stories" (an early Ware strip) between the superhero comic book-style characters and the personal, intimate subject matter. Ware's images evoke memories of comic strips such as "Krazy Kat" and "Gasoline Alley," popular favorites of the early twentieth century. But while at first glance the images and headlines seem to mimic the relentless cheerfulness of those older comics, Ware's text, which is often printed in tiny letters, is all about alienation, loss, petty cruelty, and moral emptiness. For example, one "advertisement" in *The ACME Novelty Library* offers "The Odor of Childhood . . . Just spray on sweaters, inside of arm, or just spritz into air for a fleeting remembrance of what's now long, long gone. Great for parties, feeling horrible and sad."

Moves to Chicago

Ware lived in Austin, Texas, for three years after graduating, experimenting with his visual style and with the layout of panels on the page. Characters and ideas that emerged from this period were included in his comic strips "Rocket Sam," "Quimby the Mouse," and "Big Tex," published in a variety of magazines, but he also began work on ideas that would become *Jimmy Corrigan: The Smartest Kid on Earth* (2000). He moved to Chicago in 1993 and began creating comic strips for the underground journal *New City*. He produced a volume of *The ACME Novelty Library* roughly each year in the 1990s, and it became his main source of income. But he was also working on *Jimmy Corrigan,* the book that would break him out of the "underground" world of comics and into the mainstream.

Entering the Mainstream

Jimmy Corrigan is one of the most celebrated graphic novels of all time. It picked up many of the most prestigious awards for comic books in 2000 and 2001. More importantly, though, much of the admiration for *Jimmy Corrigan* has come from mainstream literary and art reviewers. Besides picking up several Harvey Awards from the comic book industry, *Jimmy Corrigan* also won the prestigious *Guardian* First Book Award in 2001. At the time, only Art Spiegelman, who won the Pulitzer Prize for his *Maus* comic book, had been honored in this way by a major literary award.

Ware has been surprised at the critical attention and often professes real doubts about the quality and value of his work. He has also described how his art teachers looked down on comic book drawing and discouraged him from pursuing it. In fact, many of his comic strips and commentaries poke fun at art teachers and the mainstream art world, which he thinks undervalues drawing skills and "honesty" in art. It is all the more remarkable then that in 2002 Ware was featured in the Whitney Biennial of American Art, a showplace for high art, and in 2005 was among a handful of comic book artists featured in "Masters of American Comics," an exhibition at the Museum of Contemporary Art, Los Angeles, and the University of California's Hammer Museum.

Jimmy Corrigan tells the story of an underachieving office worker whose life is filled with disappointment and rejection. Jimmy Corrigan's first meeting, at the age of thirty-six, with his father, is at the center of the multiple stories in the book. Much of Ware's work could be described as confessional or at least personal, and this episode in *Jimmy Corrigan* seems to be a retelling of a similar episode in his own life. While writing the book, Ware was contacted by his own father and met him briefly, for the first time, just before he died. In the hands of another artist, that kind of personal involvement could slip easily into sentimentality, but Ware's meticulous illustrations and ruthless attitude toward his characters and their troubles will not allow it. Writing in the *New Yorker,* Peter Schjeldahl said of the book: "Ware's visual style recalls the clean-lined perfectionism of 'Tintin,' the classic adventure strip by the Belgian Hergé . . . but it is far more varied in design, with densely rhythmic layouts of small and large panels and of close-up and long views, and it is subtler in color, with moody, volatile pastels."

After *Jimmy Corrigan*

In the jacket blurb for the sixteenth volume of *The ACME Novelty Library,* Ware describes his activities following the success of *Jimmy*

Corrigan: "four years of almost exclusively repackaging his sopho-moric early work for the book trade." Ware was also busy working on a comic strip called *Building Stories* for the *New York Times* funny pages and developing new ideas for the *ACME Novelty Library* series. *Building Stories* features an apartment block inhabited by ordinary people doing mundane and ordinary things. As is the case with much of his work, what makes the subject matter appealing is Ware's simple yet intricate drawings and the heart-wrenching sto-ries of the characters who live there (for example, a woman who lies awake worrying about her husband's abuse and neglect, or a night shift janitor whose life centers on a vending machine and a pinup calendar). Like his mentor, Art Spiegelman, Ware also contributes, as he puts it "quite semi-irregularly," to *The New Yorker*.

Although he has been successful at making a living as a cartoon-ist, Ware's output is relatively small, especially compared to those working for major comic book publishers such as Marvel or DC. Because of the detailed drawings and carefully crafted text, his work is time-consuming to produce; *Jimmy Corrigan*, for example, took seven years to create. Yet Ware's record as an award winner is formidable. He has won numerous comics industry awards and has been singled out in particular for the quality of his coloring, presentation, and storytelling. A reviewer on the *Artbomb* Web site explains: "From 1995 to the present, Ware has utterly dominated the comic medium's major awards, winning dozens of Harvey, Eisner and Ignatz Awards, the comic book industry's most presti-gious awards, as well as a prestigious Reuben Award for Excel-lence." The same reviewer suggests that Ware may be the only comic book writer in history to have won more awards than he has produced comics.

Ware's work is often puzzling, shocking, and sad. His stories of loss, disappointment, and failure deal with the inner thoughts of characters who seem on the outside to be happy and settled in their lives. Because of this, and because of the sensitivity with which he addresses his characters' troubles, Ware has been com-pared to the major American writers William Faulkner and Ray-mond Carver. Like them, he creates stories of significant weight from minor, everyday incidents and makes otherwise insignificant people and events the focus of his work. Ware prefers not to present his books as stories to be read from beginning to end, spreading the strips out over every available surface and forcing the reader to construct the storylines from collected snippets of information. His success in breaking into mainstream newspapers, magazines, and review pages has been part of a wider growth of interest in graphic novels and comic strips as an art form with important things to say and elegant ways of saying them. Ware lives in Chicago with his wife, Marnie, and their daughter, Clara.

■ ■ ■

For More Information

Periodicals

Book (January 2001): p. 66.

Booklist (February 15, 1998); (November 15, 2000); (September 1, 2003): p. 76.

Bookseller (December 7, 2001): p. 7.

Comics Journal (December, 1997): pp. 15–16, 119–171.

Creative Review (July, 2001): p. 66.

Entertainment Weekly (February 23, 2001): p. 156.

Guardian (London, England) (December 7, 2001); (July 21, 2001); (October 31, 2005).

Library Journal (November 15, 2000): p. 64.

New York Times (January 21, 2001): p. 2; (April 4, 2001): p. E1; (February 8, 2002).

New York Times Book Review (November 26, 2000): p. 7.

New Yorker (October 17, 2005).

Observer (London, England) (October 16, 2005).

Publishers Weekly (September 4, 2000): p. 87; (July 19, 2004): p. 146.

Time (September 11, 2000): p. 116.

Web Sites

"Chris Ware." *Fantagraphics Books.* http://www.fantagraphics.com/artist/ware/ware.html (accessed on May 3, 2006).

"Chris Ware Profile." *Artbomb.* http://www.artbomb.net/profile.jsp?idx=6&cid=142 (accessed on May 3, 2006).

"The Inimitable Chris Ware." *Salon.com.* http://www.salon.com/books/review/2005/09/02/ware/index1.html (accessed on May 3, 2006).

"Interview with Beth Nissen." *CNN Book News.* http://archives.cnn.com/2000/books/news/10/03/chris.ware/index.html (accessed on May 3, 2006).

"Interview with Chris Ware." *Random House.* http://www.randomhouse.com/pantheon/graphicnovels/warekiddprint.html (accessed on May 3, 2006).

The Ragtime Ephemeralist. http://home.earthlink.net/~ephemeralist/index.html (accessed on May 3, 2006).

"Ware, Chris." *I Like Comics.* http://www.yakv.net/comics/artists/ware-chris/ (accessed on May 3, 2006).

Yu Watase. *Kevin Lillard.*

Yu Watase

Born March 5, 1970 (Osaka, Japan)
Japanese author, illustrator

"I feel manga is one tool that can be used to communicate to other countries in the entire world."

Manga creator Yu Watase made a name for herself in the shojo manga (Japanese comics for girls) market by refusing to limit her stories to the confines of that genre's narrow definition. Typically, shojo manga are defined as romantic stories dealing with the emotional well-being of the characters, while shonen manga (Japanese comics for boys) are a collection of action-packed adventure stories. Watase combined elements of both genres to create unique manga series with female protagonists. Watase related in an interview on the *EX* Web site that she thinks "it's kind of funny that in Japan where we have shounen [sic] manga and shoujo [sic] manga and we separate it. I feel that everybody shouldn't really separate those two, and I want to portray something that has almost everything."

While still categorized as shojo manga, Watase's works offer readers fresh perspectives; her characters deal with their emotions and love interests while simultaneously battling evil rulers, dealing with the consequences of being a descendant of a celestial being, or finding themselves transported into a magical, ancient book. *Animefringe* reviewer Patrick King's description of one of Watase's volumes applies well to her work in general: Watase writes "Shojo, the way it ought to be. Nothing too frilly, plenty of action, and an engaging romantic tale tucked in for good measure." Her series *Alice 19th, Ceres: Celestial Legend* and *Fushigi Yugi* form the foundation of her extreme popularity in Japan, as well as in the United States.

A professional by age eighteen

Born March 5, 1970, Yu Watase grew up in a small town near Osaka, Japan. Her interest in drawing and storytelling started when she was about five years old, and by age eighteen she had published her first story, "Pajama de Ojama," in a popular monthly shojo magazine. Since her first publication in 1989, Watase continued writing and drawing. Watase briefly attended an art school after high school, but by that time she was also working as a professional manga artist with her own studio in Tokyo and her own assistants. She dropped out of the art school before graduating and went on to become one of Japan's most popular manga creators by the mid-1990s.

Driven to do her best work, Watase developed a strong work ethic. She related to *EX* that she works almost every day from about noon to midnight. Her long hours were in part dictated by her insistence on drawing her manga by hand. Although interested in the capabilities of computer graphics, Watase draws her manga on paper with a traditional pen dipped in an inkwell. "I feel that using new media and computers is okay, but jarring," she told *EX.* "The traditional way has more feeling. So I want to continue in traditional ways with pen and paper."

Author Asides

Shojo manga are frequently marked by notes and asides written by the author directly to the reader. Appearing in the margins or as whole pages interrupting the flow of the story, these author communications provide readers with feelings of closeness to the author. Each shojo manga creator uses these notes in his or her own personal way. Yu Watase offers insight into her motivations for creating characters in certain ways, discusses her trips to industry conventions, or tells about her journeys for the purpose of manga research, among other things.

In volume fourteen of *Fushigi Yugi,* for example, Watase discusses a variety of things, from the differences between creating anime and manga, and how seeing the anime of her work helped her look at her drawing more "objectively"; to revelations about her manga, about which she confesses: "I've never looked at my own drawing and screamed at how good they look. In fact, I get sick of them pretty quickly." She also explains how she developed the continuing storyline for the series: "There were all sorts of ideas floating around my head, but in the end, I couldn't avoid the idea that *Fushigi Yugi* is pretty much a work that centers on Miaka and the Suzaku Celestial Warriors." She goes on to describe her characters in detail, among other things. Throughout her other manga, Watase sprinkles similar thoughts, each relating how thankful she is to her fans and offering insight into how much work is required to create manga.

Foundations of popularity

Fushigi Yugi catapulted Watase to popularity. Published in Japan between 1992 and 1995, the series made Watase one of her country's most recognized manga creators. Upon its first publication in the United States in 1999, *Fushigi Yugi* became publisher Viz's best-selling shojo title.

Fushigi Yugi tells the story of Miaka, a young girl alternately studying feverishly for her placement exam (she's not a particularly good student, so this exam is causing her great stress) and living out an incredible adventure in the pages of a magical book called *The Universe of the Four Gods,* where she discovers that she is a priestess of the god Suzaku and where she falls in love with the warrior charged with her protection. Watase centers the fantasy on Miaka. She describes her character in *Fushigi Yugi,* volume eleven: "I wanted to depict a girl who was honest, pure and innocent. A kid that is doing her best to cope with every situation she encounters, but her naivete can work against her too." To complicate matters, Miaka's real-life friend, Yui, is also living a normal school life as well as a parallel one in the same book, where she is a priestess of Seiryu, the archenemy of Suzaku. The thrill of *Fushigi Yugi* revolves around the friends' ability to solve their troubles and how these attempts play out in both their real lives and the fantasy world of *The Universe of the Four Gods*.

Fantasy added spark to Watase's next manga, *Ceres: Celestial Legend*. Originally published in Shogakukan's *Shojo Flower Comics* between 1996 and 2000, the fourteen-volume manga series weaves a tale about the marriage of a celestial being with a human and the consequences of this marriage for the couple's descendants. *Ceres* highlights the life of Aya Mikage, a descendant of the celestial maiden, Ceres. Aya, unlike some of her relatives, possesses powerful magic. Though Aya wants only to be a normal teenager, she must learn to master her powers to battle evil, which means she must even fight against the deadly plots of her own family members. The *Mangamaniacs* review noted *Ceres* as "a satisfying story that surprised . . . in a lot of pleasant ways."

Watase's third manga series, *Alice 19th*, explores relationships by highlighting the power of communication. The story revolves around Alice Seno and her older sister, Mayura. Like most siblings, Alice and Mayura have a hard time getting along, and to make matters worse they pine for the love of the same boy. Watase turns this relatively normal story of sibling rivalry into a fantastic exploration of the power of language. Alice and her love interest, Kyo, both learn they have the power to become Lotis Masters, people possessing the power to use magical words for good. In the meantime, however, Mayura becomes possessed by the evil demon Darva, who is set on destroying the world. King noted in *Animefringe* that Watase "crafted a story containing believable characters that rise to the occasion in extraordinary circumstances. This series remains realistic despite the overt slant toward the fantastic." Published in Japan in 2001, the seven-volume series began publication in the United States in 2003.

Watase has also produced short stories and various shorter manga series, including *Imadoki!* and *Absolute Boyfriend*. In the United States, Watase's work is labeled as being appropriate for mature audiences only. Though Watase's stories involve younger teenage female protagonists, the storylines often include nudity and sexual content that American readers often associate with stories for older teenage audiences. These differences are typical of many Japanese manga because the social expectations about sexual content in Japanese popular culture are different from those in the United States. The different ways cultures categorize content does not diminish the popularity of Watase's work, and she enjoys strong fan support in both Japan and the United States. Proud of her works' appeal, Watase explained to *EX* that "I feel manga is one tool that can be used to communicate to other countries in the entire world." Indeed her works have reached many: Watase's manga have spawned numerous translations, novels (written by others), anime (animated cartoons), films, and even music.

For More Information

Books
Watase, Yu. *Art of Fushigi Yugi.* San Francisco: Viz, 2002.

Web Sites
"Animazement—Yu Watase—2004." *A Fan's View.* http://www.fans view.com/2004/may2004/052904a.htm (accessed on May 3, 2006).

"AnimeExpo98—An Interview with Yu Watase (continued)." *EX: The Online World of Anime and Manga.* http://www.ex.org/3.4/11-feature_watase2. html (accessed on May 3, 2006).

"AnimeExpo 98—One of the 'Seven Stars of Anime Expo,' an Interview with Yu Watase." *EX: The Online World of Anime and Manga.* http:// www.ex.org/3.4/10-feature_watase1.html (accessed on May 3, 2006).

Arnold, Andrew. "Drawing in the Gals." *Time.* http://www.time.com/time/ columnist/arnold/article/0,9565,589081,00.html (accessed on May 3, 2006).

"Ceres: Celestial Legend Vol. 1." *Mangamaniacs.* http://www.mangamaniacs. org/reviews/ceres.shtml (accessed on May 3, 2006).

"Ceres: Celestial Legend Vol. 4: Chidori." *Animefringe.* http://www. animefringe.com/magazine/2003/08/reviews/08/ (accessed on May 3, 2006).

King, Patrick. "Alice 19th. Volume 2 Inner Heart." *Animefringe.* http:// www.animefringe.com/magazine/2004/02/review/12.php (accessed on May 3, 2006).

Andi Watson. *Courtesy A. Watson.*

Andi Watson

"I guess I noticed women got a raw deal in comics, and they still do."

Born October 1969 (Kippax, Yorkshire, England)
British author, illustrator

Few graphic novelists are as skilled at capturing the ins and outs of relationships as British author/illustrator Andi Watson. In graphic novels like *Breakfast After Noon, Slow News Day, Dumped,* and *Love Fights,* Watson expertly reveals the slow and grudging process by which people fall in and out of love. He uses words to explore the gulf between what is said and what is meant and pictures to reveal the meaning that resides in silence. Watson has earned critical praise both for the realism of his dialogue and for the retro style of his illustrations. Like many graphic novelists who receive recognition and awards for their serious or experimental works, Watson has also dabbled in writing for other, more mainstream titles. He has penned several stories in the *Buffy the Vampire Slayer* graphic novel line, and he co-wrote stories for the short-lived *Namor* superhero series published by Marvel Comics.

Working-class beginnings

Watson was born in 1969 in the Yorkshire, England, town of Kippax, on the outskirts of the larger city of Leeds. By the time of Watson's youth, the region was going through a transition brought about by the decline of the British mining industry. Watson came from a working-class family, and both of his parents held down full-time jobs in what was an area suffering from increasing unemployment. Like many kids, Watson was a fan of comics from an early age. He told Lindsay Duff in an interview for the *Ninth Art* Web site: "My first contact with comics was way back before I could read; *Peanuts* and Disney strips in the *Daily Mirror.* Then Brit humor comics, *Beano* (not *Dandy*), *Whizzer and Chips,* and all the rest, and *Star Wars* reprints, which I read until I was 13 or so and then stopped reading comics altogether."

Comics, thought the teenage Watson, were something that one gave up as he grew older and turned his attention to more mature interests—yet it was not immediately clear what Watson's interests were. "For a long time as a kid I wanted to be a mechanic, which is a big joke as I'm the least practical person on the planet," he told *Sequential Tart* interviewer Wolfen Moondaughter. He entertained the idea of ending his education after finishing secondary school (the English equivalent of high school), but realized there was one thing that he was always good at: art. "I was always drawing so don't know why I didn't realize art would be my thing," he told Moondaughter.

Watson attended Liverpool Polytechnic (now named Liverpool John Moores University), graduating in 1992 with a bachelor's degree in graphic design and illustration. It was while attending art school that Watson rediscovered his interest in comics. This time, however, it was not mainstream comics that Watson enjoyed. Instead, he found himself attracted to *Akira,* by Katsuhiro Otomo (1954–), one of the first manga (Japanese comic books) published in English, and to *Love and Rockets,* an American comic book series by **Gilbert Hernandez** (1957–; see entry) and **Jaime Hernandez** (1959–; see entry) that was proving that comics could treat adult interests. Still, he told Duff, "[I] never considered creating my own [comics] until years later—which is weird as I was always into stories and images inspired by the written word."

Opens door with *Skeleton Key*

After graduating college, Watson worked for a time as a video game developer and a commercial illustrator, providing drawings for a children's animation series and for a variety of businesses. Yet more and more, he devoted time to drawing comics. His first published work was *Samurai Jam,* which was published for four issues in 1993 by the American independent publisher SLG (Slave Labor Graphics). Though short-lived, the comic led to his creating a more successful series. Watson told *PopImage* Web site interviewer Christopher Butcher, "[I] was wondering how I could do something that totally pleased myself, wouldn't put off y'r typical comics buyer and would work for anyone unfamiliar with comics." The result was *Skeleton Key,* the story of a female high school student in Saskatchewan, Canada, who discovers a key that allows her to open a door to anywhere. That door to anywhere allowed Watson to take his two strong female characters on a variety of adventures. "I kind of poured all my love of myth, fairy tale, folk tales, pop culture, Japanese culture, comics, and all the other stuff cluttering my head at the time into that series," Watson related to *Sequential Tart*'s Jennifer Contino. But it also allowed him to develop his strengths in depicting relationships. The ongoing series, appropriate for all ages, was published as graphic novels beginning in 1996 and reached five volumes in 2000.

Watson followed up with *Geisha,* his first work that was intended to have a beginning, middle, and an end (as opposed to the episodic nature of *Skeleton Key*). *Geisha,* published by Oni Press, tells the story of an android artist named Jomi who tries—not too successfully—to fit into a society that doesn't like androids.

Working on this graphic novel freed Watson to think about creating more self-contained graphic novels, and these would make up the bulk of his work in the years to come. They didn't necessarily help him make a living, however; publishers didn't want to take risks on trying to sell a new story, and readers often were hesitant to pay for a story they knew little about. Luckily, Watson had received enough favorable reviews and comments about his work that he was able to pursue his career on two tracks: to pay the bills, he worked on several existing series for established mainstream publishers; and to pursue his real interests, he worked on a series of increasingly well-developed graphic novels.

Hits stride with *Breakfast After Noon*

Watson followed *Skeleton Key* and *Geisha* with several longer works that have earned him a stellar reputation in the field of graphic novels for older teen and adult readers. The first, published serially and collected into a graphic novel in 2001, was *Breakfast After Noon,* the story of a young couple, engaged to be married, who discover that they've been laid off from work at the local pottery factory. The pair—Rob and Louise—react very differently to the setback: Louise retrains and moves on with her life, while Rob wallows in self-pity, sleeping late, avoiding the agony of job-seeking, and alienating everyone around him. Anyone who has ever tried to solve a problem by not talking about it will sympathize with the slow erosion of the pair's relationship and rejoice when the pair reunite. The story was well reviewed: Matt Fraction, writing on the *Artbomb* Web site, called *Breakfast After Noon* a "quiet little marvel" that is "somehow both elegant and charming in the same stroke without feeling affected or trite," and Don MacPherson, in a review quoted on the book jacket, wrote that "This is one of those rare comic books that any reader can be proud to pass along to a non-comics-reading friend to show that the art form is far more versatile than one might expect."

In Watson's next two works, *Slow News Day* and *Dumped* (both published in 2002), he continued to explore the mysterious workings of human relationships. In *Slow News Day,* an aspiring American screenwriter, fresh out of college, joins the staff of a small English newspaper, where she butts heads and eventually falls in love with the embittered and cranky head reporter. The American and the Brit are instantly harsh with each other (their language is sometimes harsh as well), and their frequent clashes and cultural misunderstandings—he calls it football, she calls it soccer; she

The graphic novel *Breakfast After Noon* tells the story of a young couple, engaged to be married, who discover that they've been laid off from work at the local pottery factory. *Courtesy A. Watson.*

wants to work late, he's off to the pub—only delay their mutual realization of how much they care for one another. In *Dumped,* Watson pairs two twenty-somethings, Debs and Binny, who meet at a party and, over the course of the book, work out their insecurities and fears of growing older as they fall for each other. Matt Fraction, reviewing the work for *Artbomb,* wrote that "In the

Into the Mainstream

Graphic novel and comic book publishing in the 1990s and 2000s is generally divided into two distinct worlds: there are popular series titles, usually based on superheroes or other established characters, that sell many copies and make a lot of money; and there are independent titles that, while they may attract critical attention, have a hard time finding an audience and don't make very much money. Graphic novelists who only publish independent works are often stereotyped as "starving artists" who sacrifice financial rewards to preserve their art. Luckily, a number of graphic novelists have figured out how to succeed in both realms, producing series titles for the money while simultaneously developing their own, more personal works on the side. A good example of the success of this approach is Andi Watson.

Watson has worked on two popular series: *Buffy the Vampire Slayer* and *Namor*. The former were graphic novel spin-offs of the popular TV series *Buffy the Vampire Slayer* and were published in 1999 and 2000 by Dark Horse. Watson's other mainstream work came on *Namor*. Namor the Sub-Mariner was one of the original characters in the Marvel Comics superhero universe, and the title has been published intermittently since 1939. In 2003-2004, Watson co-wrote the script (with Bill Jemas) for a twelve-issue run of the series, and in it he explores Namor's dual commitments to the worlds above and below water.

Work on series titles like *Buffy* and *Namor* brought Watson an above-average paycheck, but it is not his first love, as he reflected to Michael Farrelly in an interview for the Web site *Bookslut*. With series books, Watson commented, "You work within parameters, you're using other people's property, characters, situations, often other people's stories laid out for you. You have to respect that, it's not yours." At the same time, he continued, "It's cool I get paid." Watson's real love is working on his own stories: "With my own work economic considerations don't come into it. I have an idea I'm really excited about and I HAVE to express it." And, he told Moondaughter, "There's such a freedom and satisfaction to doing things totally your own way."

hands of a lesser cartoonist, Debs and Binny would come off as shallow . . . little twits; Watson elevates both them and *Dumped* into a caring sketch of young lovers damaged and eager to be fixed."

Perhaps influenced by the work he had done on the superhero comic *Namor* (see sidebar), Watson set his next work in a world in which superheroes make regular appearances but are mostly a distraction to Jack, a comic book artist, and Nora, who works for a magazine that chronicles the exploits of superheroes. In what is becoming the distinctive Watson style, Jack—described in volume two of the graphic novel as "the male equivalent of the lonely lady with an apartment full of cats"—and Nora must fight through the distractions posed by work and the outside world in their quest to nourish their romance. By the end of 2004, Watson had published two volumes of graphic novels in the series; more are expected as he develops his characters with even more attention to detail and characterization than ever before.

With a number of critically acclaimed graphic novels under his belt, Watson has carved out a niche for himself as a writer who is unusually skillful at portraying the humor and the difficulty in modern romance, and as an artist with a distinctive style that often draws comparison to magazine illustrations from the mid-twentieth century. Watson's works are not strictly autobiographical, but they are certainly modeled on his life experiences: the agonies of declining industry of *Breakfast After Noon* were lifted directly from his childhood; the cross-cultural antagonisms of *Slow News Day* reflected his own experiences as a Brit working in the United States; and the emotions of young adults coming to terms with adulthood and parenthood that permeate his works are very much a product of his own life. (As he told Farrelly, "I've spent the last couple of years drawing 400 pages from the world around me.") Happily married and a loving father who spends a great deal of time with his daughter, Watson seems likely to continue mining the stuff of his life in order to turn out graphic novels that find both laughter and emotional insights in the situations of everyday life.

For More Information

Web Sites

Andi Watson. http://www.andiwatson.biz (accessed on May 3, 2006).

"Andi Watson." *Artbomb.* http://www.artbomb.net/profile.jsp?idx=6&cid=91 (accessed on May 3, 2006).

"Andi Watson." *Read Yourself Raw.* http://www.readyourselfraw.com/profiles/watson/profile_andiwatson.htm (accessed on May 3, 2006).

Butcher, Christopher. "All About Andi." *PopImage.* http://www.popimage.com/industrial/061300watsonint.html (accessed on May 3, 2006).

Contino, Jennifer M. "Andi Watson's Shining Little Star." *Comicon.* http://www.comicon.com/cgi-bin/ultimatebb.cgi?ubb=get_topic;f=36;t=004304 (accessed on May 3, 2006).

Contino, Jennifer. "From Geisha to Namor: Andi Watson." *Sequential Tart.* http://www.sequentialtart.com/archive/mar03/andiwatson2.shtml (accessed on May 3, 2006).

Duff, Lindsay. "Hold the Front Page: An Interview with Andi Watson." *Ninth Art.* http://www.ninthart.com/display.php?article=210 (accessed on May 3, 2005).

Farrelly, Michael. "An Interview with Andi Watson." *Bookslut.* http://www.bookslut.com/features/2003_06_000451.php (accessed on May 3, 2006).

Jozic, Mike. "Andi Watson: Fighting the Good Fight." *Silver Bullet Comic Books.* http://www.silverbulletcomicbooks.com/features/107292766021840.htm (accessed on May 3, 2006).

Moondaughter, Wolfen. "Breakfast, Skeletons, and Slow News Days." *Sequential Tart.* http://www.sequentialtart.com/archive/july02/awatson.shtml (accessed on May 3, 2006).

Judd Winick. *Courtesy of Mr. Duane Cramer.*

■ ■ ■

Judd Winick

Born February 12, 1970 (Long Island, New York)
American author, illustrator, lecturer

"I found daily comic strips to be limiting, not just in length and size formats or language, but creatively.... I wanted to be a story-teller."

Careers that begin on reality TV shows are not always to be taken seriously. But Judd Winick, who spent six months living in MTV's *Real World* house in San Francisco in the early 1990s, went on to win acclaim for his graphic novel *Pedro and Me* and for his work as a comic book author and illustrator. Winick, who recalls an issue of *X-Men* as one of his first comic book memories at the age of nine and admits to being a fan of the *Garfield* comic strip, began publishing his work in newspapers at the age of sixteen. By the time he became a "star" of *The Real World III* in 1993, Winick had already enjoyed success with his *Nuts and Bolts* comic strip, which ran weekly in the college paper the *Michigan Daily*; he managed to sell out 1,000 copies of a privately published collection in just two weeks. *Nuts and Bolts* was briefly picked up for national syndication, though that deal fell through. When Winick joined *The Real World*, he was unemployed and hoping his luck would change. It did.

Best-Known Works

Graphic Novels (as author/illustrator)

Terminal Madness: The Complete Idiot's Guide Computer Cartoon Collection (1997).

The Adventures of Barry Ween, Boy Genius 4 vols. (1999–2002).

Pedro and Me: Friendship, Loss, and What I Learned (2000).

Frumpy the Clown 2 vols. (2001).

Graphic Novels (as author)

Road Trip (1998).

Green Lantern 5 vols. (2001–04).

Exiles 5 vols. (2002–04).

Star Wars: A Valentine Story (2003).

Caper DC Comics, (2003).

Blood and Water (2004).

Outsiders 2 vols. (2004).

Teen Titans/Young Justice: Graduation Day (2004).

Batman: As the Crow Flies (2004).

Green Arrow 2 vols. (2004–05).

Starting early

Winick was born on February 12, 1970, and raised in Dix Hill, Long Island, New York. He attended Hollow Hills East High School, where he shunned schoolwork in favor of reading and drawing cartoons. In his early teens, Winick began working on *Nuts and Bolts,* a comic strip that was published weekly in local newspapers while he was still in high school. After graduating high school, he moved to the University of Michigan, Ann Arbor, to study drawing and art. *Nuts and Bolts* became a four-panel strip and appeared every day in the school's paper, the *Michigan Daily.* Winick graduated with a B.A. in 1992 and almost immediately landed a development contract with Universal Press Syndicate and worked for a year in Boston hoping to turn the strip into a nationally syndicated newspaper cartoon. When the contract was terminated, Winick moved back in with his parents and, in August 1993, answered a newspaper ad to audition for the third season of MTV's groundbreaking and popular reality TV show, *The Real World.* On his Web site, Winick adds that for a while *Nuts and Bolts* was in development with Nickelodeon as an animated TV show, but that deal fell through as well.

The idea behind *The Real World* is to place seven young adults from across America in a house, where they live together rent-free while being filmed at all times. After six months of interviews, screen tests, and lengthy application forms, Winick joined the other six "stars" in the house on Lombard Street, San Francisco, where he learned he would be sharing a room with Cuban AIDS activist Pedro Zamorra, who was HIV positive. The pair became great friends and went on tour together promoting sex education and AIDS awareness. When Zamorra's health began to fail during 1994, Winick took on speaking engagements in his place. After Zamorra's death in November of that year, Winick continued the tour alone. While on the show, which aired in the fall of 1994, Winick began a relationship with one of the other participants, Pam Ling, and they married on August 21, 2001; they have one son, born in May 2005.

Makes a breakthrough

Winick's personal experiences during his time on *The Real World* were significant, but there were also professional benefits. While he was filming the show, Winick began publishing *Nuts and Bolts* in the *San Francisco Examiner*. It was a badly needed career break that gave him exposure in a major city. Better still, the whole deal was filmed and aired on the show, making Winick, who was known as the "serious, geeky" member of the group, also one of the coolest. At around the same time, he also began illustrating for the *Complete Idiots' Guide* series of books, and by 2005 had illustrated more than 300 volumes. Recognizing that this area of his work was developing a fan base all of its own, in 1997 Winick published *Terminal Madness,* a collection of the best cartoons from the *Complete Idiots' Guide* computer manuals.

By 1996, Winick grew tired of *Nuts and Bolts* and began working on a spin-off cartoon strip based on one of his favorite characters from the original series, Frumpy the Clown. Frumpy moves into a suburban home and joins in with family life, much to the dismay of the adults. Frumpy's cynical attitude and frequent attempts to explain the pointlessness of human existence challenge the upbeat parents and disturb the children. In one frame, the children run a lemonade stand selling drinks at ten cents a cup; sitting next to them is Frumpy, offering "The truth about the government" for an additional three cents. From 1996, *Frumpy the Clown* was syndicated as a daily strip to thirty national newspapers. But the clown's cynical commentary proved too much for many newspaper readers, and the number of syndications dropped steadily over its two-year run. Winick himself had also begun to turn his attention to other projects, and Frumpy was dropped in 1998.

Despite its edgy subject matter, in 2000 *Barry Ween* won a "notable graphic novel citation" from the Young Adult Library Services Association (YALSA). *Oni Press.*

Publishes *Pedro and Me*

While he was still churning out daily *Frumpy* comic strips, Winick began developing a comic book about a boy with an IQ of 350, *The Adventures of Barry Ween, Boy Genius.* The first volume of *Barry Ween* appeared in 1999 and was widely acclaimed. Winick told the *Needcoffee* Web site that *Barry Ween* emerged as a reaction to the end of Frumpy: "And Barry was a response to finally quitting doing . . . a family comic strip. I went and did the filthiest thing I could possibly put my hands on. I mean, you look at it, it's still comic strip art, it's about little kids—but what are they doing? They're cursing and blowing [stuff] up." Despite its edgy subject matter, in 2000 *Barry Ween* won a "notable graphic novel citation" from the Young Adult Library Services Association (YALSA).

In the late 1990s, Winick also began working on *Pedro and Me,* an autobiographical graphic novel about his friendship with Zamorra. When he first discovered he would be sharing a room with HIV-positive Zamorra, Winick was surprised to find himself uncertain and afraid. Describing the process of writing the book, Winick told *The Advocate,* "So I began to write about the two of us. I wrote about myself, warts and all, not as the completely open-minded liberal I tried to be on television. I wrote about Pedro's dealing with being gay and with learning that he was HIV-positive. I wrote about our friendship, and I described the journey we all took together through his illness and his death." Encouraged by noted gay writer Armistead Maupin (1944–), Winick submitted what was then a vast, rambling manuscript to more than thirty publishers without success. He finally reduced the length to 180 pages with help from an editor at Holt.

Pedro and Me tells the stories of Zamorra and Winick as parallel tales. It focuses on their friendship, Zamorra's declining health, and Winick's own journey from ignorance and fear to understanding and affection. It is unusual subject matter for a graphic novel, but the book was well reviewed. *Publishers Weekly* called it "powerful and captivating," while *School Library Journal* declared "This is an important book for teens and the adults who care about them. Winick handles his topics with both sensitivity and a thoroughness that rarely coexist so seamlessly." After the book's publication, Winick appeared on TV and radio shows to discuss Zamorra's life, death, and the disease that killed him. He also visited schools and college campuses campaigning for AIDS awareness organizations.

Goes back to comics

Pedro and Me made Winick well known as an AIDS campaigner but it also enhanced his reputation as a comic book artist. He won many awards for the book from a wide range of organizations.

HIV/AIDS in Mainstream Comics

After his experiences with Pedro Zamorra and the publication of *Pedro and Me,* Winick continued his career as a comic book writer. But he managed to introduce the difficult issue of HIV/AIDS even in *Green Arrow,* one of his mainstream comics. Winick is hardly a pioneer in this area— Kevin Smith introduced an AIDS storyline to the *Daredevil* series—but in the past it had always been done with minor characters, and often in a less than realistic way. Mia Dearden, who is revealed to be HIV positive in *Green Arrow* no. 43, is one of the series' major figures. Winick has justi-fied making Mia HIV positive on the grounds of realism, saying "We got Mia as someone who had an abusive boyfriend; she'd obviously lived on the streets and was getting by as a prostitute. It's not an unlikely progression." *The Comic Wire* dis-cussed the issue in 2004: "While the sub-ject of HIV and AIDS has been discussed in mainstream comics before, this story is a bit different as we now have a starring hero, not a throw-away supporting character, who's infected with the virus . . . . Winick plans on portraying her life and struggles with HIV in as realistic a way as possible."

These include the National Association for Latin American Studies Programs and the Gay, Lesbian, Bisexual, Transgender Roundtable. It was also praised by more traditional comic book award organ-izations: he won a 2000 GLAAD Media Award for Best Comic Book; and in 1999, he received Eisner Award nominations for talent deserving wider recognition, best humor artist/writer, and best original graphic novel.

In 2001, having decided to move on from the material covered by *Pedro and Me,* Winick began writing for the *Green Lantern* series published by DC Comics. He also produced further installments in the *Barry Ween* series between 2000 and 2002 and collected *Frumpy the Clown* strips into two volumes. Since *Pedro and Me,* Winick has worked for several major comic book publishers, including DC, Marvel, and Dark Horse. Although he has declared an intention to put *Pedro and Me* behind him, his work on *Green Arrow* has sometimes drawn on similar material. In issue 137 of *Green Lantern,* for example, one of the main characters is revealed to be gay and in a later issue suffers a homophobic attack. In *Green Arrow,* a character called Mia turns out to be HIV positive. Winick has won two GLAAD awards for his *Green Lantern* stories as well as attracting media attention for his willingness to cover these diffi-cult issues in mainstream comics.

Winick became known as one of the most successful comic book writers of the late 1990s and early 2000s. His realism, humor, and humanity have endeared him to an audience that extends well beyond regular comic fans; books such as *Pedro and Me* have shown that graphic novels can succeed in territory usually held by more conventional books. Since his experience on *The Real World,* Winick was lured back to TV in 2000, co-hosting several MTV *Real World* spinoff shows with his partner, Pam Ling. In 2005, he made his debut as a producer and writer of an animated TV show, *The Life and Times of Juniper Lee,* which appeared on the Cartoon Network.

■ ■ ■

For More Information

Periodicals

The Advocate (February 1, 2000): p. 20; (September 12, 2000): p. 61.

Billboard (September 7, 1996): p. 100.

Booklist (September 15, 2000): p. 230; (December 1, 2000): p. 693.

Entertainment Weekly (July 23, 2003): p. 79; (December 19, 2003): p. L2T22; (June 10, 1005): p. 28.

Library Journal (November 1, 2003): p. 63.

Publishers Weekly (September 11, 2000): p. 92; (September 18, 2000): p. 37.

School Library Journal (October 2000): p. 192.

USA Today (September 18, 2000).

Washington Times (November 13, 1994); (January 11, 2003): p. B2.

Web Sites

"A Conversation with Judd Winick." *Needcoffee.com*. http://www.need coffee.com/html/convo/jwinick1.htm (accessed on May 3, 2006).

"Interview with Judd Winick." *Comic Book Resources*. http://www.comic bookresources.com/news/newsitem.cgi?id=4298 (accessed on May 3, 2006).

"Judd and Me." *Sequential Tart*. http://www.sequentialtart.com/archive/ feb01/winick.shtml (accessed on May 3, 2006).

Judd Winick. http://www.juddwinick.com/ (accessed on May 3, 2006).

"Judd Winick." *Artbomb.net*. http://www.artbomb.net/profile.jsp?idx=6 &cid=209 (accessed on May 3, 2006).

Marv Wolfman. *Albert L. Ortega/WireImage.com.*

"Comics are a synthesis of writing and art."

Marv Wolfman

Born May 13, 1946 (Brooklyn, New York)
American author, editor

Comic book writer Marv Wolfman has built a distinguished career working in the industry mainstream. He has authored stories for established characters from Superman to Batman to Captain Marvel, revamped popular characters including Robin and Lex Luthor, and created his own characters, the best known of which is Blade, the Vampire Hunter.

While expert at conjuring up cleverly devised, action-packed scenarios, Wolfman also creates characters that are more than one-dimensional superheroes or villains defined by their fighting skills. He is adept at spotlighting characterization, and his creations often must deal with inner demons and conflicts. In a *Library Journal* review of the 2003 release of *The New Teen Titans: The Terror of Trigon,* which includes reprints of five of his early *New Teen Titans* stories, Steve Raiteri observed, "Even in such an action-filled story, Wolfman keeps the characters' inner lives in the spotlight."

Best-Known Works

Graphic Novels

Doomsday: The Fantastic Four (1979).

New Teen Titans 5 vols. (1991, 1999–2005).

Tomb of Dracula (1991).

Spider-Man 3 vols. (1995).

Crisis on Infinite Earths (1998).

Batman: A Lonely Place of Dying (1998).

Blade II (2002).

Gene Pool (2003).

Superman: The Man of Steel 3 vols. (2003–05).

Essential Tomb of Dracula (2004).

Blade: The Vampire Slayer, Black and White (2004).

Curse of Dracula (2005).

Essential Ghost Rider Volume 1 (2005).

Essential Spider-Woman Volume 1 (2005).

The Oz Encounter (2005).

Fantastic Four Visionaries (2006).

Defex (2006).

Wolfman is also the author of countless comic books, as individual issues and series, many of which are collected in the graphic novels listed above. He is also a prolific author of screenplays and treatments for television shows and movies.

From reader to writer/artist

Marv Wolfman was born on May 13, 1946, in Brooklyn, New York. As a child, he was an avid reader of comic books. *Superman* was a favorite, and he savored the work of Harvey Kurtzman, Julie Schwartz, John Broome, and particularly Stan Lee. He also devoured science fiction novels by Ray Bradbury, Isaac Asimov, and Robert A. Heinlein, and horror-suspense stories by Edgar Allan Poe and Shirley Jackson. As he explained to Vincent Zurzolo in a 2005 interview on *World Talk Radio,* "I loved creating stories in my head. I would create endless ones (set in) in-depth-type universes, with all these different types of characters interrelating, (along with) complicated storylines."

By age ten, Wolfman had decided to pursue a career in the comics industry. In his early teens, he began writing and drawing in fanzines (amateur magazines produced by comics fans). They included *Super Adventures,* which featured superheroes; *Stories of Suspense,* a horror fanzine; and a comedy fanzine titled *The Foob.* "My intent was to be an artist," he told Zurzolo. "I was drawing stories as well as writing them, but everyone kept (telling me) that my writing was far better than my art. In point of fact, it was."

Early credits

In 1968, Wolfman was hired as a writer by DC Comics. Meanwhile, he attended Queens College, where he earned a bachelor of fine arts degree in 1971. That year, he put in a four-month stint as story editor at horror magazine publisher Warren Magazines, where he edited *Creepy Eerie* and *Vampirella*—magazines that usually featured several unrelated short narratives. Wolfman, however, conjured up the idea of linking the stories by populating them with the same characters or themes.

Also in 1971, Wolfman married. (He divorced his wife, Michele, in 1987, and has one daughter, Jessica.) The following year, he began working for DC's rival, Marvel Comics, where he became a highly successful writer and editor. While at Marvel, he wrote issues of *Amazing Spider-Man, Doctor Strange,* and *Fantastic Four,* but his most significant credit was *Tomb of Dracula,* which was created in 1972 by Gerry Conway and Gene Colan. The comic employed the essence of the Bram Stoker vampire novel in which the character originated, but presented Dracula in a modern-day setting.

Wolfman took over writing *Tomb of Dracula* with its seventh issue, at which point he transformed the comic into an eerily gothic horror series highlighting multifaceted storylines. "The difference between me and most of the other people who had written *Dracula* was that I had never seen a *Dracula* movie," he explained to Zurzolo. "My knowledge of the character came from the novel ... for that reason, I was able to approach it from a character-driven (point of view)." Wolfman credits his work on *Tomb of Dracula* with allowing him to develop as a writer by discovering what he called "subtle writing tricks" relating to plot, dialogue, and story structure. He also was allowed complete artistic freedom. Working on what was the first continuing horror series, noted Wolfman, "There was no template, I was making it up. That allowed me to create (from) what was inside me."

One of Wolfman's more intriguing projects during the decade was his first novel: *The Oz Encounter,* which debuted in a 1977 edition of *Weird Heroes: A New American Pulp.* In *The Oz Encounter,* he merged Doctor Raymond Phoenix, a parapsychologist-hero created earlier in the decade by science fiction writer Ted White and L. Frank Baum's celebrated *Oz* stories. In the resulting narrative, Phoenix penetrates the mind of a comatose girl and discovers an Oz-inspired fantasy world.

The Origin of Blade

While at Warren Magazines, Wolfman conjured up the character who would become his most celebrated creation: Blade, the Vampire Hunter. "His origin, personality, and look actually came to me in a flash," Wolfman explained on his Web site. However, he left the company before committing a Blade story to paper. The character first appeared in *Tomb of Dracula,* debuting in the comic's tenth issue, dated July 1973.

"Blade was one of the earliest black comic book heroes, and the first Marvel hero not to wear the typical comic book spandex costume of the time," Wolfman added. "Since *Tomb of Dracula* took place in a semi 'real world,' I wanted Blade dressed in somewhat realistic clothes: leather bomber jacket, pants, boots and his special goggles which, because he had vampire blood running through his veins, would let him see in daylight. Yes, he wore a bandolier complete with wooden knives (the better to kill vampires with, my dear), but they were only a fashion accessory."

As a slayer of vampires, Blade predates the popular Buffy character (of *Buffy the Vampire Slayer* fame), who debuted onscreen in 1992 and graduated to her own TV series in 1997. And Blade was not Wolfman's lone Marvel concoction. Another of his characters—Hannibal King, a 1930s-1940s-style detective who also is a vampire—debuted in issue number 25 of *Tomb of Dracula.* In 1976, he and Bob Brown created the character Bullseye, a psychotic villain who mostly does battle with Daredevil, Stan Lee's and Bill Everett's superhero.

From Marvel to DC Comics

Before leaving Marvel in 1979, Wolfman moved up the ranks to become editor-in-chief, a position that allowed him to supervise the creation of all of Marvel's titles. In 1980, he returned to DC Comics as a writer-editor and immediately co-created (along with artist George Pérez and editor Len Wein) and wrote the *New Teen Titans* series. *New Teen Titans* was an updating of the *Teen Titans* comic books, which debuted in 1965. Both involve a band of teenaged superheroes who unite to battle evil. The *New Teen Titans* characters were a mixture of holdovers from the original series— Robin, Kid Flash, Wonder Girl, and Changeling (who originally was called Beast Boy)—and newly created superheroes Raven, Cyborg, and Starfire. *New Teen Titans* became the first genuinely successful DC Comics series in years, an achievement that allowed the company to challenge Marvel as the industry's leading comic book publisher. One of the keys to the success of *New Teen Titans* was its multidimensional characterizations. Writing in the *New York Times* in 2003, George Gene Gustines described the stories as "both epic and emotional."

Wolfman wrote *New Teen Titans* for sixteen years, through the mid-1990s, and he is justifiably proud of the series. "I've got a very bizarre attitude when it comes to the Titans, which a lot of fans don't understand," he noted in an interview with Daniel Robert Epstein on the *UnderGround Online* Web site. "I've never looked at an issue of the Titans once I got off it. I never was interested in seeing what other people had done. In many ways, they were my babies, and I knew no matter how good or poorly others did it, they wouldn't be the same, and they couldn't be. I had very specific speech patterns, viewpoints for every character."

Landmark series

New Teen Titans was not Wolfman's lone DC Comics project. In 1985, he and Pérez created *Crisis on Infinite Earths,* a milestone series in which the publisher's most celebrated characters—including Batman, Superman, Wonder Woman, Aquaman, and the Green Lantern—unite to thwart the Anti-Monitor, a strange being who is determined to cause the demise of life on earth. As he conjured up *Crisis on Infinite Earths,* Wolfman reorganized and restructured the characters' pasts. He established that they lived concurrently, but on assorted earths. Writing in the *Tampa Tribune* in 2005, Jared Eaton observed, upon the release of a hardcover version celebrating the series' twenty-fifth anniversary, "*Crisis on Infinite Earths* was the pivotal comic book miniseries of the 1980s that ultimately redefined, as well as re-created, the DC Comics universe as fans knew it." And finally, in 1989, also for DC Comics, Wolfman conjured up the character of the "third Robin" (following Dick Grayson and Jason Todd): Timothy "Tim" Drake, who remains Batman's associate but is a superhero in his own right. "My take was that the previous Robins all wanted to be Batman," he explained to Zurzolo. "I wanted (a Robin) who thought being Robin was the coolest thing ever."

During this period, Wolfman occasionally penned and edited stories in other well-established DC Comics series, including *Batman*, *The Adventures of Superman*, *Green Lantern*, *Avengers*, and *Captain Marvel*. "One of my favorite ideas was coming up with the revised version of Superman's arch foe, Lex Luthor," he recalled on his Web site. "When I was growing up, Luthor was a mad genius who wore prison grays every time you saw him. The typical story began with him breaking out of jail, finding one of his old hideouts, and usually building a giant robot or something equally preposterous in order to fight Superman. I turned Luthor into a brilliant businessman who lived on top of the highest mountain in Metropolis, so its citizens would have to look up at him while he looked down on them." Wolfman's Luthor is brainier than Superman: He is a villain whom the world's strongest man must outwit, rather than out-punch.

Branches out to new line of work

In 1980, as he was settling in at DC Comics, Wolfman made his first foray into television production when he co-scripted *Yami no Teio Kyuketsuki Dracula*, produced by Japan's Toei Animation Company and based on *Tomb of Dracula*. Through the decade, he penned episodes of a range of animated series, including *Transformers* (broadcast from 1984–87), *G.I. Joe* (1985–86), *Jem!* (1985–88), and *Superman* (1988). He continued into the 1990s and beyond with *Batman: The Animated Series* (1992–95); *Monster Force* (a 13-episode series from 1994, which pitted teenagers doing battle against Dracula, Wolfman, the Mummy, and the Frankenstein monster); *Spider-Man* (1994–98, with his Blade character appearing in several episodes that aired in 1996 and 1997); *Beast Wars: Transformers* (1996–99); *Shadow Raiders*, also known as *War Planets* (1998–99); *Godzilla: The Series* (1998–2000); and *The Legend of Tarzan* (2001–03). His live-action credits include *Captain Power and the Soldiers of the Future* (1987), a science fiction series that incorporated computer-generated special effects.

Additionally, Wolfman was executive script consultant for *The Transformers*; served as story editor of *Superman* and *Monster Force*; produced *Pocket Dragon Adventures*, a 1998 animated series; and developed the animated TV series *Beast Machines: The Transformers* (1999–2001). He branched out into feature filmmaking, co-scripting, and executive producing *Elfquest* (2002), based on **Wendy and Richard Pini's** (see entry) comic book.

Even more significantly, several of Wolfman's creations were popularized on the big and small screens. His Blade character first came to the movies in *Blade* (1998), a New Line Cinema production with Wesley Snipes cast in the title role. "I was lucky enough to visit the set (during the film's production)," Wolfman recalled on his Web site. "It really is a thrill to watch your creations come alive." The box office success of *Blade* resulted in a pair of sequels, *Blade II* (2002) and *Blade: Trinity* (2004). Seeing Blade on the big screen was not a completely fulfilling experience. In 1998, Wolfman sued Marvel and Time-Warner, New Line's parent company, for $35 million, claiming that he owned the character's copyright and trademark. He asserted that, when he created Blade, he was an independent contractor, rather than a Marvel employee. After a three-year legal battle, Wolfman's suit was dismissed.

Wolfman's Hannibal King character (played by Ryan Reynolds) also appears in *Blade: Trinity*. Another of his creations, Catherine "Cat" Grant, a reporter/police officer/press secretary who first appeared in *The Adventures of Superman* in 1987, was an ongoing character on the *Lois & Clark: The New Adventures of Superman* television series (1993–97). Bullseye (played by Colin Farrell) menaced the title character on the big screen in *Daredevil* (2003). Also in 2003, Wolfman's *Teen Titans* became a hit animated TV series, produced by Warner Bros. Animation and the Cartoon Network.

"I started writing because of my love for comics, so it's great fun to realize that so many of my characters have been turned into movies, TV, toys, and animation," Wolfman explained on his Web site. "Fact is, I've been told that I've created more characters that have been adapted into movies, TV, and animation than any other comics writer with the exception of Stan Lee." Not all of Wolfman's projects have been successfully transferred to the big and small screens, however. In 2002, he and Len Wein created *Gene Pool,* spotlighting a group of unwilling superheroes who link up when their survival is jeopardized. It originally was written as a screenplay, but ended up as a graphic novel published the following year.

Maintains a prolific output

Even as Wolfman was immersing himself in television and motion picture production, he still found time to create new comic books. With Shawn McManus, he created *The Man Called A-X,* first published by Malibu Comics in 1994. The title character was a strong, silent hero who arrives in the city of Bedlam and takes on the criminal clans that rule the metropolis.

In the mid-2000s, as he was approaching his sixtieth birthday, Wolfman continued to conjure up new superheroes for emerging generations of comic fans. In *Defex* (2006), he created a group of heroes who start out as college biology students recruited by their professor to work in a state-of-the-art laboratory. Unbeknownst to them, they are being used as guinea pigs—and emerge with super-powers. *Defex* also is a typical Wolfman creation in that each of the heroes has personal issues with which he or she must deal.

■ ■ ■

For More Information

Periodicals

Eaton, Jared. "Silver Age Hero Flashes Back to Dawn of Time and Re-Creation of 1 Earth." *Tampa Tribune* (May 22, 2005).

Gustines, George Gene. "Adventures of Robin and His Merry Band of Mega-Friends." *New York Times* (July 20, 2003).

Raiteri, Steve. "*The New Teen Titans: The Terror of Trigon.*" *Library Journal* (November 1, 2003).

Web Sites

Epstein, Daniel Robert. "Teen Titans: Marv Wolfman." *UnderGround Online.* http://www.ugo.com/channels/freestyle/features/teentitans/ (accessed on May 3, 2006).

Marv Wolfman. http://www.marvwolfman.com/ (accessed on May 3, 2006).

Zurzolo, Vincent. "Marv Wolfman Interview." *World Talk Radio.* September 27, 2005. http://www.worldtalkradio.com/archive.asp?aid=5105 (accessed on May 3, 2006).

Where To Learn More

Books

Baetens, Jan. *The Graphic Novel*. Louvain, Belgium: Leuven University Press, 2001.

Crawford, Philip Charles. *Graphic Novels 101: Selecting and Using Graphic Novels to Promote Literacy for Children and Young Adults*. Salt Lake City, UT: Hi Willow Publishing, 2003.

Eisner, Will. *Comics and Sequential Art*. Tamarac, FL: Poorhouse, 1985.

Eisner, Will. *Graphic Storytelling*. Tamarac, FL: Poorhouse, 1996.

Goldsmith, Francisca. *Graphic Novels Now: Building, Managing, and Marketing a Dynamic Collection*. Chicago: ALA Editions, 2005.

Gorman, Michele. *Getting Graphic!* Worthington, OH: Linworth, 2003.

Gravett, Paul. *Graphic Novels: Everything You Need to Know*. New York: HarperCollins, 2005.

Gravett, Paul. *Manga: Sixty Years of Japanese Comics*. London: Laurence King Publishing, 2004.

Lent, John, ed. *Themes and Issues in Asian Cartooning: Cute, Cheap, Mad and Sexy*. Bowling Green, OH: Popular Press, 1999.

Lyga, Allyson A.W., and Barry Lyga. *Graphic Novels in Your Media Center: A Definitive Guide* Westport, CT: Libraries Unlimited, 2004.

McCloud, Scott. *Making Comics*. New York: Harper Paperbacks, 2006.

McCloud, Scott. *Reinventing Comics*. New York: Perennial, 2000.

McCloud, Scott. *Understanding Comics*. Northampton, MA: Kitchen Sink Press, 1993; reprinted, New York: HarperPerennial, 1994.

Miller, Steve. *Developing and Promoting Graphic Novel Collections*. New York: Neal-Schuman, 2005.

Sabin, Roger. *Comics, Comix & Graphic Novels: A History of Comic Art*. London: Phaidon Press, 1996.

Schodt, Frederik L. *Dreamland Japan: Writings on Modern Manga*. Berkeley: Stone Bridge Press, 1996.

Schodt, Frederik L. *Manga! Manga! The World of Japanese Comics*. Tokyo: Kodansha, 1983.

Weiner, Stephen. *Faster than a Speeding Bullet: The Rise of the Graphic Novel*. New York: NBM, 2003.

Weiner, Stephen. *The 101 Best Graphic Novels*. New York: NBM, 2005.

Witek, Joseph. *Comic Books as History: The Narrative Art of Jack Jackson, Art Spiegelman, and Harvey Pekar*. Jackson, MS: University Press of Mississippi, 1989.

Wright, Bradford W. *Comic Book Nation*. Baltimore: Johns Hopkins University Press, 2001.

Periodicals

Amazing Heroes. Seattle, WA: Fantagraphics, 1981–92.

Back Issue Magazine. Raliegh, NC: TwoMorrows Publishing, 2003–.

Comic Book Artist. Raliegh, NC: TwoMorrows Publishing, 1998–.

Comicology. Raliegh, NC: TwoMorrows Publishing, 2000–01.

Comics International. Brighton, United Kingdom: Dez Skinn and Quality Communications, 1990–.

Comics Journal. Seattle, WA: Fantagraphics, 1976–.

Comics Spotlight. Clifton, CO: Ground Zero, 2002–.

Graphic Novel Scene: The Guide to Trade Paperbacks, Manga, and Original Graphic Novels. Florence, KY: Blue Line Pro, 2004, 2006–.

Indy Magazine. Bellefonte, PA: Calliope Comics, 1993–.

Time. Published regular feature called "*Time*.comix" by Andrew Arnold. 2001–.

Wizard. Congers, NY: Wizard, 1991–.

Web Sites

ArtBomb. http://www.artbomb.net/home.jsp (accessed on June 9, 2006).

Broken Frontier. http://www.brokenfrontier.com (accessed on June 9, 2006).

Bussert, Leslie. "Comic books and graphic novels: Digital resources for an evolving form of art and literature." *American Library Association (C&RL News).* http://www.ala.org/ala/acrl/acrlpubs/crlnews/backissues2005/february05/comicbooks.htm (accessed on June 9, 2006).

Comic Book Resources. http://www.comicbookresources.com (accessed on June 9, 2006).

Comic World News. http://www.comicworldnews.com/cgi-bin/index.cgi (accessed on June 9, 2006).

Comicon.com. http://www.comicon.com/index.html (accessed on June 24, 2006).

Comics International. http://www.qualitycommunications.co.uk/ci (accessed on June 9, 2006).

The Comics Journal. http://www.tcj.com (accessed on June 9, 2006).

Graphic Novel Review. http://www.graphicnovelreview.com (accessed on June 9, 2006).

Graphic Novels. http://graphicnovels.info (accessed on June 9, 2006).

Indy Magazine. http://www.indyworld.com/indy/index.html (accessed on June 9, 2006).

The International Comic Arts Association. http://www.comicarts.org/index.php (accessed on June 9, 2006).

Movie Poop Shoot. http://www.moviepoopshoot.com (accessed on June 9, 2006).

Ninth Art. http://www.ninthart.com (accessed on June 9, 2006).

No Flying, No Tights: a website reviewing graphic novels for teens. http://www.noflyingnotights.com/index2.html (accessed on June 9, 2006).

Pop Matters. http://www.popmatters.com (accessed on June 9, 2006).

Sequential Tart. http://www.sequentialtart.com/home.php (accessed on June 9, 2006).

Sidekicks: a website reviewing graphic novels for kids. http://www. noflyingtights.com/sidekicks/index.html (accessed on June 24, 2006).

Silver Bullet Comic Books. http://www.silverbulletcomicbooks.com (accessed on June 9, 2006).

Index

Italic type indicates volume number; **boldface** type indicates main entries and their page numbers; (ill.) indicates photos and illustrations.

B

G

H

J

K

N

Sakai, Stan, *3:* 455, 457, 458–60

Takei, Hiroyuki, *3:* 512–13

See also Bushido

Sand Land (Toriyama), *3:* 572

Sandman (character), *1:* 131, 132 (ill.)

The Sandman (Gaiman and McKean)

American success of, *2:* 356

Gaiman, Neil, *1:* 127–28, 131–33, 132 (ill.)

McKean, Dave, *2:* 317, 320

The Sandwalk Adventures (Hosler), *1:* 221, 225 (ill.), 226–29

Sarajevo, *2:* 259–60

Satrapi, Marjane, *3:* **465–72,** 465 (ill.)

Sava, Scott Christian, *2:* 266, 269

Savage Sword of Conan (comic series), *1:* 78

Scandalous (Torres), *3:* 578

Scarlet Pilgrim (Robbins), *2:* 425

Schodt, Fred, *1:* 204

School Is Hell (Groening), *1:* 186

Schulz, Charles

on Aragonés, Sergio, *1:* 11

Hosler, Jay and, *1:* 222

Schwartz, Julie, *3:* 628

Science

Gonick, Larry, *1:* 159–62

Ottaviani, Jim, *2:* 395–403

Science fiction

Ellis, Warren, *1:* 107

Gaiman, Neil, *1:* 129

Pini, Richard and Wendy, *2:* 413–19

See also Steampunk

Scorsese, Martin, *1:* 7, 21

Scream Queen (Anderson), *1:* 8

SD Hyakkaten (Takei), *3:* 511

Secret War (Bendis), *1:* 25

Seduction of the Innocent (Wertham), *3:* 498

Seijin manga, *3:* 498

Seinen manga, *1:* 124

Sendak, Maurice, *2:* 322

Sequential art, *1:* 93–94, 96, 99

Seuss, Dr. *See* Dr. Seuss

Seven Against Chaos (Chadwick and Ellison), *1:* 57–58

The Seven Samurai (film), *1:* 58; *3:* 457

Seven Soldiers of Victory (Morrison), *2:* 278

Severin, John, *2:* 283

Sgt. Rock (Kubert), *2:* 253, 256 (ill.), 261

Shades of Gray Comics and Stories (Gownley), *1:* 178, 179, 180

Shadow of the Torturer (comic series), *2:* 391

Shakespeare, William, *2:* 415

Shaman King (Takei), *3:* 511, 512–14

Shamray, Gerry, *2:* 409

Shauna, Queen of the Jungle (comic series), *3:* 548

Sheena (Eisner and Iger), *1:* 94

Sheldon, Phil (character), *1:* 40–41

Shelton, Gilbert, *1:* 159; *2:* 286

Shin Seiki Evangelion (television series), *3:* 448, 449–50

Shin Takarajima (Tezuka). *See New Treasure Island*

The Shining Knight (character), *2:* 378

Shirt Guy Dom (character), *1:* 143

Shockrockets (Busiek and Immomen), *1:* 45–46

Shogakukan, *3:* 505, 608

Shojo Flower Comics (publication), *3:* 608

Shojo manga

CLAMP, *1:* 59–65

history of, *3:* 586

Robbins, Trina, *2:* 427

Soryo, Fuyumi, *3:* 481–85

Sugisaki, Yukiru, *3:* 495, 496, 497–98

Taniguchi, Tomoko, *3:* 531–35

Tezuka, Osamu, *3:* 540

Ueda, Miwa, *3:* 583–87

Watase, Yu, *3:* 605–9

Shonen Jump (publication)

Kishimoto, Masashi, *2:* 233, 234, 235

Takei, Hiroyuki, *3:* 511, 512, 514

Togashi, Yoshihiro, *3:* 560, 561, 563

Toriyama, Akira, *3:* 566, 568, 569

Shonen manga

Fujishima, Kosuke, *1:* 123–24

in Japan, *3:* 498

Sugisaki, Yukiru, *3:* 495, 496, 497

Takei, Hiroyuki, *3:* 511–14

Togashi, Yoshihiro, *3:* 559–63

Shonen Shojo Shinbun (publication), *2:* 346

Shonen-ai manga, *3:* 498

Shooting Star Comics, *1:* 81

Sidekicks (Torres), *3:* 575, 577, 578

Signal to Noise (Gaiman and McKean), *2:* 323

Silvestri, Marc, *2:* 314

Sim, Dave, *1:* 178; *3:* 477–78

Simmons, Al (character). *See* Spawn (character)

The Simpsons (Groening), *1:* 159, 183–84, 187, 187 (ill.), 188, 189

Sin City (film), *2:* 339, 340 (ill.), 341

Sin City (Miller), *2:* 339, 340 (ill.), 341

Sin City 2 (film), *2:* 341

Sinclair, Alex, *1:* 45

Sinclair, Upton, *2:* 277

Skeleton Key (Watson), *3:* 613

Skuld (character), *1:* 123, 124

Slave Labor Graphics, *2:* 392; *3:* 576, 613

SLG Publishing. *See* Slave Labor Graphics

Z